PARTING THE CLOUDS

THE SCIENCE OF THE MARTIAL ARTS

A Fighter's Guide to the Physics of Punching and Kicking
for Karate, Taekwondo, Kung Fu and the Mixed Martial Arts

GRENVILLE HARROP

An imprint of Dark Matter Books

www.darkmatterbooks.com

For Rebecca & Grenville

Copyright © 2011 Grenville Harrop

FIRST EDITION

PARTING THE CLOUDS: THE SCIENCE OF THE MARTIAL ARTS

A Fighter's Guide to the Physics of Punching and Kicking

for Karate, Taekwondo, Kung Fu and the Mixed Martial Arts

GRENVILLE HARROP

www.partingtheclouds.com

ISBN 978-0-9837041-0-2

Hatsuun Jindo
Parting the Clouds, Seeking the Way
Master Gichin Funakoshi (1868 - 1957)

Bring me my spear; O clouds, unfold!
Bring me my chariot of fire!
William Blake (1757-1827)

Warning

The techniques described or referenced in this book can be dangerous and must be practiced or used in an appropriate and responsible manner. The author is not responsible for any actions or consequences that may result from any person's choice to use any of the content of this book.

Acknowledgements

First and foremost my thanks to Rebecca Harrop, the most wonderful daughter a man could hope for, a Shotokan karate black-belt, and the wizard that helped me to turn a basic manuscript into a book that could be understood and published. Thank you Rebecca for everything.

The martial arts community in general, and I know this of karate in particular, is full of generous individuals, with people who are willing to give their time and energy to teach, learn or practice the way of that art. I know of no other craft, sport or vocation in which the seniors and masters of the art or profession are so accessible and amenable.

My thanks therefore to all those who have helped me along the way for they provided a foundation from which this book could be built.

Although my very first instructor in karate was Sensei Mike Toze, of the Rochdale Shotokan Karate Club, my predominant and long term instructor has been Sensei John Cheetham originally of the Lymm & Altrincham Karate Club in England. My first decade and more in Karate was under the direct instruction of John within an organization headed by Master Enoeda, who was aided by a group of outstanding instructors. My shodan certificate bears the signatures of Master Nakayama and Master Enoeda.

When moving from England to Boise, Idaho, USA in 1996 I was at first unable to locate a Shotokan club and trained with a good Taekwondo instructor (J. Stinnett) before finding Sensei Joe Shuter's Shotokan School. Relocation to Idaho Falls in 2000 brought me into contact, in every sense of the word, with Shotokan black belt Randy Hubbard and we became long term training partners and good friends. This prompted a more active connection to Master Nishiyama's organization and I benefited from the instruction and training with some of the best karateka in the US, including Sensei (Dr.) Tim Hanlon, who encouraged me to finish this book. Moving to Pittsburgh in 2006 brought me to the Pennsylvania Shotokan Karate Club of Sensei Dustin Baldis, a former international champion and a current USA National Team coach, and I train at his clubs as often as possible. I was also introduced to a small but dedicated group of mature black belts, from Master Viola's Allegheny Shotokan Karate Club, and I accepted their kind invitation to train at their advanced class on Saturday mornings.

I return to England several times a year and each time find my way back to the watchful eye of John Cheetham and a small group of training partners who have known each other for over thirty years. I suspect that I will be with my bare footed brethren until my journey is over and then may ask my younger brother and best friend Chris (3rd Dan Shotokan) to make sure the belt sees a few more years.

I remain a student of the martial arts and always will. My occupation has always involved travel and occasional periods away from home. This has allowed me to train in places that would otherwise have been inaccessible—from the JKA Honbu Dojo in Tokyo to the SKA Caltech Dojo in Pasadena; from a Master Nishiyama seminar in Windsor, England to a dawn session in a park in Shanghai. Whenever I attend a special course or train at a different club or in another country I am reminded of the global family within which I reside. The true martial artists, those that now train with a tempered ego, open their doors to others that follow similar paths with a non verbal welcome that is as deafening as it is inaudible. For this we should all be grateful.

It has been my experience that the martial arts are available, at all levels, for those that are prepared to apply the effort expected. It is as though the void reaches out to those who are deserving; all it asks is that you pay for the privilege. It is a simple equation, when you enter a training hall and stand amongst fighters you either have to have earned the right to be there or you have to pay later; or both.

If you understand, things are just as they are
If you do not understand, things are just as they are
Zen proverb

CONTENTS (DETAILED ON 261)

"In the instance a warrior confronts a foe, all things come into focus"

Morihei Ueshiba
The Art of Peace

INTRODUCTION

'The mind needs to be freed'
Master Funakoshi

Purpose

I have been privileged to spend decades training amongst the mass of karateka who simply practice the art. These men and women just train. Year in, year out, they just train. They don't aspire to be high-ranking masters, they don't hope for any financial gain, trophies or recognition—ego has long since been beaten into its proper place. They train for their own reasons: karate has become part of them and they a part of karate. There is no point in asking why they do it, why they are apparently obsessed, for as the saying goes:

> *'To those that know, no explanation is necessary.*
>
> *To those that don't know, no explanation will suffice.'*

This book is for them, it is for you and for me. This book is for the martial artists who will spend months or even years struggling with the minutest detail—trying to get a foot, hand or body position right when performing a certain technique, working to co-ordinate the breathing in a particular kata but failing and accepting that perfection is elusive—yet nevertheless they continue to strive for that perfect moment. It is for those that thereby come to understand that there are no goals, no objectives, and the revelation is therefore clear: this is simply a journey, a way. It's a journey that takes a lifetime, no matter how long the life; there is nothing more—'Mu' or 'Wu'—nothing, no mind.

This work may be of interest to others but it is essentially for those that want to supplement their years of dedicated training. No book can ever be a substitute for training under expert tuition but books can provide help. This one aims to help those in the martial arts to better understand the laws of physics as they relate to the fighting techniques being practiced. In so doing it can help an instructor explain why a technique is taught in a particular way and help a fighter understand what's important to its effectiveness. Science has many purposes, perhaps the most important is to provide explanations of the way things are.

If this book helps just one person to better defend themselves against an evil intent then it will have served a fundamental purpose. Fighting is an extremely important matter. Fighters know that there is no room for empty promises and that the teaching of techniques that probably do not work in real circumstances is unacceptably dangerous. Those that pass on knowledge that could be used in hazardous conditions must do so with an understanding of the associated responsibility.

Background

The traditional martial arts invite passion in the pursuit of excellence. Often where there is passion there is controversy - and conflict is at the very essence of the martial arts. Throughout the centuries there has been debate and discussion about the effectiveness of one technique or another. Arguments have raged over the particular ways of applying a move, about the consequences of training a certain way or the advantages of a specific body position when engaged in a strike, block or evasion. Different styles and schools have emerged from the heat of these discussions. Progress has been made, and sometimes stilted, because of differing views on the optimal way of training or fighting. Examples of these questions and debates could include:

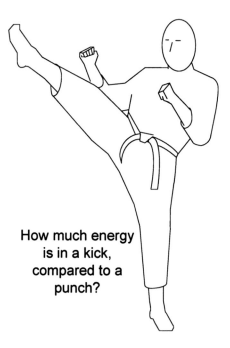

- What's the maximum impact that can be attained by a trained fighter?
- How do I become more powerful?
- How do I know that the style I am studying is effective?
- Does a mixed martial art provide the ultimate fighting skills?
- How much more force is felt from a kick, compared to a punch?
- Which has more force: a thrust or snap kick?
- How does the speed of a strike affect its force or power?
- How important is the contact time of a strike?
- Do you need to be grounded in order to be effective?

How much energy is in a kick, compared to a punch?

Debate and discussion is healthy. It invokes thought and deliberation over the topic of interest and prompts communication and exchange of views between individuals or groups. In many cases science can be used to help settle these debates or disputes. However, in some circumstances, science can also be misused and misquoted; which does not assist in finding the truth.

The problems associated with the application of science in the martial arts forum are numerous. In the past there has been limited formal research undertaken that produced reliable results to allow objective analysis and the formulation of clear conclusions. Despite the multitude of great books that have been written to help those dedicated to the pursuit of the martial arts, there are still only a limited number of authoritative texts that relate the art to the science.

Yet the fundamental principles of physics that apply in the martial arts are completely developed. Newtonian mechanics is sufficient to mathematically describe the forces in action. For example, the conservation of momentum and energy can provide the insight needed to understand what is happening when two bodies collide. After all, fighters are basically most concerned with what happens when two objects, such as a projectile and a target, collide. In our case the projectile may be a fist or foot and the target may be someone's stomach or head.

There appears to be a gap in the collective knowledge of the scientific principles that underpin the martial arts and for many fighters this leaves their understanding clouded. This book aims to show how known scientific principles apply to the martial arts; to provide the 'science behind the art' and thereby help part those clouds and fill that gap.

Prior to around the year 2000 there were relatively few numerical results from martial art orientated studies that had been undertaken in a rigorous scientific manner. In particular, the reliable and repeatable measurement of the force of a punch or kick was very limited. Simply put, the accurate measurement of force is difficult. Much of what we learn in training is based on anecdotal or subjective experience that provides qualitative (rather than quantitative) evidence. This book therefore attempts to explain the underpinning scientific principles, review some of the important available data and summarize the more useful results. The recent upsurge in the interest of fighting, due mainly to the popularity of the Mixed Martial Arts competitions, has prompted a renewed interest in the determination of how hard we can punch or kick. This has fuelled the production of television shows that are measuring 'who' can hit the hardest. The use of the internet allows easier access and review of these studies and insight can be gained by looking at the performance of expert fighters hitting a target.

A fighter does not need to be a physicist to be proficient at, or a Master of, their chosen art— far from it. For most practitioners the answer to the majority of questions can be found by simple examination of good practice. Indeed, many of the academic debates can be ignored by those who simply want to train under the guidance of a good instructor. However, the martial arts encourage contemplation and analysis and the serious fighters should have the opportunity to apply their minds to the numerous questions that emerge in training.

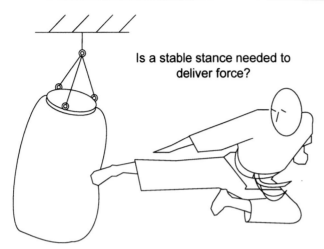

Is a stable stance needed to deliver force?

Frequently asked questions can often be answered by simple analysis of the techniques being practiced. This is mainly a contemplation over what 'feels' right, with time spent thinking about what it is that makes the difference between a technique that appears effective compared to one that seems weak or slow. As an illustration, during one post-training discussion I was asked if you really needed to be rooted in a good stance to be able to deliver power. The fairly high-ranking karate instructor that asked has a very impressive side thrust kick. It is even more impressive when you see this kick hit a bag as he 'hops' through the stance to strike, and better yet when the kick is delivered in mid air in a flying sidekick fashion. Anyone who witnessed his technique striking the bag saw the force of impact and power being delivered as the bag is blasted. So why would this person of intelligence have to ask if you need to be rooted to hit hard, given that he had seen and felt his own power being demonstrated when his feet were not even on the ground? If you need to be on the ground to be rooted, and only a technique delivered from a routed stance can provide power, then a flying kick can have no power. We know this is not true - and some of us may have even carried the bruises from such a kick.

Of course he used the floor to launch his attack and in so doing has found a way to 'lift-off' and get a massive push from the earth. The floor will have been the source of much of the power but when in the air you are in the air and no longer grounded. An arrow, cannonball or bullet has no connection to the ground when in flight but it carries immense energy and destructive power. Why then should anyone believe you can *only* be effective when *in* a solid stance? Why are the practical, every day, experiences ignored?

For good reason a beginner to the martial arts will be told to remain connected or even rooted to the ground when delivering a strike. This is good instruction but it can be stressed to the point where students become confused or conditioned into believing this is the *only* way to be forceful. This conditioning can be so ingrained that individuals will unwittingly 'bend' or misuse science to try and justify a belief that is actually inaccurate. In the following chapters I will therefore try to unravel some of these puzzles or 'mysteries'.

Why Study the Science?

The book "Karate: The Art of "Empty Hand" Fighting, by Hidetaka Nishiyama and Richard C. Brown states: *"The remarkable strength manifested by many individual karate techniques, both offensive and defensive, is not the mysterious, esoteric thing many observers, as well as certain proponents of the art itself would have you believe. On the contrary, it is the inevitable result of the effective application of certain well known scientific principles to the movements of the body."*

Master Nishiyama was one the foremost experts on karate. He was taught by Master Nakayama and dedicated his life to Budo or 'the way of the warrior'. Those fortunate enough to have trained with this Master will attest to his immense knowledge, insight and unfailing enthusiasm in our art. In his book, published decades ago, Master Nishiyama is telling us that in karate the basic laws of science are used to attain the maximum benefit by the correct application of a technique.

To help explain these fundamentals of physics and the way they apply to fighting techniques this book will start at first principles and progress through to the advanced application of the science. Most of what follows, viewed with the right perspective, is 'only' a technical explanation for what is experienced in real life.

Why should a martial artist want to study the underlying scientific principles that underpin, explain and quantify the effectiveness of fighting techniques? The reasons are numerous and the following five suggestions are only a start; different people will have different focal points:

1. Knowledge of the related scientific principles provides a true understanding of the reasons why a technique should be performed or implemented a certain way.

2. Understanding the 'why' helps enormously with the study and improvement of the methods employed. This then assists with personal practice and the instruction of others.

3. With an understanding and proper application of science we can further develop and improve our art. Understanding is crucial to future development and progress.

4. The understanding of science will assist in the critical examination of all techniques, including any new innovations that may be promoted.

5. We are at a point where technology can be more easily used to measure the effectiveness of technique and thereby provide impartial judgment. Instructors may soon be able to start numerically measuring their student's abilities and progress.

And yet . . .

The martial arts allow a path of self-awareness where neither fighting ability nor technique is the ultimate goal. This path to self-awareness needs more than an understanding of the history of the chosen art or the study and practice of technique and forms - and it is certainly not restricted to fighting ability. This book is not intended to be a guide to an esoteric goal; it does not enter into philosophical discussion that may help a martial artist that is seeking to achieve the perfection of character. This book merely wants the readers to be better equipped to be able to understand their training and techniques.

Summary

Understanding the scientific principles that underpin the martial arts can provide an insight into the reasons why we practice and apply techniques in a particular way. This can help fighters to fight, instructors to teach and advanced students to work things out for themselves. A lack of understanding of the theory and physical laws can cause difficulties for even the best instructors when trying to explain why a kick or punch is done a certain way. The use of 'loose' or inaccurate terminology by an instructor can cause a student to become confused. Many martial arts students are science graduates for whom force, power and energy are three completely different yet interconnected and well defined terms. An instructor may understand on a physiological level why a technique has to be done a particular way but can have difficulty putting that insight into words. Yet such instructors will typically strive to be accurate with both their strikes and their words.

This book explains the basic laws of physics and how they relate to the martial arts. It provides a summary of some of the key available data, including numerical values of the speed and force of kicks and punches. Chapters are devoted to the study of how to strike with maximum force, the penetration and timing of strikes, the determination of the energy needed to break boards, the pros and cons of different stances - and more. All this is aimed at promoting a true understanding of our art and helping people explain or even quantify some of the more subjective 'feelings' that they may have experienced in training or fighting.

Don't worry about the math—just look at what's being told at a fundamental level.

CHAPTER 1:   HOW HARD CAN WE HIT?

'When two tigers fight one is certain to be maimed and one to die'
Master Funakoshi

1.1   Introduction

Many years ago I was asked how hard an expert fighter could hit; what would be the force felt from such a punch or kick? Having been trained as an engineer it bothered me that I did not have a numerical answer. I couldn't easily turn to a report that reliably showed what specific level of energy or force a human can hit with. There are references such as the Guinness Book of Records that can show how fast Olympians can run or high they can jump but answering the simple question "What force can an expert martial artist generate?" proved more difficult than I expected. That basic question, more than anything else, prompted the production of this book.

In future chapters we will be looking at the physics—the mechanics—of the forces involved in various strikes and discussing how we might improve a technique for maximum effectiveness. In the first instance however let us simply ask the question "how hard can we hit?" and review several studies that attempted to measure the force of a strike; to see the level of agreement amongst them. The amount of published material that's relevant is now growing and a review of this accessible data reveals a great deal. What follows in this chapter is a summary analysis of numerical data contained in a selection of reported studies. This analysis tries to provide answers to the questions of how fast or forceful a weaponless fighter can strike, or the difference between a punch and a kick. These quantifications and comparisons can help us to assess techniques that have developed from age-old principles and the life works of past masters. In the end only numerical evidence, reliably collected under controlled conditions, will objectively answer the most basic questions such as how hard can we punch or which is the more powerful technique; for accurate measurements help remove subjectivity.

Serious fighters will want to know if the techniques they are being taught are fundamentally the same as those that have been shown to achieve maximum effect. Knowing which techniques can create a maximum force, plus a few of the related physical laws, can help supplement our understanding of our art.

Most of us that train in the art of fighting will not get very close to the maximum achievable strike force—and really don't care. We just want to know that we are striking as hard as we personally can. Aiming to achieve a maximum recorded force is not a sustainable reason to train in the martial arts, just as millions of runners in this world have no ambition to compete in the next Olympics; they simply run because it makes their lives better.

1.2   Lies, Damn Lies and Statistics

One or two words of caution are appropriate, about matters that are all too often neglected. The first warning is associated with the principles of statistics and the concept of representative samples. For results obtained from a limited number (or sample) of subjects to be truly indicative of a much bigger population the sample used has to be large enough to be representative. There are statistical tests that show how large the sample needs to be to ensure that the results are reasonably accurate. It is unfortunate that in so many walks of life there are examples where these tests are not always rigorously applied, for instance by those that may be in marketing or even politics. In our own field all too often you see or hear about a comparison or competition between (say) a karate practitioner and a Tae Kwon Do expert being held up as indicative of a fundamental difference in the effectiveness of the two styles. This is simply statistical nonsense.

Imagine comparing one white cat with one gray cat and finding that the gray cat can run faster and then suggesting that this indicates that all gray cats can run faster than white. What nonsense! Questions such as each cat's age, condition, health, history of accidents and so on are all relevant. It is only by a study of a very large population of each type of cat that an appropriate hypothesis could be tested and conclusions drawn. If that was successful and we did show, statistically, that on average a gray cat can run faster than a white one, what then? Shouldn't someone ask what is it that causes one type of cat to run faster than another? And here we may get into the business of correlation, causality and hypothesis testing. An illustration of such a questioning approach may be along the following lines: By measurement we have shown that one set of students, from the style of Gray Cat Do, can punch faster than a set of students from the style of White Cat Do. We have analyzed the measurement data and know that it is statistically valid and does indeed show a significant difference in speed. We may now have to design an experiment to test the hypothesis that the uniquely Gray Cat practice of licking the fist before punching makes the strike faster.

So beware of any report that starts out by stating something like 'we tested this 2nd Dan against this 5th Kyu and the results showed . . . ' Such results, alone, are only indicative of the specific comparison between the actual two people, who may be of vastly different ages, condition, body type or even gender. The results alone provide no reliable indicator of a general comparative nature between the majority of 2nd Dan and 5th Kyu karateka. I know of no experiment that provides reliable, statistically significant and replicable results from a comparison of major styles of the martial arts. If such a scientific experiment were to be conducted then it would need to be designed carefully. The population tested, to be representative, would need to be very large. This is obvious; imagine comparing the members of two clubs, one Tae Kwon Do and the other Karate. Assume now that the results showed that Club A is better than Club B at front snap kick. Does this prove a general difference in standard between taekwondo and karate on this technique? Or does it more accurately reflect the difference in the specific capability, attributes and preferences of the instructor and students tested? Or does it reflect the fact one club has been established longer and has more advanced students? Or that one club practices that specific kick every lesson because it was their founder's favorite? And so on.

The second warning is that people are only human and those involved with tests can allow bias to unwittingly creep into test results. This is usually completely unintentional but if someone is expecting a particular result then they are already biased and tend to attribute a debatable observation as supporting their expectation: They give the 'close call' to their bias. A disinterested observer, on the other hand, may see things differently. This is one reason why medical tests use 'blind' and 'double-blind' routines, where neither the subject nor the observer are aware of the test details—such as which patient is receiving medication rather than a placebo.

My final warning comes from spending so much time examining the existing data on the martial arts. Certain measurements are relatively straightforward and therefore can be more easily accepted as accurate and precise. In these cases measuring the same type of variable somewhere else with different people and equipment should provide similar comparable results; within an acceptable tolerance. In other words the measurement is repeatable. We are all familiar with this concept; we trust the speedometer of the car we drive, even when it is a new or different vehicle being driven on different roads. However some measurements are not so straightforward and are therefore prone to error and misinterpretation. One such example is the determination of force and some of the technical papers that record these numerical data are unclear on the applied methods of force measurement. Force may be quoted without qualifying if it is average or peak, or it may be unclear if it is measured or calculated. In some instances a comparison of quoted forces can give unreliable results and cause suspicion over the methods of measurement of one experiment compared to another. Measurement of force requires sophisticated equipment and set up. By comparison measurement of speed is relatively straightforward and the more recently available, experimentally derived, velocity data is reasonably consistent. For these reasons the following review of available data mainly quotes force quantities that appear to be reliable; looking for supportive evidence that provides confidence in the results quoted. This means that some of the other, previously published, force data is not repeated here.

1.3   *'Fight Science'*: One of the Best Experiments So Far?

As indicated above, even within the strictest of scientific fields reports can be produced that lack clarity and prompt unanswered questions: A paper may quote a force but not specify if that force is peak or average; measured or mathematically determined. It may compare two fighters of differing styles but the individual participant's details, such as weight, may not be quoted; yet we know that a well trained heavyweight can usually punch 'heavier' and more forceful than a lightweight. Hence the comparison of results between one fighter and another can be difficult.

So much more value could be gained by being present during the tests and thereby being able to see and get a feel for the comparative order of forces achieved. Watching a test being conducted can be so useful to an experienced martial artist. For example, being able to see from where (or how far back) a punch was launched can be insightful to a fighter who has 'an eye' for such detail—whereas with only words on paper a written report is limited.

That is one reason why I consider the television special **Fight Science** to be of particular importance. This feature first aired in America on television's National Geographic Channel in August 2006. In this program researchers can be seen using advanced technology and biomechanical concepts to compare different methods of punching and kicking. This high technology equipment included the following:

- A $150,000 US Government certified crash test dummy with the following modifications:
    - Additional sensors were installed in the dummy.
    - Load cell sensors were placed in the upper neck, lower neck, chest, and knee.
    - A potentiometer was placed in the chest of the dummy, to measure the displacement of the chest cavity caused by a strike.
- Thirty two (32) infrared motion cameras.
- Three (3) high definition cameras.
- Three (3) ultra-high-speed cameras.
- Reflective markers fitted to the fighters.
- Sensors in the shoes of the fighters.

This equipment, electronics and software allowed the scientists to measure the speeds and forces of different fighters. The researchers mapped out the fighters range and movements and created three dimensional models of their bodies in motion. This was then used to produce animations of the fighters' movements—showing computer graphic displays of bone, muscle, tissue and tendons. This allowed video to be generated that gives an insight into how and from where the body generates its force and energy. (It should be no surprise that the program shows how important pushing against the floor is in generating power.)

This is a program to watch and watch again. The practitioners used in the tests are real and an expert observer will generally be able to tell which technique is more effective before even looking at the numerical data. The results match our own experiences and general 'common sense' types of conclusions. The following sections draw upon some of these findings.

1.4   How Hard Can We Punch?

1.4.1   'Fight Science' - First Set Up

In the *Fight Science* experimental setup described above a primary aim was to determine which of four fighters could punch and deliver the most force. The participants were experts from each of the following backgrounds or styles: Boxing, Tae Kwon Do, Karate and Kung Fu. Each was invited to hit a crash test dummy as hard as they could. Unfortunately, the physical details of these participants—specifically their weight—are not quoted. It is however visually clear that the Wushu (Chinese-style) expert was a lot lighter than the others. This is important when recognizing that although this individual has extremely fast hand speed the others all punched with significantly more force. A trained heavyweight hits hard, very hard. A comparatively well trained lightweight may be able to hit faster and more often but with a single strike more trained muscle can cause more damage. In other words, *bulk does count*.

Fight Science Results:

Style	Punching Force		
	lbs force	*kg force*	*Newtons*
Boxing	993	450	4417
Tae Kwon Do	917	416	4079
Karate	816	370	3630
Kung Fu	612	278	2722

These numbers show the force differences between the fighters, not the fighting styles.

As can be seen, in the lead is a boxer with approximately 1,000 pounds of impact force (450 kilograms force or 4,400 Newtons). This is a massive punch! According to the program, the sensors revealed that the punch started in the feet pushing against the floor and traveling up the legs through the hips to the chest and shoulders—gaining energy as it passed up the body.

1.4.2   'Fight Science' - Second Set Up

Subsequently, the National Geographical setup tested a mixed martial-artist fighter, namely former Heavyweight Champion Bas Rutten, a 5th Degree in Kyokushin Karate, and a 2nd Degree in Tae Kwon Do. With apparently similar equipment and test set up, Rutten's measured force from a punch was an impressive 941 pounds force (4186 Newtons). This is only 5 percent lower than the boxer referenced; a difference that has no statistically significant difference. We should therefore conclude that there is nothing significantly discriminating about the style/background shown here and that the best in Boxing, Tae Kwon Do, Karate and the full spectrum of Martial Arts or Mixed Martial Arts (MMA) can all hit really hard.

Facts for Fighters

A human can punch and cause over 4,000 Newtons of peak force.

This is equivalent to being hit on the head with a 12 pound mallet swung at 20 mph!

It was pointed out earlier that one of the positive things about these tests is that they were recorded and are currently available to watch via the internet. Looking at the Heavyweight boxer and MMA fighter it is clear that these punches are 'reverse' in style (as opposed to jabs) which is what you would expect, and that the punch or fist does not originate at the hip. In other words the fighters each stood in an easy free style stance with the left leg and hand forward, allowing the right handed punch to start from somewhere around the right pectoral or chest muscle. Furthermore, there was virtually no 'pull back' of the opposite hand—the left hand did not pull back towards the left hip or shoulder. Breaking down the way that the Mixed Martial Artist punched shows the following:

a) The fighter started with the left side forward, as though he had just delivered a left jab or the left hand has 'sighted' the target. Hence the upper body is turned 'side on' with the right shoulder back and right fist at about chest height. The punch did not start from the hip.

b) The fighter then exploded from the floor, up and through the body, allowing the upper body to drive the fist out towards the target.

c) On delivery everything—the whole body—seemed to be intent on hitting the target. The arm starts to straighten out and the fist strikes and tries to go into the head of the dummy. The body at this stage is twisted into the target, so that the right side is now foremost, the back leg has straightened and the heel is up—everything is driving into the punch.

The boxer in the first *Fight Science* set-up delivered his punch in a similar manner, but had a slightly more relaxed style with a little less follow through of the punch into and beyond the dummy's head.

1.4.3   *Verification of the Punching Force Results*

Several years ago the starting point for me writing this book was a very simple question: How hard can we punch? The more research I did the more dissatisfied I became with the range of numerical answers seen in the literature. It was therefore particularly pleasing to see the program that's described above. True to scientific reasoning, what was then needed was verification of the figures that *Fight Science* had measured. It was considered essential to find a completely independent well-conducted study that produced results which aligned with the figures recorded by the crash test dummy experimenters. This is the way of science: looking for independent confirmation, within reasonable experimental limits, of results obtained. Independent confirmation provides confidence in the measurement process, techniques and instrumentation applied.

Research revealed an excellent paper by Smith et al (2000) reporting on work that was sponsored by the UK Sports Council as a joint venture between University College Chichester (UK) and the Amateur Boxing Association of England. Results were obtained using a sport specific (boxing) dynamometer comparing the maximal punching force of seven elite, eight intermediate and eight novice male UK boxers. The elite team was composed of England's 1996 European Championship team and the results were as follows:

Punching Force *Newtons*	Training Level					
	Elite (n=7)		Intermediate (n=8)		Novice (n=8)	
	Rear	*Lead*	*Rear*	*Lead*	*Rear*	*Lead*
Peak Force (N)	4800	2847	3722	2283	2381	1604
+/- limits (N)	227	225	133	125	116	97

The results show that for the elite boxers the maximum force was recorded with a rear (reverse) type of straight punch, and that this force (on average) was 4800 Newtons plus or minus (+/-) 227 Newtons. Hence we have a force of between *4600 to 5000 Newtons* as measured using a completely different set-up, experimenters and participants to those employed in the *Fight Science* investigation. This elite boxing data set compares favorably with the force determined in the *Fight Science* studies of around 4,400 Newtons.

And why the difference—can these elite boxers really hit harder than the other fighters? We don't know! We don't know because they were not measured on exactly the same test rig. They used different gloves and struck different targets that had different characteristics that resulted in different impulse force curves and therefore different peak forces were recorded by different instruments. Yet... the results are close. Close enough for me at least to have confidence that a human can punch and cause over 4,000 Newtons, or about 900 pounds force. An astonishing figure.

The other interesting feature of these results is that the lead hand punch was measured at around 60% of the force of the rear hand punch. The paper referenced, by Smith et. al., comments that *"Such a difference between the forces produced by the rear and the lead hands may be related to the forces generated by the legs, body rotation and the distance over which the long range straight rear punch is thrown."* Now where have we heard that before? More on this later.

1.4.4　　　The Peak Force of a Punch? – Other Results

1　Frank Bruno:

Frank Bruno, the 1995 WBC heavyweight champion boxer, was measured to have a peak impact force of over 4000 Newtons (Atha et al, 1985); with an impact velocity of 8.9 m/s and the peak force attained within 14 milliseconds of contact. The punching time, from start to impact, was approximately 100 milliseconds or 0.1 second.

2　Ricky Hatton:

In 2007, one time WBA Welterweight Champion Ricky Hatton, was measured as having almost a 3,900 Newtons peak impact force right hand punch. This study was conducted at England's University of Manchester, School of Mechanical, Aerospace and Civil Engineering (MACE); where sensors were reported to have been attached to a 30kg (66lb) punch bag wired up to a laptop containing software to measure and analyze the data.

3　Professional Boxing Matches:

A study by Pierce et al (2006) measured the actual forces associated with punches during six professional boxing matches. This showed a number of punches with a maximal punch force of over 3,500 Newtons and just two punches of over 5,000 Newtons force. This was within a professional fight and therefore the target was not a fixed, inanimate, object. The very high punch forces could therefore have been influenced by the opponent moving into the strike and being caught with perfect timing. The study showed that the majority of punches delivered were around the 1,000 N level—significantly lower than can be achieved in ideal test conditions. This is because a fight in the ring is dynamic in nature and the opponent does not normally stay still and just allow the punch to strike.

4   What about the Ladies? Lucia Rijker:

Lucia Rijker, a former (undefeated) Welterweight Champion boxer was measured in a *"Sport Science"* program to punch with around 4000 Newtons (approximately 900 pounds of force). This is from a lady of 5 foot 6 inches (167 cm) height and 140 pounds (63 kg) weight. Again, this is available to view on the internet and although the measurement details are not elaborated upon, watching the body mechanics and dynamics of Lucia is very impressive, particularly the hip action. The way in which this fighter transmits speed and power through to the fist is extremely efficient. The hand speed achieved is reported to be 36 feet per second, or just less than 11 meters per second.

1.4.5   Other References

1   Feld, McNair and Wilks:

An exceptional source of data and insight was provided in an article by Feld et al published in Scientific American in 1979. Although only a few subjects were studied the article is still very relevant and worth reading, despite its age. It determined that it takes around 2000 Newtons to break a 'typical concrete slab' and since these slabs are being broken regularly we know that a reasonable martial artist can deliver over 2000 Newtons of force with hand strikes.

2   Pieter & Pieter:

A paper by Pieter and Pieter (1995) reports on the study of members of the 1988 US Olympics Taekwondo teams undertaking a variety of kicking and punching techniques. The forces reported in this work are only quoted as average or mean forces, not peak. In my view, the results are therefore of more use in a comparative rather than an absolute value manner. The following table summarizes the ranking of the techniques in descending order of force (highest first).

Technique	Male Forces Ranking/Order		Female Forces Ranking/Order	
	Right Side	*Left Side*	*Right Side*	*Left Side*
Spinning back kick	First	First	First	First
Reverse punch	Second	Third	Fourth	Fourth
Round kick	Third	Second	Third	Second
Side thrust kick	Fourth	Fourth	Second	Third

Assuming the same set up was used we can compare the male results to female, the right to left side techniques and the force of a kick to a punch.

1.4.6   Summary Conclusion: How Hard Can We Punch?

Facts for Fighters
Results show that for elite fighters the maximum peak force recorded with a rear (reverse type) of straight punch was between 4600 and 5000 Newtons or around 1,000 pounds force!

Clearly there will be those that will exceed this standard and others that can only aspire to the challenge.

1.5   The Most Force From a Kick?

1.5.1   'Fight Science' Results

The *Fight Science* experimental set up referenced in section 1.4.1 was used with three of the participants kicking the same car test dummy. These kicking results were as follows:

Style (Type of Kick)	Kicking Force		
	lbs force	*kg force*	*Newtons*
Tae Kwon Do (Spinning Back Kick)	1572	713	6992
Karate (Side Thrust Kick)	1023	464	4550
Kung Fu (Flying Kick)	981	445	4363

Over 1,500 pounds of impact force (~7,000 Newtons) was delivered by a spinning back kick! This is a lot of force. If you get a chance watch these demonstrations; the spinning back and side-thrust kicks are a positive pleasure to watch.

1.5.2   Comparison of Kicking and Punching Power

With such a small sample we have to be careful with any conclusions but it is interesting to note how this 'Fight Science' study shows that each individual's best kick can be 25 to 70 percent more forceful than his best punch. A kick being more forceful than a punch makes intuitive sense. An experienced fighter can relate to this—it's the kind of 'feel' you get from striking a bag and seeing the effects for yourself when comparing a punch to (say) a good back kick. Section 8.10 of this book delves into this subject a little deeper.

Style	Force of punch	Force of kick	Percentage difference
Tae Kwon Do	4079N (917lbs f)	6992N (1572lbs f)	70
Karate	3630N (816lbs f)	4550N (1023lbs f)	25
Kung Fu	2722N (612lbs f)	4363N (981lbs f)	60

1.5.3   Force of a Kick – Other Results

Forces in general, including the peak forces of kicks, are not particularly well documented. Some studies measure the force but are not clear if it is the average or maximum force that is being recorded. Some studies measure the speed of the kick and then determine, rather than measure, the force of the strike. Such a determination assumes the mass behind the strike and the contact time of the strike—which are prone to error. The *Fight Science* results referenced earlier recorded a top measurement of over 1,500 pounds of impact force (6,992 Newtons) being delivered by a spinning back kick. That's the highest force I have found (so far) within reputable references. A paper of the late 1990's by Professor Hitoshi Ohmichi of the International Budo University provided numerical results from systematic experimentation. In this paper entitled 'The Body's Centre of Gravity in Budo: Science from the Biomechanical View', Professor Ohmichi describes how he set out to compare the kicking and punching abilities of several practitioners of the martial arts and quotes a peak force with a front kick of a 3rd Dan karateka at around 950 pounds force (4200 Newtons).

1.6   The Most Force From Any Single Technique?

The *Fight Science* program declared that a knee strike to the chest was a most forceful and damaging technique. Delivered by a former two-time Muay Thai world champion, this knee to the chest at close quarters resulted in a chest compression of around five centimeters or almost two inches — as measured by the chest displacement sensor. The program noted that this was the equivalent of a thirty five mile per hour (56 km/hr) car crash — and a car test dummy should know! Like the punch previously described, the energy from this strike was shown to start from the floor and move up to the knee. The blow was delivered to the soft tissue below the rib cage while the fighter held and pulled down the opponent's head. Disappointingly, the actual force was not quoted; which I assume is because it was not measured. Perhaps there were insufficient sensors within the chest of the dummy and the TV program had the integrity not to quote a figure that was inconsistently derived, when compared with the other forces impacted to the head strikes. (Even so, the experimental designer could have arranged to measure the forces of a knee strike to the head, but I complain only because this experimental set-up was otherwise so very good.)

And then:

Subsequently the technical team asked Mixed Martial Artist fighter Bas Rutten to kick the same type of dummy, in the same chest area. He did so using a roundhouse type of kick and striking the dummy's chest with his tibia or shin. The result was a deflection of 67 millimeters, or over 2.6 inches — more than the Muay Thai demonstration referenced earlier. Try searching the web (e.g. under National Geographic or YouTube) to view this: I would recommend watching the act in slow motion to get a true appreciation of the potential damage to an opponent.

And then:

In a related manner, the program *Sport Science* reported on the determination of the force required to break two different types of baseball bats, one of ash and the other of a harder, maple, wood. This was determined to be approximately 740 and 790 pounds of force respectively. The measured force of the roundhouse kicks of Muay Thai master, Melchor Menor, was measured as between 740 and 1000 lbs and he did break each of the two bats. It is therefore reasonable to assume that his roundhouse kick, when breaking a baseball bat, is capable of a force impact in excess of 800 pounds force or about 3560 Newtons.

1.7   Hand Speed – How Fast Can We Punch?

In the *Fight Science* program the experimenters measured the speed of the subjects using an accelerometer. The hand striking speed of a Wushu (Kung Fu style) practitioner was shown to be 12.2 meters per second or over 40 feet per second. This is entirely consistent with other data referenced in this book. The producers of the program were keen to point out that this is about four times faster than a snake can strike, which averages at around three meters per second. There are other studies and references, for the recent *Fight Science* program was not the first to examine the speed of a punch and nor will it be the last. For completeness let us look briefly at some of these and see what can be concluded.

1   Pieter & Pieter:

The Pieter and Pieter (1995) study of members of the 1988 US Olympics Taekwondo teams undertaking a variety of techniques included measurements of velocity. In summary the results showed that the mean (or average) male subject's reverse-punch speed was measured at approximately 11 meters per second and the female mean was approximately 9 m/s.

2   Stull & Barnham:

In 1988 studies undertaken by Stull and Barnham obtained kinematic data, analyzed the movement patterns, and provided an analysis of the work and power produced by different martial arts styles in the application of a reverse punch whilst in front stance. In terms of similarities, rather than differences, it can be noted that the velocity of strike (wrist speed) achieved by all practitioners ranged from 7 to 10 meters per second, which is about a 30% difference from slowest to fastest.

3   W.C. Whiting

Other studies by Whiting et al (1988) have demonstrated that the peak speed of a boxer's punch reached up to 12.5 meters per second, with an average velocity on contact range of 5.9 to 8.2 m/s. Note that this range covers a variety of punches being thrown at a practice bag.

4   Feld, McNair and Wilks

With hand strike speeds measured via photography and strobe light flashing at 60 or 120 cycles per second, the 1979 article by Feld et. al. provides evidence that:

A beginner's "karate chop" speed = 6 meters / second or 20 feet / second

An advanced "karate chop" speed = 14 meters / second or 46 feet / second

Note that this 14 m/s hand speed result is considerably higher than the 10 m/s punching speeds referenced elsewhere in this chapter but these are techniques where the hand arcs downward to the target and follows a completely different trajectory to that of a punch. The Scientific American article provides a useful listing of peak speeds of other karate techniques, as follows:

Hand Maneuver	Peak Speed (Meters / Second)
Front Forward Punch	5.7 – 9.8
Downward Hammer-Fist Strike	10 – 14
Downward Knife-Hand Strike	10 – 14

1.7.1 Summary conclusion: How Fast Can We Punch?

The fastest speed for a stationary, rather than stepping, punch is around 12 meters per second. Expert downward strikes can be faster with an upper speed of around 14 meters per second. Clearly there are those that can exceed this standard and others that can only aspire to the challenge.

Facts for Fighters

A highly trained and skilled martial artist should aspire to a reverse punch of around 10m/s.

1.8   Foot Speed – How Fast Can We Kick?

(A) Pearson: Roundhouse Kick

A trawl of the internet will find some extensive work by a Jake N. Pearson (1997) as published in his Bachelor of Physical Education Honors degree dissertation entitled "Kinematics and Kinetics of the Tae Kwon Do Turning Kick".

Speed

The highest (toe) speed at 16m/s was achieved by a 22-year-old subject with ten years experience and a weight of 72kg. The second highest (toe) speed at 15.7m/s was achieved by a 32-year-old subject with ten years experience and mass of 69kg. The third highest (toe) speed at 15.6 m/s was achieved by a 27-year-old subject with six years experience and weight of 62kg. Note that all these speeds are fairly close.

Velocity profile of the kick

The work by Pearson also records the measurement of the linear and angular velocities of the kicking leg joints. The graphical plots produced by Pearson shows the average linear velocity of the toe, knee and hip, from commencement of the kick (0%) to the point of impact (100%). Although most indicators on these curves are reasonably predictable, a particularly striking feature is the virtual straight-line relationship between the velocity of the striking foot and the distance traveled. The foot speed just keeps on getting faster and faster—at an almost linear acceleration—from floor to target. The body of a martial artist has found a way of near perfect efficiency: a truly remarkable feat. Note also that the work done by Pearson shows that the hip has the  highest initial speed, followed by the knee and then the foot. This indicates the way in which the kick is performed, with the body leading the transfer of momentum through to the thigh of the leg with the lower leg waiting to 'take over' as the knee almost reaches alignment with the target. This is a near perfect sequential transfer. It is akin to an athlete throwing a javelin, where the body and limbs lead and are ahead of the throwing arm, with a transfer of momentum through to the arm, hand and then spear.

Chapter 8, section 8.9, reproduces the round house kick velocity profile referenced above.

(B)   Serina and Lieu: Roundhouse, side thrust and back thrust kicks

A paper by Serina and Lieu, published in 1991, reports on the results attained using three male black belt competitors from the University of California, Berkeley, Taekwondo Club to examine the dynamics and effects of roundhouse, side-thrust and back-thrust kicks. The authors developed mathematical models to simulate the motion and kinematics of thrust and 'swing' (including roundhouse) kicks. These models were used to predict the probability of serious injury due to thoracic (the twelve vertebrae in the middle section of the backbone) compression. A selected summary of the results follows.

On foot speed:

- The roundhouse or swing kicks possessed greater foot velocities than the thrust kicks.
- The average velocity of the roundhouse kicks, at about 16m/s was 80% greater than the average foot velocity of the thrust kicks— at approximately 9 m/s.

On energy content:

- The leg 'energy content' was greater for the thrust kicks than the round kicks. This additional energy was generated by using the entire leg instead of the lower leg and foot. The greater effective leg mass of the thrust kicks contributed to this difference.

On contact time:

- With a roundhouse type of kick a high-speed video observation of impact against a chest protector showed the duration of contact between the foot and the target to be typically less than 10 milliseconds (0.01 second).

On chest injury:

> **Facts for Fighters:**
>
> On a side thrust kick the effective mass increases as the leg *extends* and greater mechanical advantage is available.
>
> Hence, for maximum effectiveness: hit the target at the point in the kick that is about six inches (15 cm) from full extension of the leg.

- Swing or round kicks are faster and have a greater potential for soft tissue damage.
- Thrust kicks can generate larger chest compressions and thus may have more potential for skeletal injury than swing kicks.
- There is a significant probability of serious injury with all kicks, with thoracic deflections from 3 to 5 cm, when no protective body equipment is used. [This aligns with the *Fight Science* results quoted earlier; where a round house kick caused 6.7 cm deflection of a test crash dummy chest. See section 1.6]

(C)   Pieter and Pieter: Roundhouse, side thrust and back thrust kicks

Pieter and Pieter (1995) reported on the study of members of the 1988 US Olympics Taekwondo teams undertaking a variety of kicking and punching techniques.

In summary the results showed that:

- Of the techniques tested the highest speed attained was for the roundhouse kick, with males achieving around 16 m/sec and females around 13.5 m/sec.
- The most forceful kick for both men and women was the spinning back kick.

In descending order the speeds achieved are as follows, the units are meters per second:

Technique	Male Speed m/s (mean and approximated)	Female Speed m/s (mean and approximated)
Round kick	16	13
Reverse punch	11	9
Spinning back kick	9	7
Side thrust kick	7	6

(D)   Feld, McNair and Wilks: Roundhouse, front kick, and side thrust kicks

Feld et al (1979) provided data on the measured peak speeds of a number of kicks, punches and strikes. This work was accomplished with relatively few subjects and is therefore not to be considered as representative of a more general population. However, it is interesting to compare these figures with those quoted in the other articles referenced in this book. For example the peak roundhouse kick speed of an advanced karate exponent of 1979 at 11m/s compares with a USA Olympian Taekwondo expert of 1988 of 16m/s; whereas the same comparison with the side kick is 14m/s compared with 7m/s for the 1988 US team. Perhaps this Olympian team concentrated on competition winning techniques and favored roundhouse over a side thrust kick?

Maneuver	Peak Speed (Meters / Second)
Front Forward Punch	6 – 10
Downward Hammer-Fist Strike	10 – 14
Downward Knife-Hand Strike	10 – 14
Roundhouse Kick	9.5 – 11
Wheel Kick	7 – 10
Front Kick	10 – 14
Side Kick	10 – 14

1.8.1   Summary Conclusion: How fast can we kick?

With reasonable consistency the roundhouse kick emerges as the highest striking velocity, at around 16 meters per second. The other kicks have a maximum reported velocity of up to around 14 meters per second, significantly less in some studies.

1.9 Speed Summary From Another Reference

The Textbook of Karate by Okazaki and Stricevic is a classic text that sits on many a martial artist's bookshelf, particularly those belonging to serious Karate students. This is rightly so as Master Okazaki is known throughout the world for his Shotokan skill and dedication. Perhaps less well known is that Milorad V. Stricevic, along with other co-authors published a book in 1989 entitled *Modern Karate*. Together with a wide range of technical material related to techniques, tactics and training this book contains speed measurement data. A summary tabulation of their work is reproduced below. It can be seen that their results are in good agreement with the other results reported in this book. One exception is the speed of the roundhouse kick, quoted as 9 to 12 meters per second. This is a very similar range to that measured by Feld et al but lower than that reported by either Pieter & Pieter or Pearson, where both sources gave a higher figure of up to 16 meters per second.

Summary speed results from 'Modern Karate'; reference by Stricevic et al (1989)		
Category	**Technique**	**Speed (m/s)**
Punching Techniques	*Straight Punch*	5.5 to 10
	Short Punch	6 to 11
	Vertical Punch	8 to 11
Striking Techniques	*Downward Hammer-fist Strike*	10.5 to 14.4
	Downward Sword-hand Strike	10 to 15
Kicking Techniques	*Front Kick*	10 to 15
	Roundhouse Kick	9 to 12
	Side Kick	10 to 15

1.10 'Do It Yourself' Experiments, Tests and Trials

All senior instructors have an obligation to use practical illustrations to demonstrate the degree of effectiveness of techniques and the progress being achieved by the students. Some of the martial arts are taught in a theoretical way, for we cannot easily and safely prove by demonstration a debilitating or disabling blow and hence that efficacy may need to be taken on trust. The use of demonstrative tests is useful in allowing students to gain personal experience that indicates in a tactile sense the effect of various techniques.

A question of the type 'how hard can I hit?' can be answered in a relative manner, rather than having to use an 'absolute' or accurately measured approach. Producing an absolute answer, with numeric values, tends to require expensive equipment, particularly if trying to determine force values. In this present era of accessible digital cameras with video and computer software to examine, image by image, time stamped video frames it is not that difficult to measure the speed of a punch displayed against a calibrated set of distance markers. However, force transducers are needed for a student to be accurately informed that they can now hit a target with 'this much' force and assess if that is a measured improvement from (say) six months previously.

A relative answer, however, is often reasonably easy to provide without the need for expensive equipment. Asking one student to hold a target pad while another strikes with, say, a thrust kick allows insight into effectiveness. The sound that the kick makes on the target, the displacement seen, the force felt by the student holding the target are all useful indicators. The training partner holding the pad can talk to the person kicking, telling them how it felt and whether the kick had penetration or was just superficial. Comparisons can be made, using these indicators, between two or more fighters using the same techniques, or between two or more ways of performing a technique. We do this for ourselves when using a punch bag—continuously judging our performance and abilities by the feedback provided by the bag. We take note of the reactive forces, the sounds made, the indentation and bag swing seen, the level of force felt on the knuckles when punching.

Shotokan Karate Magazine (SKM) occasionally reports on studies undertaken by senior instructors with the objective of testing a particular view or hypothesis. As examples:

- Issue 77 in October 2003 carried an article by John Cheetham entitled "The Proof of the Pudding". This looked at results from performing both (a) *uraken* (back-fist strike) and (b) *gyaku zuki* (reverse punch) in two different ways. No calibrated, hi-tech measurement instrumentation was used, the results gathered were simply based on what was heard, seen and felt. Where there was a significant difference in impact, then that difference could be 'felt'.

- SKM issue 80 in July 2004 carried an article by Tony Terranova entitled "We Are What We Experience, Not What We Learn". This reported on how the forces seen and felt on a kick shield target pad had been used to show the effectiveness of different ways of performing roundhouse kicks.

- SKM issue 81 in October 2004 carried an article by Bill Burgar entitled "Does the front leg really pull?" This article describes a couple of experiments to enable students to see for themselves how little the front leg (only) can pull a karateka forward when in forward stance and the effect of relaxation of the front leg and knee.

- SKM issue 82 in January 2005 carried an article by John Cheetham entitled "The Power of Kage Zuki". This study looked at the differences in perceived power from the application of *kage zuki* (hook punch), starting from horse stance, compared with reverse punch in forward stance. The same article looks at the different perceived results based on the way in which *kage zuki* was performed – with variations of hip movement and 'snap-back'.

These studies used simple equipment, such as target pads, to provide feedback and allow a comparative perception to be formed of effectiveness of technique. Although subjective, such practical feedback is of value to all martial artists, at all grades. A student hitting a bag can see, hear and feel the efficacy of his or her techniques. That same student can notice the differences made by changes or corrections to technique. The regular use of punch bags or target training is recommended. Fighters need to hit things, that's all there is to it.

Final DIY example: I happen to have a cell phone with a timer. If I set it to 15 seconds and count the number of right hand back-fist strikes I can accomplish in that time the number is greater than 60. Hence the time taken to strike and return averages at around 0.25 seconds; so I can approximate that the time to strike (only) is about 0.125 seconds. If I measure the distance from my elbow to the closed fist as 15 inches or 0.38 meters, then the outward circumferential distance travelled is estimated at about 1.1 m and the average speed can calculated as about 8.5 m/s. The peak will be a lot higher— and that too can be estimated.

1.11 A Few Personal Comments

It may be useful to record a few comments related to this chapter and the remainder of the book: Firstly, when discussing the 'best', fastest or most forceful we tend to be thinking about the 'knock–out' blow: The single, disabling, strike that brings an end to a conflict. This is a classical 'one-strike' concept that is embedded in some of the traditional martial arts; the Japanese 'Ippon' principle that may have originated from swordsmanship. (One strike from a sword should be the end of the affair.) This one-strike concept may be what a person is aspiring towards within their chosen martial art. Others may be working more on the multiple strike approach to winning a contest. Most fighters will be doing both, knowing the value of being able to set up an opponent for the final blow yet still appreciating the physical and spiritual side of seeking the perfect strike. Remember that whenever this book discusses the 'best' of anything, perhaps looking at how a technique may be best accomplished, it is with latent recognition that there are alternative strategies to a 'single strike' approach.

Forgive me for a moment's digression: I came through a UK Shotokan apprenticeship as a member of the Karate Union of Great Britain (KUGB). As such I was encouraged to train with the KUGB and JKA Senior Instructors and although all were incredible teachers and inspirational martial artists I always particularly enjoyed being taught by Sensei Terry O'Neill. Some of his 'throw-away' lines of wisdom stay with me even today, such as: *"If someone grabs you, hit 'em! Then do the fancy stuff."* So often I see techniques being taught to combat grabs or holds that just could not be relied upon to work, unless you were to hit the opponent first. On one course Sensei O'Neill was teaching a partner drill where one strike followed another, which flowed into the next and then the next until the opponent was, frankly, devastated. His point, he explained, was to get into a mode of completely overwhelming the opponent. He paused for a moment to show that the first strike may be more than enough to finish the fight—by him delivering a controlled strike that could take out a baby rhino—and went on to say that this was good but you shouldn't assume that the one blow would be enough. His closing line was along the lines of *"Hit 'em loads of times and make 'em go down. You can always tell your mates later that you dropped 'em in one".* Terry was experienced, very experienced. He knew what survival in the street entailed.

Secondly, the 'best' values are usually attained in 'ideal' circumstances. When you ask a person to strike a crash test dummy to record the maximum force that can be delivered, or break more wooden boards than has previously been achieved, you allow them time and space. The crash test dummy doesn't bob and weave and try to evade or block the attack, the boards stay at the same distance and don't suddenly jump out of range. The point is that in a real fight fighters will very rarely be able to deliver their best.

An excellent study by Pierce et al (2006) measured the actual forces associated with punches during six professional boxing matches. These measurements showed that the vast majority of real 'in the ring' punch forces are substantially less than the maximum levels measured with professional boxers hitting inanimate, non-moving, targets.

Hence the report by Pierce et al notes: "Size and musculature may determine the force that can be delivered, but proper techniques of delivery and defense likely determine the force that is received." This observation is so important I recommend reading it again.

Finally, numerical values are often included for reference purposes, to indicate the 'best' values achievable and to allow comparisons that provide insight. From a traditional martial artist perspective we who study the art as a lifelong endeavor don't aim to be the very best and above all others; we simply aim to be the best that we can be. I am not as fast as I once was; age has an effect that no one escapes. Accepting the inevitable we can only ask are we now, right now, doing all that we should?

1.12   Summary

Punching Statistics:

- **Force:** The maximum peak force of the punch of an advanced martial artist has been measured at between **4500 to 5000 Newtons** (around 1000 pounds).

- **Speed:** With a standing reverse punch the maximum speed attained tends to be around **8 to 10 meters per second.** (Around 20 miles per hour.)

Kicking Statistics:

- **Force:** The peak force of a spinning back kick from an advanced martial artist has been measured at almost **7,000 Newtons** (more than 1,550 pounds force).

- **Speed:** With the more popular or classical kicks the range of speeds attained are as follows:

Maneuver	Peak Speed (Meters / Second)
Front Kick	10 – 14
Roundhouse Kick	13 – 16
Side Kick	9 – 14

Contact Duration:

- A hammer strike used to break a concrete slab had a measured contact time of 5 milliseconds or 0.005 seconds (Feld et al. 1979).

- A roundhouse kick striking a chest protector was measured by Serina and Lieu (1991) as having a contact time of 10 milliseconds (0.01 sec.).

- A roundhouse kick striking a water filled bag had an average measured contact time of approximately 100 milliseconds or 0.1 seconds. (J. Pearson, 1997) This reference noted that such contact duration time is an order of magnitude greater than that experienced when kicking a football, due to the elasticity of the ball compared with that of a water filled bag. (A football, when kicked, is designed to immediately respond as a projectile.)

- With a fast strike to the head the peak force has been measured as being attained within 14 milliseconds of contact, in this instance with an impact velocity of 8.9 m/s. (Atha et al, 1985).

Time Duration of the Striking Hand:

- As early as 1966, Master Nakayama was quoting measurements showing that a range of martial artists, of different styles, can complete a reverse punch in 200 milliseconds (0.2 seconds) or less.

- This is comparable to findings by Atha et al (1985) where the punching time of one time heavyweight boxing champion Frank Bruno, from start to impact, was measured as approximately 100 milliseconds.

- In the study by Feld et al (1979) a hammer-fist strike used to break a concrete slab was measured to have a hand travel duration of approximately 150 milliseconds or 0.15 seconds.

The laws of physics don't care if a martial arts master or an untrained amateur is delivering a punch, for such laws apply equally—being only interested in the properties of the strike and the characteristics of the target.

CHAPTER 2: THE LAWS OF PHYSICS

> 'The outcome of the fight all depends on the maneuver'
> *Master Funakoshi*

2.1   Introduction

This is a book of many parts, including a set of technical references. Most fighters are dynamic, active individuals that learn by putting the theory explained by their instructor to test. Lessons are not normally designed for the coach or instructor to talk for 45 minutes and then for the students to practice. Fighters are usually shown a technique and then asked to practice it; to gain an immediate understanding and feel for how to make it work. This is food for thought as you read through this and other chapters. There is no rule that says a reader has to wade through all the material in the order provided. Feel free to thumb through the contents, note what is covered, review what's of current interest and return to the detailed text when in need of a deeper understanding of the basics that are being applied in subsequent chapters.

Nevertheless, to gain an understanding of the fundamental scientific principles involved in our martial art we are eventually going to have to get through the basics. In physics, karate, taekwondo or life in general you have to be good at the basics before the advanced can be practiced properly. This chapter therefore provides useful definitions and descriptions of technical terms. All too often you can find yourself in a class where loose terminology is used. To paraphrase Lewis Carroll, from his famous book 'Alice in Wonderland', it is important to "say what you mean and mean what you say". In a pre-arranged type of attack it would be unacceptable to mistakenly name one target and then aim to strike another. Yet many people use terms such as energy, force and power almost interchangeably. Becoming better informed will help you to 'say what you mean and mean what you say'.

2.2   Mathematical Formulae—Have No Fear!

2.2.1   Mathematical Relationships

It has been said that any book that contains mathematical formulae will be ignored by the majority of readers. Stephen Hawkins' bestselling book *A Brief History of Time* deals with the most difficult of subjects and does so without using any equations other than Einstein's $E = mc^2$. Within the acknowledgments of that book Stephen Hawkins admits to having been influenced by the view that each equation in a book could halve the sales!

This book is aimed at another class of reader: Those that spend months or years working on a single technique, studying the minutest of detail in an effort to improve efficiency and effectiveness. These individuals should not be too fearful of a mathematical formula. They can work to see through it and allow it to reveal its value, truth and beauty.

Mathematical equations are used to describe a relationship between two or more variables— such as pressure, force and area; or speed, distance and time. In most instances the value or insight that the equation contains is reasonably clear. Clarity is often helped by looking at equations with a 'simple mind' that asks what does this tell us? If I increase this variable, this value or number, what happens? If I decrease this number what is the effect?

Let's start with a relationship that we are familiar with: Most of us can easily determine that if we walk and cover 4 miles in one hour then our overall speed has been 4 miles per hour or 4 mph, we can also work out that on average it has taken 15 minutes to cover each mile. Similarly, if we have to drive to a place that is 90 miles away and we travel at an average speed of 30 miles per hour then the journey will take three hours. In our mind we may compute that with a speed of 30 mph we will travel 30 miles each hour and therefore we need to travel for 3 hours to cover 90 miles. Or we may know that the time taken is equal to the distance to be traveled (90 miles) divided by the speed (30 mph). Writing this in a mathematical form, we state that time equals distance divided by speed:

Back to School?

Remember that if:

$$Speed = \frac{Distance}{Time}$$

then

$$Time = \frac{Distance}{Speed}$$

and

$$Distance = Speed \times Time$$

Or if:

$$a = \frac{b}{c} \text{ then } c = \frac{b}{a} \text{ and } b = a \times c$$

Or if:

$$a = b + c \text{ then } b = a - c$$

and

$$a - b = c$$

Just as, if 12=8+4 then 8=12-4 and 12-8 = 4

Time = Distance / Speed

So, if the distance equals 90 miles and speed equals 30 mph then the time is 90/30 hours, or three hours. In another example if the distance was 15 miles and we traveled at 45 mph then the time would be 15/45, which equals one third of an hour or 20 minutes.

Note that since   *Time = Distance / Speed*

Then   *Distance = Speed × Time*

And   *Speed = Distance / Time*

What we are doing here is transposing an equation and looking to see what it reveals.

It is technically more appropriate to use the term *velocity* rather than *speed,* and from here on that's usually what will be used. Science students will know that the term velocity has a speed component (such as 30 mph) *and* a direction component, such as due west; it is a vector rather than scalar unit. If you are not a science major don't worry about the difference.

Using the abbreviation of v for velocity, d for distance and t for time, then the equation that velocity equals distance divided by time becomes $v = \dfrac{d}{t}$ and therefore $t = \dfrac{d}{v}$.

This shows that if the distance is increased then to cover the increased distance in the same time the velocity also has to increase. We know this from experience (if you have further to go, it takes longer to get there unless you drive faster) and can use this kind of thinking to help understand some of the equations we will come across in this book.

Hence, if the distance 'd' is 100 miles and the time taken to cover that distance was 5 hours then the average velocity 'v' was 20 miles per hour. If d increases to 200 miles then for the traveling time to stay the same then v must increase to 40 mph (= 200/5). If the distance stays at 100 miles but the time taken has to reduce to 2 hours then the average velocity has to rise to 50 mph (=100/2), and so on. It helps to understand that velocity is *directly* proportional to distance and is *inversely* proportional to time: Directly proportional since, with no change in time, as the distance increases then the velocity has to increase to keep up. The velocity is inversely proportional to time since, for the same distance traveled; to get there in less time the velocity must increase; if you travel slower then it takes longer to get there.

This is the crux of the matter, faced with an equation such as pressure = force divided by area (or *pressure* $= \dfrac{force}{area}$ or $= \dfrac{F}{A}$) recognize that the larger force is then the larger the pressure and conversely the bigger the area then the lower the pressure. If the force hasn't changed but the area over which the force is felt has increased then the force per unit of area, or pressure, must reduce. In other words hitting someone with the edge of a table tennis bat will do more damage than striking them with the face of the bat, even though the striking energy level is unchanged.

Please do not be discouraged by an equation; just keep asking what does it really show?

2.2.2   *Mathematical Notation*

One of the most famous equations of all time is $E = mc^2$, where E is short for energy, m is mass and c is the velocity or speed of light. Allow me to use this equation to illustrate a few points about the notation used within this book: "$E = mc^2$" is usually translated and described as E equals m c squared. Elaborating, this means that E equals m multiplied by c multiplied by c. Hence there are different ways of writing or describing such an equation and different notation can be applied, including:

$$E = mc^2 \qquad or \qquad E = m.c^2 \quad or \quad E = m \times c^2 \qquad or \qquad E = m \times c \times c$$

Within this book the notation adopted is that seen with the equation $E = mc^2$. If just the abbreviating letters are being shown in a multiplication type of equation then the times sign or '×' will be omitted and the equation will be similar to the $E = mc^2$ shown. When numerical values are involved the multiplication sign, '×', will be incorporated, such as in a calculation that $E = 0.001 \times 299{,}792{,}458 \times 299{,}792{,}458$, to show the theoretical energy content in one gram of material (~ 90 tera joules or 90×10^{12} joules).

If an equation was literally described then $E = mc^2$ would become 'energy equals mass multiplied by the velocity squared'. Occasionally such a description could refer to the 'product' of two variables. This simply means the value of one variable multiplied by the other, so that $E = mc^2$ could be quoted as 'energy equals the *product* of the mass and the velocity squared' or even 'energy equals the product of the mass and the square of the velocity'. In this sense, the term 'product' is just another word for multiplication.

It is confusing: Pure mathematics may be an international language but it's not one that everyone understands. Within this book I promise to try and be respectful to a reader who may not be fully familiar with the idiosyncrasies of mathematics and physics.

2.3 Definitions

2.3.1 Energy

Energy is simply the ability to do work. When work is done there is always a transfer of energy. Hence the unit for energy is the same as the unit for work: the joule or the calorie. The joule is a metric unit named after James Prescott Joule (1818 – 1889); a brewer and scientist from my original hometown of Manchester, England, who laid the foundation of the conservation of energy concepts (see section 2.4.1). The calorie is an (old) British unit used to measure work or energy and equals 4.2 joules. There is confusion in the use of the term 'calorie' for the word 'Calorie', with a capital C, is familiar to us all because of its widespread use in the listing of the energy value of foods, but this actually means a kilocalorie, 1,000 calories - or 4187 joules. Those that exercise in a gym with a stair-climber, treadmill or elliptical training machine will be familiar with the electronic kind of readout that states you have used, say, 350 Calories in the last 30 minutes of exercise. These are also kilocalories, or 'nutritional' calories, to allow those training to relate the exercise to food intake. It's not too difficult to show that 4187 joules, or 1 kilocalorie, is about enough energy to raise a 71 kg (156 lb) person 6 meters (or just under 20 feet). [This can be calculated from the potential energy equation in the following section and the word 'raise' means just that – the object is lifted up through a height of 20 feet, not carried forward for 20 feet.] The 350 nutritional calories mentioned in regards to the treadmill could theoretically have lifted a 71kg person up by 2100 meters or around 1.3 miles (see the next section, 2.3.2). Whereas if a person had used about 350 Calories when running on the treadmill for 30 minutes they would have covered about three miles. (This is another way of saying that it takes less energy to run a mile on a flat trail than it does to run a mile uphill).

The technical definition, for the scientifically minded, of a calorie is as follows: It takes one calorie (small 'c') to raise the temperature of 1 milliliter of water by one degree Centigrade. One nutritional Calorie (which equals 1,000 calories) will therefore raise the temperature of 1 liter (a thousand milliliters) of water by one degree centigrade. The joule is not a large unit – it's the energy used to raise a small apple by about one meter (or one yard).

Facts for Fighters
When you punch someone the fist carries a certain amount of energy, the more energy carried then the greater the impact and damage that can be inflicted.

2.3.2   *Potential Energy*

Push a rock up a cliff and the height that the rock has been raised provides it with the *potential* to do work by rolling back down under the influence of gravity: It has *stored energy*. The downward force from such a rock is equal to the product of the mass and the gravitational pull (or acceleration that would be experienced due to gravity).

In other words: Force = m g   *Equation (2.1)*

Where m is mass (in kg) and g is the acceleration experienced due to gravity (at 9.81 meters per second per second). Work is equivalent to energy and is the product of force (mg) and distance (d) moved. Therefore, the work done in pushing a boulder up a regular straight incline of height 'h' is given by the equation:

Energy (= Work)   =   Force × Distance
Energy or Work   =   (mg) h   *Equation (2.2)*

Applying equation 2.3 and noting that since the resultant potential energy of the rock at the top of the incline must be the same as the work done in pushing it up through a height of 'h', then:

$$\text{Potential energy} = mgh \qquad \textit{Equation (2.3)}$$

In other words, the larger the mass of the rock the greater the potential energy: Similarly, the further the rock has to fall, the greater the potential energy. (Drop a small stone from shoulder height onto a hardwood floor and no harm is done, drop a huge rock from the same height onto the same floor and it's a dent and scratch to be fixed, maybe even a broken floorboard. Drop the same large rock from only an inch and the damage is far less.)

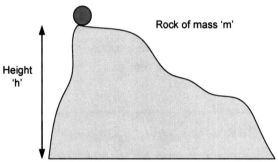

Rock of mass 'm'

Height 'h'

Figure 2.1 Potential energy of a rock at height

Placed at the top of the cliff, the rock has the potential to roll down. Once it has started rolling it has energy associated with that movement. This is dynamic or kinetic energy. Section 2.4.1 discusses the conversion of energy and how a compressed spring has potential energy that can be released into kinetic energy that can then cause damage if the spring strikes something; similar in concept to a punch or a kick.

A Fighter's Insight

A sweep of someone to the ground can be followed by a downward punch to the fallen opponent or with an axe kick where the leg is raised high and the heel comes down with force.

In a bar fight an alternative 'technique' may be applied—here the person on the ground can face an opponent who effectively jumps in the air and drops onto the fallen victim with a knee to the chest. The opponent thereby feels the full force of the opponent's falling weight hitting his chest via a knee that has a small area of impact and a hard surface. This is a good example of potential energy being converted and applied - and probably signifies the end of the dispute.

(The above idea came from an old *Fighting Arts International* interview with a fighter named Gary Spiers.)

2.3.3   *Kinetic Energy*

Kinetic energy is the energy an object has because it is moving. Get in the way of a large rock rolling downhill and you will painfully feel the transfer of that energy. All moving objects have kinetic energy and a force needs to be applied to stop such an object; the greater the energy the object has the more force needed to bring it to rest. The next chapter describes Sir Isaac Newton's laws of motion that are related to this topic.

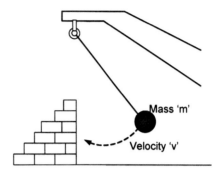

Figure 2.2: Destruction by a wrecking ball of high mass

Consider the example shown in figure 2.2, representing the destruction of a wall by a wrecking ball swung from a demolition crane. The force used to smash down the wall comes from the motion of this massive steel ball as it swings down and into the bricks. In this case the speed may be relatively low, but the huge mass of the ball results in immense force. (Imagine trying to stop such momentum.) A bullet, on the other hand, has a very low mass and relies on its enormous speed to be forcefully penetrative. If I throw a 7 gram metal object to you then you would simply catch it; if the same bullet is fired from a gun then it is deadly – because of its speed.

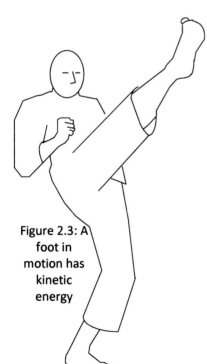

Figure 2.3: A foot in motion has kinetic energy

An object in motion has kinetic energy. The energy level depends on the mass (m) of the object and square of its speed, or more precisely its velocity (v). In mathematical form:

$$Kinetic\ Energy = \frac{1}{2}mv^2 \qquad Equation\ (2.4)$$

The derivation of this equation is shown in appendix A. Look at the powerful insight within this equation: Double the striking mass and we double the energy, kick or punch twice as fast and the energy of the foot or fist has been increased by a factor of four. This feature will emerge again and again throughout this text. How a huge sumo wrestler running at you will knock you off your feet because of his mass; how a lightweight boxer will hit you with a lighting fast strike that has a devastating and penetrative effect due mainly to the speed of the blow. Fighters continuously try to perfect the combination of striking speed and 'weight'.

Moving away from empty hand techniques think how in centuries past warriors and armies tried to develop the ultimate weapon: a balance between speed, maneuverability, type of impact, length and mass. As a warrior which would you choose: a heavy battle-axe or a lightweight sword? How would your own build and strength or your opponent's armor influence the choice? Why was the 'Halberd' weapon of the 14th and 15th centuries so successful?

Facts for Fighters

The concept of kinetic energy is of vital importance to understanding the physics of the martial arts: It is the energy of a moving object, such as a punch or kick. Science shows the relationship between mass, speed and energy content of a striking object to be: $E = \frac{1}{2}mv^2$

Increasing the striking mass of a punch by 40% will increase the energy by 40% but strike with 40% more speed & the energy of the fist will have doubled!

2.3.4 The Conversion of Potential Energy into Kinetic Energy

A comment was made earlier that work and energy are synonymous; they are scientifically defined as the same. An equation we applied in section 2.3.2 showed that the potential energy of an object at height was the same as the work done to get the object that high and equaled force multiplied by distance.

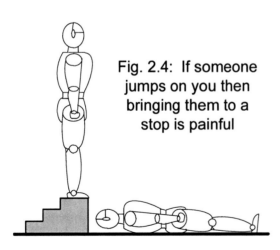

Fig. 2.4: If someone jumps on you then bringing them to a stop is painful

Climb up a flight of 6 stairs each of 6 inches (15 cm) in height and you have done the work needed to get your mass 3 feet (91 cm) higher, which has given that mass the equivalent potential energy. If you were to jump down off the stairs this potential energy would transfer to kinetic energy, which would then be a measure of the amount of work needed to bring that body to rest. In other words if you jump on someone from a height of 3 feet he is going to feel a lot of pain in bringing you to a stop.

Work = force x distance =   Energy

There are times when we "drop" into a strike. Imagine a downward elbow strike and note that fighters can deliver this strike in one of several ways: (a) They can bring the hand to the ear while lifting the elbow and then bring it down onto a target such as the collar bone. (b) They can bring the hand and arm up high and then forcefully bring the elbow down from this elevated position into the target. (c) Repeat of (b) but just before the moment of impact the fighter will bend the knees and allow the body mass to drop down into the focused point of impact. (d) They can jump into the air, raise the arm as high it will go and bring the elbow forcefully down into the target while the body is still falling to the floor; maintaining connection between the arm and body mass, through the contraction of certain muscles, at the moment of impact. The above shows the potential for a progressive increase in energy of the impacting elbow by the fighter raising the elbow higher and then converting that potential energy into motion and impacting the target with increased speed and mass. The strike force is raised because of the increase in the energy of the weapon at impact.

A Fighter's Insight

A head butt is usually done with just the force of the upper body, particularly the neck muscles. But if you have lived in the rougher part of a town you may have witnessed a brawler leap up and into an opponent - bringing the head down with both the force of the neck muscles and the added bonus created by speed, height-increase and the extra stored energy that can be converted to increased kinetic energy as the head 'drops' into the victims face with maximum 'weight'.

2.3.5 Power

Power is the ability to do work in a given amount of time:

$$Power = \frac{work}{time} \qquad Equation\ (2.5)$$

A high power machine, or person, can do a lot of work in a short period of time; a less powerful machine or person takes longer to do the same amount of work. The 'man mountain' in the gym next to you may be able to move a lot of weight through a lot of distance in just three sets of ten lifts. That does not mean you cannot push the same amount of weight through the same distance, but it takes you longer, using smaller weights and more repetitions, since the more powerful person is able to shift more weight in a single lift.

A pump equipped with a 3 kilowatt (4 horsepower) motor may be able to drain a ditch in an hour; a pump with a 1 kilowatt (1.3 horsepower) motor may take three times longer to drain the same ditch. If the drainage fluid is heavy, viscous and mud like then the lower power pump may not have the suction power to even start to move it. In summary, when you introduce the term 'power' then time usually becomes a factor. Energy equals the product of power and time, that's why electricity is metered in kilowatt hours.

Martial arts instructors can benefit from being aware of the differences imbedded in terms such as force, power or energy.

Energy is the ability or capacity to do work. One joule is the work done or energy used by a force of 1 Newton acting through a distance of one meter.

Work is done on an object when energy is transferred to that object. When a force moves an object then work is done on that object by that force.

Power is the ability to do work in a given amount of time. A power of one watt will do 100 joules of work in one second.

2.3.6 Mass and Weight

Weight and mass confuses almost everyone, including some junior science students. We live in a world where almost everyone uses the term weight when they really mean mass. For most practical purposes it doesn't make much difference—since gravity is fairly constant around the world. However please let me try and clarify:

The mass of an object is determined by the amount of matter within that object. That matter is attracted to the earth by the earths' gravitational pull. To an unsupported object this gravitation pull of the earth will give rise to an acceleration of 32 feet per second per second (or 9.81 meters per second per second), ignoring air resistance.

The weight of an object is a measure of the gravitational pull or force on that object and is linked by the equation:

	W (weight)	=	mass multiplied by the acceleration due to gravity
or	W (weight)	=	mg *Equation (2.6)*

So if an object has 1 kg of mass it experiences a force due to gravity of 9.8 Newtons. A girl of 50 kilograms (110 lbs) mass will experience a force, due to gravity, of about 490 Newtons. (Weight = mass x acceleration = 50 x 9.81 = 490N). This would be a different force experienced on a different planet, with a different gravitational pull but the mass, or the amount of material, would be unchanged. The girl of 50 kg mass and 490 N weight (110 lbs force) would weigh about 80 Newtons (18 lbs force) on the moon since it has only sixth the gravity of the earth, but she would still be made of the same amount of matter; her mass would be unchanged. In summary, simply be aware that when we say that something weighs one Newton or 2.2 pounds then that is a measure of the force experienced by the mass due to gravity. In the equations we are to apply it is the mass not the weight that is usually of interest.

2.3.7   Inertia

Having come to terms with mass as a measure of the quantity of material in an object let's cover the concept of inertia. In the next chapter, in dealing with Newton's Laws, we will formally describe how a body wants to stay at rest and that it needs a force to change this state of rest. We call this natural tendency of a body to stay at rest 'inertia'. There is no mystery here. As a fighter you will have had firsthand experience with punch bags. You know that the heavier a bag is the harder it is to move. More force is needed to make a larger, heavier, bag move and swing. The larger bag has more inertia, it's that simple.

Also, a moving body wants to remain in motion; an external force is required to reduce or stop that movement. This is another common phenomena that's seen when a fighter stops an in-swinging heavy punch bag - the heavier the incoming object, the more difficult it is to stop.

Before Newton this fact that a force is required to bring an object to a stop was not a popular concept. People thought that all moving bodies would eventually come to a state of rest, that a force was needed to keep objects moving and that the stopped state was natural. They didn't understand that objects would keep on doing what they are doing until a force was applied to them. This is somewhat understandable since we continually see objects come to a halt apparently without an external force being applied, but in reality it's usually because of the resistive force of friction. Hence this stopped state could easily be considered to be natural, especially in a time when people could not imagine a world without friction and so had no alternative explanation to bring to mind.

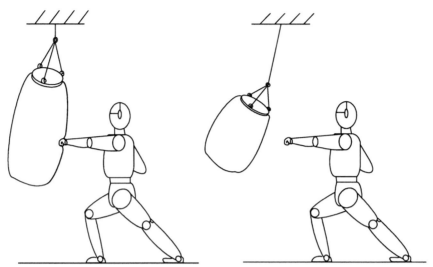

Figure 2.5: Hit two bags with the same force and the lighter one will move further - it has less inertia

There are fighters that exclusively practice free-style sparring and some that also use 'one step sparring' methods that emulate defending against an attack while standing in a natural (upright) stance. When you are in an active free style stance it is easy to move. When you are static it takes an effort merely to start the motion of the body, to overcome its inertia— and this is *before* you have actually moved it out the way of an attack. Hence a defender caught by surprise can be in difficulty, especially if the attacker is in range. Watch professional tennis players as they face a serve, they are moving, swaying from side to side, they are not static and neither are fighters in battle. Fighters that practice evading a fast strike from a nearby attacker, while standing still and upright, know the value of this training. They know how difficult it is to move from this position and avoid or block a committed attacker. They know it to be real training. Outside the training hall you are more likely to be attacked while in a natural, standing, posture rather than being 'switched on' and prepared to fight from a free-style stance, distance and state of readiness.

2.3.8   Acceleration

The term acceleration is known and intuitively understood by most. A car's performance is often related to its ability to reach a high speed in a certain amount of time – such as 0 to 60 miles per hour (mph) in 10 seconds. Here the overall acceleration equals the change in velocity (0 – 60) divided by the time taken (10 seconds). In this example, since 60 mph is 88 feet per second the average acceleration achieved would be 8.8 feet per second per second. Hence, assuming linear acceleration, after 5 second you are at a speed of 44 feet per second (30 mph) and after 10 seconds the speed has doubled to 88 ft/s (60 mph).

Velocity can here be considered as equivalent to speed and equals 'the distance covered divided by the time taken'.

Velocity = change in distance / change in time $= \dfrac{\Delta d}{\Delta t}$ *Equation (2.7)*

 and

Acceleration = change in velocity / change in time $= \dfrac{\Delta v}{\Delta t}$ *Equation (2.8)*

An acceleration of 0 to 60 mph in 10 seconds can be expected of a Jeep Wrangler. A Porsche 911, on the other hand, can be made to reach 60 mph in 4 seconds or less, it has over twice the acceleration of the Jeep Wrangler.

It is just as important to appreciate the concept of deceleration as it is to understand acceleration. Deceleration is the negative of acceleration, it is the slowing down or reduction of speed with time, as experienced in a car as the brakes are applied – or more forcefully when the vehicle is brought to a sudden stop by hitting something. When we punch a bag our fist is brought to a fast stop by the bag and the higher the rate of deceleration the greater the peak force impact to the bag. It is the same when striking an opponent, for a high peak force you are looking for rapid deceleration. Just as decelerating the car by the steady application of the brakes is harmless but hitting a tree can cause serious injuries.

2.3.9 *Force*

A force is something that can cause a change – a force acting on an object can change the state, speed, acceleration or the direction of that object. The relationship between force, mass and acceleration is discussed in the next chapter on Newton's Laws of Motion. Newton's law tells us that a pull or push force can change the speed or direction of an object and his pivotal 'force equals mass times acceleration' equation is a working definition of force that is of great interest to the martial artist. But all of that is dealt with in detail later. Fighters are mainly concerned with the way two colliding bodies or objects (such as a punching fist and a target) will interact. On contact, for example, we want to know the forces that each object experiences; what force a fighter's strike can exert on an opponent. Later in this book force impact curves are introduced, showing how the characteristics of a target will affect the peak force experienced – how the difference between a soft and hard target can influence the choice of strike or technique.

A force is something that can cause a change.

2.3.10   *Force, Pressure and Area*

Force is not the only thing of importance in the martial arts, there are other related variables that may be dominant, such as how a strike will penetrate, how that force is focused or what pressure is exerted onto a target. Pressure is inversely proportional to the area over which the strike is delivered; the smaller the area the more intense the pressure, for the same force. That can be visualized by picturing how high heel shoes will cause indentations on floors while snow shoes allows the weight to be so spread out that a person can walk on top of a deep soft snow surface. We all know that a knife will cut better when it's sharpened or that a dart needs a point to penetrate into a dart board.

The formal equation for this relationship is:

$$\text{Pressure} = \text{Force divided by Area} = \frac{Force}{Area} = \frac{f}{a} \qquad \text{Equation (2.9)}$$

This is why you will see a car's tire pressure referred to as say 30 pounds per square inch or psi (2 bar) which is 30 pounds force experienced by each square inch of the tire's internal surface area. If you were to put the same force into a tire and wheel with half the internal surface area then the pressure would be doubled to 60 psi – which may be too much for the tire fabric to tolerate and thereby cause early failure. The point being that the pressure has now been increased because of the reduction in applied area, not because of an increase in force, and this can cause damage and destruction. Put another way, for higher pressure strikes either increase the force (hit harder) or decrease the area over which the force is experienced.

The importance of this relationship to a fighter should be obvious. This is one reason why some fighters are taught to strike with only one or two knuckles when punching, or the edge of the hand with a 'knife-hand' strike, etc. The physics here enables an untrained, out of condition, maniac with a sharp knife to be capable of achieving far more penetration of tissue and bone than any punch delivered by a trained expert.

A Fighter's Insight

Reduce the striking area of impact to increase the penetration of a blow.

Match the strike to the nature, characteristics and area of the target. When appropriate, choose a vulnerable target.

A Numerical Example – The effect of area on the force of a strike

Let's reinforce this theme with a few numbers: Some expert fighters can achieve a punching speed approaching 10 meters per second (33 feet per second or 22 mph) and are thereby capable of delivering over 2000 Newtons of force (~ 450 lbs force).

A male hand is typically about six inches long and just over three inches across, so it has a total area of about 20 square inches. Hence if you were to slap someone with the full area of the hand and equal dispersion of the 450 lbs of force then the pressure felt, or force delivered per unit of area, is given by:

$$Pressure = \frac{Force}{Area} = \frac{f}{a} = 450 / 20 = \quad 22.5 \text{ pounds per square inch (psi) } [\sim 1.5 \text{ bar}]$$

If, on the other hand, you were to use a knife-hand strike and deliver with the edge of the hand of about 2 inches in length and about 1 inch in width (thereby having an area of about 2 square inches) then assuming equal and consistent dispersion, the force per unit area, or pressure, has increased to 450/2 or about 225 pounds per square inch (15.5 bar). Finally, if your strike is with only one or two knuckles, having a total area of about 0.4 square inches, then the force per unit area has increased to 450 / 0.4 or over 1100 pounds per square inch. Simply by changing the striking method we have moved through a pressure range from 22 psi to over 1100 pounds per square inch. This upper pressure is sufficient to inflict significant damage. *(22 psi is ~1.5 bar and 1100 psi is ~ 75 bar.)*

The use of mitts or gloves:

These numerical examples also indicate why we put on mitts or padded gloves to reduce the chance of injury to our training partner due to lack of control or accidents during sparring. The padding of the glove increases the surface area of a strike, spreading the load with no 'single knuckle' type of effect and has cushioning that elongates the contact time and reduces the peak forces.

While we are considering the effects of padding, think of the following occasional event: You have parked your car, got out and pushed the door so that it will swing and close - but in this case the door does not completely close or fully latch. So you turn your back to the car door, push with the hips and let your gluteus maximus (backside) hit the door to close it. Works every time, the backside is a near perfect match for closing a car door. So, here's the question – why? Why not swivel, twist the hips and drive a low reverse punch into the door? Because you will dent the panel of course - you will have evidence of lots of damage to testify just how strong the punch was, but the door may still not be fully closed and latched. Consider what is happening here and then ask yourself why, in a street fight, a head butt is so effective.

2.3.11 Momentum

Section 2.3.6 described inertia and its direct relationship to mass. The more mass in an object the greater the inertia and the more force that is required to change its position, path or velocity. An object in motion has momentum, and the measure of that momentum involves the velocity and mass of that object. Momentum is related to the concept of 'mass in motion' and technically the term momentum equals the product of an object's mass and velocity.

Momentum = mass x velocity, $\rho = mv$ *Equation (2.10)*

Where ρ is momentum, m is mass and v is velocity

For illustration; a truck of several tons of mass, even at a low velocity, has immense momentum; a bicycle at the same speed has only a small fraction of this momentum. (The fraction is equal to the ratio of the mass of the bicycle to the truck.) Stopping a bicycle requires far less force than stopping a truck. This we know from experience and observation, we would all rather be hit by a bicycle than a truck – particularly if both were traveling at the same speed. Being hit hard by a heavyweight is usually more devastating than being hit at the same speed by a lightweight. An object of small mass can have high momentum because of its very high velocity; such as a bullet.

To bring an object to a stop we can apply a large force for a short time period or a smaller force for longer. Frequently in the martial arts we want to apply a large force in a short time – the very essence of a fighter's strike to a bony target. Sometimes we want to minimize the peak forces involved with a change in momentum, for example when we try to 'break' a fall by rolling and being 'soft and compliant'. We try to avoid the fall impacting the solid body parts, such as our head, or with locked joints such as our knees. It is better to make our body 'soft', to *prolong* the time of impact and *reduce* the peak forces, rather than hit the floor hard, decreasing the momentum too fast and suffering the high resultant forces. These high forces do damage; ask anyone that has had the misfortune to fall from even a moderate height and hit the floor feet first with locked knees and no ability or chance to roll – or the skateboarder that has suffered a broken wrist.

A Fighter's Insight

An appreciation of momentum and the conservation of momentum will help to provide understanding and insight into why we apply techniques in a certain way.

A fighter is continually trying to 'change momentum'.

2.4   Physical Laws and Relationships

There are innumerable physical laws and relationships—textbooks fill academic libraries on the subject. For now let's restrict ourselves to the consideration of just two that will enter into our discussions and considerations repeatedly.

2.4.1   The Conversion of Energy

Continuously and all around us energy is being converted from one form to another. In its simplest form a car is a machine to convert the energy content of gasoline or diesel into motion. When the conversion of energy occurs there is no creation or destruction of energy or mass, although wastage of energy is to be expected. When objects collide energy is also conserved—the total amount of energy before the strike is the same as the total energy after the strike. This fact, coupled with the conservation of momentum relationship described next, allows us to determine a great deal about what effects are experienced by the objects involved in the collision. This will be seen in later chapters.

Most punches and kicks basically apply muscle power and energy conversions. Continuously, in karate at least, students are taught the importance of contraction and expansion, or compression and release; of the 'wind-up' and 'let-go' types of applications. Many of these can be considered as analogous to a spring action and we have only to recall how, as children, we bounced on a spring mattress and felt firsthand the kind of effect being described.

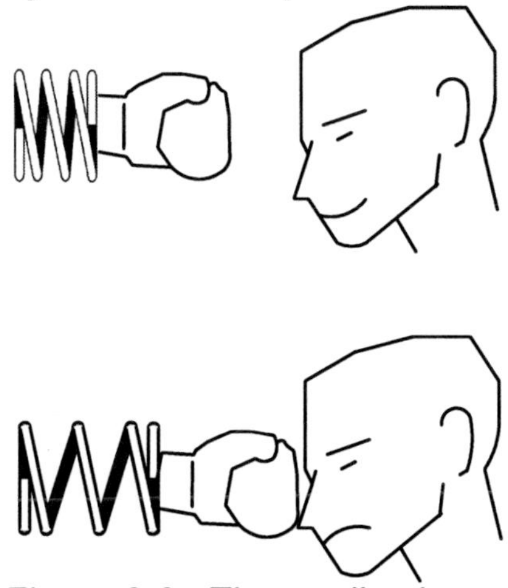

A spring can be compressed by the application of force; a force that could be mechanical, pneumatic or hydraulic etc. When a spring is compressed the nature of the material of the spring makes it want to return to its normal (expanded) state – which gives the spring its driving force. Release the compressive hold or force and the spring will expand. If the spring is robust and significant material compression has occurred then the expansion will be fast and forceful. The release of the holding force allows the expansion of the spring—creating movement and kinetic energy (and pain if it hits you).

Figure 2.6: The application of a force to compress a spring provides potential energy that can be released as kinetic energy

---

Facts for Fighters

The conservation of energy is a fundamental concept. In a collision energy is neither created nor destroyed. Energy can be converted from one form to another but the total amount of energy remains constant. There is no such thing as a free lunch. Mass can neither be created nor destroyed—at least not with bare hands!

2.4.2 The Conversion of Momentum

The conservation of momentum is a fundamental concept of physics, sitting alongside the conservation of energy to illustrate that nothing in life is free. The conservation of momentum means that the amount of momentum remains constant; momentum is neither created nor destroyed, but only changed through the action of *forces*, as described by Newton's laws of motion. When two objects collide the total momentum after the collision is the same as the total momentum before collision.

$$p_{1i} + p_{2i} = p_{1f} + p_{2f} \qquad \textit{Equation (2.11)}$$

Where:

p_{1i} is the initial momentum of object '1',

p_{2i} is the initial momentum of object '2'

p_{1f} is the final momentum of object '1',

p_{2f} is the final momentum of object '2'

See figures 2.7 and 2.8 for illustrations.

If, before collision:

(a) Object one has a mass of m_1 and an initial velocity of v_{1i} and the second object has a mass of m_2 and an initial velocity of v_{2i}.

And after collision:

(b) The first object still has a mass of m_1 but a new (final) velocity of v_{1f} and the second object still has a mass of m_2 and a new final velocity of v_{2i}. Then:

$$m_1 v_{1i} + m_2 v_{2i} = m_1 v_{1f} + m_2 v_{2f} \qquad \textit{Equation (2.12)}$$

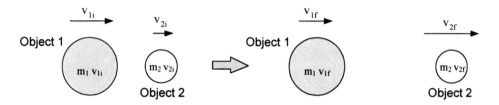

Figure 2.7: A baseball hits a pool ball, causing both balls to change their initial speeds, but the total momentum remains unchanged.

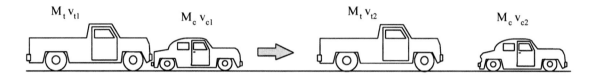

Figure 2.8: A truck hits a car, causing both vehicles to change their initial speeds, but the total momentum remains unchanged.

Dealing with momentum can be difficult because momentum is a vector quantity having both a magnitude and a direction but in this example we keep things simple with everything traveling in a straight line and no deflection angles involved.

Later you will see this type of equation being used to examine the collision of a fist as it breaks a wooden board. In that kind of circumstance the object being struck has no initial velocity, it is simply 'at rest' and therefore has no momentum. This simplifies equation 2.12 to:

$$m_1 v_{1i} = m_1 v_{1f} + m_2 v_{2f}$$

If you recall the principle of the conservation of energy and note that the wooden board has no kinetic energy then you may be able to determine that in these circumstances the following equation applies:

$$\frac{1}{2} m_{1i} (v_{1i})^2 = \frac{1}{2} m_{1f} (v_{1f})^2 + \frac{1}{2} m_2 (v_{2f})^2$$

By combining these momentum and energy equations a real insight can often be gained into what is going on. The next chapter deals with some of the most famous Laws of Physics, each of which is of direct relevance to our martial art.

2.5   Summary

This chapter and the next are meant to serve as a reference of how physics can be applied to fighting; a reference that can supplement the insights gained through instruction and practice. Great fighting expertise is attainable without a full understanding of the associated science but to properly explain what is happening it helps if the related descriptive terms and definitions are appreciated. This assists with dialogue on subjects such as power, energy or force. Chapter 2 here provides the scientific definitions and explanations of important terms such as kinetic energy, momentum or power and thereby lays down a foundation for the work ahead.

The principles of conservation play an important role in explaining how things work. Put simply these principles say there is no magic, that material isn't mystically created or destroyed without trace and that mass, or matter, remains constant. After some mechanical collision or chemical reaction, individual objects may have changed but there is still an energy balance – no material is mysteriously lost or found. Energy that is no longer available or visible will have been converted into something

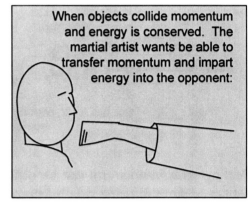

When objects collide momentum and energy is conserved. The martial artist wants be able to transfer momentum and impart energy into the opponent:

less apparent, such as heat or sound. Energy and momentum remains constant after a collision. There is no such thing as a free lunch—you get what you give.

This chapter describes potential energy as stored energy that can be released, and kinetic energy as the energy that something has because of its motion. Reference is made to how a combination of both can increase the effectiveness of a strike. It covers the concept of inertia; something that needs to be overcome before we can move and engage in combat or defense. The relationship between force, pressure and area helps explain why the martial arts have developed techniques that use small area strikes and why boxing gloves reduce the risk of facial cuts.

This chapter has outlined how energy and momentum relationships influence the impact forces experienced when a strike hits a target. Chapter 3 next describes Newton's Laws and provides a fuller explanation of, and insight into, these forceful interactions.

'Do not forget the control of the dynamics, the elasticity and the speed'
Master Funakoshi

3.1 Introduction

The seventeenth century saw the publication of some of the greatest books ever written. Alongside the works of William Shakespeare and the King James Bible came the completion of *Principa Mathematica* by Sir Isaac Newton; a book that forever changed the world of science and mathematics. Newton's laws allowed scientists and engineers to predict with great certainty the behavior of machines that would be invented over the next few centuries; helping to create an industrial revolution and change the planet. These laws also allow fighters to understand the physics of the martial arts and are therefore described below.

3.2 Newton's First Law

A body stays at rest or continues to move with unchanged velocity unless acted upon by an external force.

In other words, nature lets sleeping dogs lie. This law has two major parts and states:

(1) That an object that is at rest or stopped will stay that way unless a force comes along to disturb it.

Secondly:

(2) An object that is moving in a straight line at a particular speed will continue along that path and at that speed unless something knocks it off its path, slows it down or speeds it up.

If the object were a car, then it may be another car that knocks it off its path, it could be friction of the road surface that slows it down or it could be a downward change in incline that would cause the car to go faster.

In general, forces are associated with acceleration or deceleration. We know this from common experience; put you foot down on the

The bag stays at rest until a force is applied

Figure 3.1: Newtons' 1st Law - Punch a bag and it moves

accelerator of a moving car and you can feel the resultant forces pushing you back into the seat. Come to a sudden and abrupt stop in the same moving car and the forces associated with this deceleration (or negative acceleration) can throw you through the windscreen if the seat belt isn't being worn or an air bag doesn't stop you. All of which demonstrates the preference of a body to continue to move with uniform or unchanged velocity. Any skier or snowboarder will have experienced the difficulty of learning how to change direction or stop on alien surfaces with little friction or traction, while wearing strange footwear such as skis or having boots that are bound onto a snowboard.

Side note:

Sir Isaac Newton acknowledged that his first law was basically a formalized summary of the ideas of Galileo (1564 – 1642) that related to forces associated with the motion of an object subjected to friction. This prompted Sir Isaac to say:

> *"If I have seen further it is because I have stood on the shoulders of giants."*

The intellectual giant he was referring to here was Galileo. This is an image fit for a martial artist. We are repeatedly invited to stand on the shoulders of giants and thereby see further than they were able to. We have access to some of the best instruction anyone could wish for. Our techniques, kata or forms contain the wisdom and experience of *those that have gone before* – through centuries of devotion to excellence within times of war and circumstances of conflict. We have an obligation to acknowledge this generosity and use it wisely. We see further or perform better because we stand on the shoulders of giants.

3.3 Newton's Second Law

If an object of mass (m) is acted upon by a force (F) then the magnitude of the resultant acceleration (a) is equal to the ratio of force to mass.

This is given by the equation: $a = \dfrac{F}{m}$ [or $F = ma$]

Hence: Force equals mass times acceleration: **$F = ma$**   *Equation (3.1)*

We know that if we push a stationary car (with no handbrake applied and the vehicle in a neutral gear) then we can cause it to move. Put another way, if we apply a force to an object we can cause a change in acceleration of that object: The heavier the object the less acceleration (change) we achieve for the same force. These are not surprising laws, they match our everyday experiences.

This equation is so important to the martial artist. If you want to know how much force you will feel when hit think about this equation and the following:

- o The force will be proportional to the mass behind the strike; the heavier the blow the worse it is. This is one reason why a large opponent has to be taken so seriously.
- o The force will be proportional to the deceleration experienced by the punch or kick when it strikes you. When you are hit then *you* are the cause of the reduction in speed of the punching fist as it drops from its impact velocity to a complete stop. You are the barrier that absorbs its energy and consequentially it's you that feels the pain and damage. The greater the deceleration the more force felt.
- o Therefore, the higher the initial speed of the strike the more damage done.
- o The less time taken to stop the blow the more damage done. If you can't avoid being hit then try and 'ride the punch'; elongate the impact time; make the deceleration take longer, with a consequential lower peak value of force felt.

The equation *F* = *ma* shows that when you hit a hard object, which makes the deceleration more rapid, then the peak force will be higher. You know this – you have felt the difference between falling onto soft ground compared with a concrete road. It shows that if the big guy can put weight behind his strike and also has a very fast punch you really don't want to be hit by him. It shows that if the smaller opponent can strike with high speed and put mass behind her punch you don't want to be hit by her either.

Facts for Fighters

Force = Mass times Acceleration

To hit hard - hit with mass and speed

If you are punched, don't try to stop the punch with your face - ride it!

All of this insight from just one equation! An equation suitable to calculate the force associated with a collision. For example, assume that I hit you with an effective mass of 6 kilograms, a speed of 7 meters per second and that the contact time that brings my strike to an end is 15 milliseconds (0.015 seconds). I can use this equation to show that the force involved is 2800 Newtons or approximately 600 pounds force.

$$[F = ma = m\frac{\Delta v}{\Delta t} = 6 \times (\frac{7}{0.01}) = 2800 \text{ Newtons}]$$

Understanding that *F* = *ma* and knowing that energy equals the product of force and distance helps to see how this law can be used to derive the relationship between energy, mass and velocity described in section 2.3.3: See appendix A for this derivation.

3.4 Newton's Third Law

For every action there is an equal and opposite reaction.

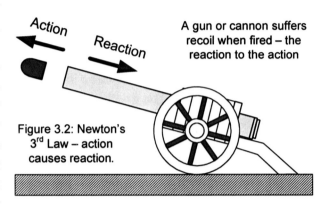

Figure 3.2: Newton's 3rd Law – action causes reaction.

A gun or cannon suffers recoil when fired – the reaction to the action

This is probably the most quoted of Sir Isaac's laws. To try and explain in a tactile way imagine lying still on a bed. Since you are not moving all the forces must be equal. If some force was pushing you up that exceeded your own downward force due to your weight, then you would move up. If the force due to your own mass was not met with an equal force pushing back you would fall downward. You are not falling because the bed is pushing back with exactly the same force as you and your weight are exerting on the bed. Occasionally the forces are not equal; as you turn over in bed springs are compressed or released until equilibrium is regained. You may have sat on a chair that collapsed because it was not strong enough to take your weight. Since it could not 'push back' with sufficient force you ended up dropping towards the floor. Similarly, when you hit something, such as a punch bag, there will be forces that are reactive to your action. *The bag pushes back.* The bag also deforms (absorbing or transferring energy), the bag moves (transferring energy) and sound is generated – using up some of the energy you imparted. Punching and kicking in free space is very different from hitting a bag or a person. The air does not 'push back' — well not much.

Let us look at another aspect of this law, one that provides insight of particular importance to a martial artist. For the purpose of this exercise, assume that you are a rickshaw handler with a passenger to pull. As you pull the rickshaw forward you need to overcome the initial inertia of the cart and get the rickshaw up to the desired walking speed. Now let's spare a moment to think on how the cart is kept moving and the nature of the involved forces.

Assuming that the road is flat and smooth then once the cart is moving you basically only need to overcome the backward pull from the frictional effects, particularly the friction of the wheels in contact with the ground. And what pushes you forward? The ground does. As your muscles push through the legs and feet to the earth then the ground pushes back with an equal force allowing this walking pace to be maintained. If you push with a force greater than that needed to overcome the effects of friction then the surplus force will cause an acceleration of the cart; this will increase the speed to a new level. Similarly, if you reach an uphill stretch of road then to keep the same speed you will need to apply more force, to overcome the extra effort needed in raising the cart, passenger and yourself through the increase in height.

Figure 3.3: To pull a rickshaw the feet push against the ground and the ground pushes back.

Of particular importance is the observation that the force to pull the rickshaw comes from the ground. There is an equal and opposite force exerted by the earth on the human/rickshaw system. Imagine trying to pull such a thing on an ice rink and as you push against the surface you simply slide; the ground cannot push back, cannot react, because you can't get the grip. Think on this in respect to the range of fighting and training stances adopted in different circumstances. In the sketch labeled figure 3.3 is it an accident or coincidence that the person pulling the rickshaw is shown in forward stance?

A Fighter's Insight
The force comes from the floor. Punch from the floor.
Explode forward from the earth!

3.5 Reactive and Impulse Forces

Newton's Laws tell us that to accelerate forward we push against the floor and the earth pushes back. This resultant push-back force can cause us to propel our bodies with great acceleration and this concept will be developed throughout this book. For now, having been reminded of Newtons Laws, consider the simple act of a standing jump. Physically act out or imagine standing in one place, allowing the knees to bend, pushing with the legs and... springing off the floor... landing in the same spot, allowing the knees to bend to absorb the impact... and coming to a complete rest: See figure 3.4. If you did this on a force plate (a form of robust electronic weighing machine) that recorded the forces experienced then you would see the following kind of results:

o   A starting force, on the floor, of say 650 Newtons—equivalent to the subject's weight. [650 Newtons is 66kg force or 146 pounds force.]

o   This measured force of 650 N momentarily reduces as she bends the knees in preparation for the 'push off' or spring upwards. (If the subject were to stop and remain on the force plate with the knees bent then the measured force would quickly return to the standing weight force of 650 N.)

o   The force dramatically increases as she forcefully straightens the knees to push against the force plate, to provide the jumping force needed for takeoff.

o   The force drops rapidly to zero as she takes flight and is no longer in contact with the plate. For a few tenths of a second the subject is in flight and therefore there is no force on the 'floor' or force plate.

o   A massive impact is felt by the force plate (and the subject) as she lands: An impact much greater than the starting force that was due to her weight only.

o   The measured impact drops rapidly and the deceleration forces are reduced as the knees are bent to cushion the landing; leading to the force level momentarily dropping below the final amount as the bent knees release the weighting effects.

o   A return to a stable, final, position and state occurs as the standing force due to body weight (only) is reestablished, and the force plate again measures 650 N.

All of this is schematically depicted in figure 3.4, which provides a display of the force that would be felt by the floor during a standing jump. The text above provides a description of what's happening: How movement (jumping height) comes from forces that are caused by the jumper bending her knees, which release her weight, and then pushing off from the floor.

What is also being introduced here is the relationship between momentum, force and time: That for the body to come to a complete stop the momentum of the jumping body needs to be reduced to zero, which as we now know requires a force to be applied. As the body hits the ground the reactive force is applied over a period of time. A later chapter will point out that this product of force and time, that is required to change momentum, is called the impulse of force, or force impulse. If I punch a target then the stoppage of my fist requires a reactive force to be applied, acting over a finite period of time. If the object that I hit cannot cope with these forces then excessive deformation and damage may result; for example the wooden board may be broken or my opponent could be incapacitated.

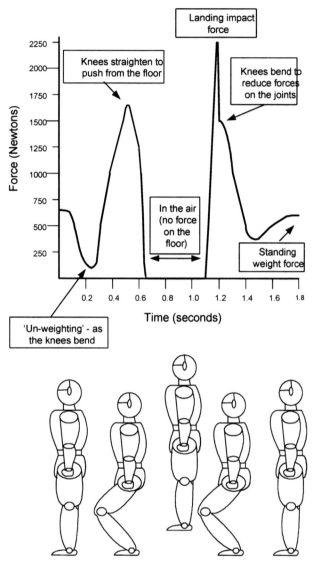

Figure 3.4: Ground reaction forces
during a vertical jump

Martial Arts Demonstration:

When teaching, ask the class to jump up into the air. Now ask the students to do the same without bending their knees. Point out how this shows that they get their movement by pushing against the floor.

3.6   Summary

Things want to stay as they are. Objects will stay where they are until something forces them to change or move. Moving objects tend to continue traveling in the same direction unless something forces them to change their path. They stay at the same velocity unless additional forces make them speed up or slow down. For something to change you have to apply a force. To make a punch bag move push or hit it. This is Newton's First Law.

Apply a force to an object and you will make it accelerate at a rate that is directly proportional to that force and inversely proportional to the object's mass—the bigger the force then the bigger the acceleration. An object of lower mass will accelerate more than an object of larger mass, for the same force. A force applied against a moving object will cause deceleration. Deceleration is just negative acceleration. When you punch and hit a target your fist has a certain velocity at the point of impact. The target or opponent that is hit applies an opposing force which decelerates and stops the punching hand. The greater the punching speed the higher the consequential deceleration and the greater the resultant force. The greater the mass or weight behind the punch then the greater the required force to stop that punch, and the more pain felt. This is Newton's Second Law and if the target being hit cannot cope with the consequential forces then it will deform and may break.

To jump up and away from the floor you first need to push against the floor, to make it push back and allow you to go airborne. The pushing force just prior to a person lifting off can be two and half to three times the standing force due to that person's weight alone. Different people will display different results; an Olympian high jumper will use more muscle to create enormous pushing force just prior to lift-off. Fighters push against the floor to move forward to deliver a high force kick or punch. And whatever you hit, hits back. This is Newton's Third Law in action, and reaction.

(Newton's) Facts for Fighters

Things stay as they are unless forces intervene: that moving object or fist should keep traveling if you don't get in its way.

The more mass and speed behind a punch or kick the greater the energy it carries and hence the greater the force needed to stop it.

Whatever you push—pushes back!

CHAPTER 4: THE COLLISION OF BODIES

> *'Imagine ones arms and legs as swords'*
> *Master Funakoshi*

4.1 Introduction

Any object that is in motion, including a fist or a foot, has kinetic energy. As that object collides with another body, such as a head or a stomach, it will transfer energy to that other body. For the moving object to come to rest it has to lose or transfer its kinetic energy. In collisions where this energy is mostly transferred to the target then this causes a state change in the receiver and the target is moved and/or deformed. Think of the demolition squad wrecking ball shown in section 2.3.3. It hits a wall while in flight and the smashing of the bricks and mortar allows it to lose, or give away, sufficient energy to come to rest.

As objects collide in these ways the equations related to the conservation of momentum and the conservation of energy can help us to understand the effects of that collision. It is a fact that even in a most violent collision between two bodies the overall momentum (before and after the event) doesn't change. It is also known that there is a conserved balance to the amount of energy and mass before and after the collision.

4.2 Small & Fast or Big & Slow: Which is More Dangerous?

Many of us have faced opponents at the two ends of the body form spectrum. We have fought against the large and the smaller fighters and come away with different lessons from each experience. To apply a little science to these experiences let's address a simple, non personal, question:

Given a choice between the lesser of two evils, which would you prefer: to be hit with a sledgehammer weighing 2 kilograms (4.4 pounds) and traveling at half a meter per second (m/s), or be hit with a pin hammer weighing 0.1 kg (4 ounces) and traveling at ten m/s?'

To answer the question let's start by looking at both the momentum and the kinetic energy of both objects.

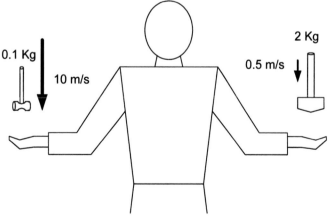

Fig 4.1: What's worse, being hit by a 0.1 kg hammer falling at 10 m/s or a 2 kg hammer at 0.5 m/s speed?

Momentum:

Section 2.3.11 introduced the principles of momentum and equation (2.10) [$\rho = mv$] shows that both hammers have the same momentum—each would stop the other in a head to head collision, as follows:

(1)   Momentum of the sledgehammer   =   2 x 0.5   =   1 kg m/s
(2)   Momentum of the pin hammer   =   0.1 x 10   =   1 kg m/s

So if they both have the same momentum is there a difference in the effect of being hit by one rather than the other and if so does it matter? This question, and understanding the implications, is vitally important in the martial arts—it is another arrow in the quiver of applicable knowledge. Even though the momentum in each case is the same, the masses and speeds are not and therefore the kinetic energies are very different, as follows:

Kinetic Energy:

(1)   Kinetic Energy of the sledgehammer $= \frac{1}{2}mv^2 = \frac{1}{2}2 \times 0.5^2 =$ 0.25 Joules

(2)   Kinetic Energy of the pin hammer $= \frac{1}{2}mv^2 = \frac{1}{2}0.1 \times 10^2 =$ 5 Joules

And here is the point: The higher the kinetic energy of a moving object, then the greater the penetration it can have if it hits you; in this case the difference is 20 times worth. This difference is caused by the relatively higher speed of the lighter hammer. Consider a well known example of low momentum but high energy: A bullet may weigh as little as 5 grams (0.005kg) but travels at around 300 meters per second. Hence it has a momentum of 1.5 kg. m/s, which is not very dissimilar to our hammer example, but in this case it has an energy content of 225 joules. This low momentum figure is not a surprise—the recoil felt from a hand gun is suitably modest—but it has a deadly level of energy. The bullet's energy content is, by design, high and concentrated in a small and focused package. A bullet is designed to be penetrating.

Facts for Fighters

The higher the kinetic energy of a moving object, the greater the penetration.

[Remember that $E = \frac{1}{2}mv^2$ - so increasing the striking mass of a punch by 10% will

increase the energy by 10% but increasing the speed by 10% will raise the energy level of the fist by 20%]

And why, specifically, should a fighter be interested? Throughout this book you will be reminded of the importance of speed and there should be no doubt that instruction and practice increases the hand speed of fighters. The downward 'chopping' type of strike action can get much faster with training, from around 7 meters/ second as a beginner to up to about 14 m/s at an advanced stage. Let's assume the expert is a lightweight and able to put 5 kg behind a strike of speed of 14 m/s. The beginner, on the other hand, strikes at a reduced speed of 7 m/s but is a heavyweight and can double that expert's mass, at 10 kg. The momentum in each case is the same (5 x 14 = 7 x 10), but the energy content of the expert's strike is twice that of the heavier beginner. By increasing the speed of the technique through training the penetration effects are increased dramatically.

Tools for the job: A lightweight pin hammer is used to drive light, thin, nails through wood. A sledgehammer is typically used to smash and demolish heavy concrete slabs or similar. Use a pin hammer on a concrete slab or paving stone and the effect will be negligible: Use a sledgehammer on a thin nail or tack and the likelihood is that the nail will bend rather than penetrate true. In each instance the weight of the hammer should suit the weight of the object to be struck and the resultant speeds or forces in collision conditions. As a fighter we know that there are times to use a light, fast, deflection against a punch and there are times to attack the incoming strike: We choose to smash the attacker's arm rather than brush it aside. There are times when we will use an open hand strike rather than a closed fisted punch. Knees and elbows have their place in the battlefield. Although we all have our favorite techniques better fighters have a greater armory of weapons.

Sportsmen involved in rugby, American football or soccer may have felt this 'penetration' effect when running into an on-rushing opponent. Hitting a member of the opposition that is heavy and fast is bad enough but after running into someone who is small, bony and lightning-fast and you can get up off the floor feeling really hurt. Both guys may stop you in your tracks, and big guy may take all of your breath away, but the impact from the lightning fast thin man seems to go right through you.

A Fighter's Insight
Expert fighters intuitively understand the tools they have and how the right weapon can be applied—because of training no pause for thought is needed.

4.3 Penetration

Why should the lighter hammer in the previous section be so much more penetrating? How can I visualize what's happening here? Allow me to try and assist—this is so important that the end is worth the journey.

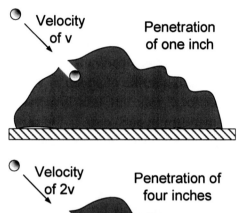

Image your fist, or your finger, pushing through an inch of some soft, mud like material. To do so requires a certain amount of force; let's call that force one unit. Rather than thinking of some gruesome fleshy images let's pretend to be bakers: Bakers of bread to be precise. As such we have just poured out a large lump of dough. Bread dough requires to be kneaded, pummeled, manipulated and generally bashed about. Now imagine throwing an object into that dough, perhaps a nut, and it penetrates by one inch. How much do I have to increase the speed of

Figure 4.2: Speed & Penetration

that object so that when I throw it at this faster rate, it will penetrate by four inches? The answer suggested by the above is twice as fast. Let's use this dough-like mental image to try to picture what's going on:

To push through an inch of this dough requires a certain amount of force to be applied. So, to push through four inches needs this unit of force to be applied through each of the four inches. We have shown previously that the product of force and distance is work and that work is equivalent to energy. [Force x distance = work = energy.] So in this case the amount of energy needed is four units. It takes four times as much energy to push through these four inches as it does to push through one inch. This makes sense.

Returning now to our original image of an object being thrown in to the dough, the next step should not be too much of a leap. We can see from the last paragraph that to increase the penetration fourfold demands four times the energy. And we know from our new friend $E = \frac{1}{2}mv^2$ that to increase the energy fourfold only requires that the speed is doubled.

Double the speed, quadruple the penetration.

Later in this book is a discussion on the differences between a rubber bullet that bounces off a target and a metal one that penetrates. If the muzzle velocity of a bullet is doubled, assuming no change in type (mass) of bullet, then the momentum is doubled. This means the bullet is twice as capable of knocking something over, however, if the bullet penetrates then it will go up to four times deeper than one with half this speed.

Before we leave this subject, be aware that when the penetration is quadrupled, because the speed is doubled, the time taken to penetrate is only doubled. This may appear obvious, from the (linear) observation that with twice the speed and twice the time an object can cover four times the distance. The same basics apply with linear decelerations also. Think on what this means, the contact time has only doubled, but the strike has four times the potential penetration. Imagine the implications to the peak forces normally seen or felt.

Earlier in this book is an outline of the relationship between force, pressure and the area over which that force is applied. Essentially it describes what we already know; that a pointed object such as a dart will penetrate more easily than a blunt object that has a larger area of contact; that a sharp knife will slice better, that we need snow shoes or skis to avoid sinking into deep snow, or that the strike of a bare knuckle punch will create greater impact pressure (or force per unit area) than a full hand slap carrying the same energy. The slap may bruise a cheek but the punch can crack the cheek bone. It is important to know that penetration depends on several factors, including the strike area.

The previous explanatory example described the penetration of an innocuous material, namely dough, to work through the science. Such a material, when penetrated, does not really 'push back'. Push your finger into such a material and it does not (significantly) push back trying to get rid of the finger. Unlike pushing against a spring you do not have to sustain the force to stop the material from returning to its original position or level. In the main, the human body is not dough-like, and empty hand strikes to the body do not pierce the flesh and tissue in a manner similar to that shown in the sketched example. The muscles of the body will, when struck, exhibit 'push back' or reassertion tendencies, as will bone and joints – until breakage causes major loss of such protective characteristics.

It is not within the scope of this book to delve in to the human anatomy and analyze the differences between bone, muscle, fatty tissue and the like. But all of us can recognize that the differences exist, that the physical characteristics of the skull (or jaw or ribs) are not the same as the stomach, chest or neck. We can explore our own bodies and gain insight into the degree of tolerance that these different parts have to an impact from being hit. This tolerance depends upon the strength and nature of the structure, its compliance and health. Certain body parts, such as bone, are tough but with enough impact are prone to breakage or

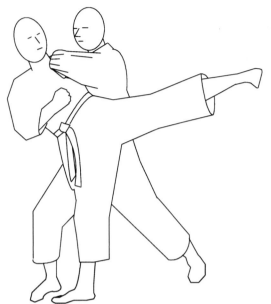

Figure 4.3: Develop a range of weapons or "tools" for the job and distance.

fracture, other parts are prone to trauma, bleeding or rupture; joints can be dislocated and ligaments torn.

Just as a carpenter would use different tools for differing tasks, the expert martial artist will understand how particular strikes can be used to match the target being struck. There are a wealth of striking weapons—open hand, closed hand, edge of hand; ball, side or instep of foot; elbow etc. plus a spectrum of striking techniques: snap, thrust, straight or round trajectory etc. This combined range provides choices from which to select for the striking 'focus' that's wanted, depth of penetration or impact time. The expert fighter will become intuitively proficient at matching the choice of technique to the target and the desired effect.

A Fighter's Insight

Some martial artists are well known for the lightning fast speed of their strikes and their ability to 'penetrate', break boards or cause severe injury. These attributes are complimentary, one follows the other. The traditional martial arts never ask that fighters become bigger or more massive but rather to make the most of what they have naturally. The techniques of the martial arts are designed to help the smaller person succeed against a larger attacker.

A fighter may not always use a sledgehammer to crack a nut—but she may choose the destructively safe option if there is uncertainty about the opponent and the stakes are as high as they get. Other sections of this book discusses the conservation of momentum and points out that with an elastic collision of objects of equal mass there is a complete exchange of momentum. In other words if you match the 'weight' of the strike to the 'weight' of the target the effectiveness and efficiency is improved. However, faced with a thug on a dark night the defender can be forgiven for striking with as much speed and mass as she can muster. There are indications that an aggressor on particular drugs may be less susceptible to pain, so a 'pain compliance' hold cannot be relied upon and that such an opponent can be hit hard but still continue to attack. This creates difficulties in academic discussions on the application of reasonable force, for if you cannot easily judge what force is needed to stop an individual from doing you harm then how can you try and apply only that much force to protect yourself, and no more? Hence in my view an innocent defender can be forgiven for striking as hard as she judges, in impossible circumstances, with the hope that the attacker is dissuaded or temporarily but sufficiently incapacitated to provide her an opportunity for escape to safety. The appropriate authorities can then be notified. Reasonable or legal force in the eyes of most law will allow for a person to instinctively use force, even if it is likely to cause great bodily harm, providing that person reasonably believes that such force is necessary to prevent a forcible felony or violent crime.

4.4   The Time and Energy to Punch

You cannot get something for nothing. Stating that a fighter should aim to strike faster is easy and obvious. Pointing out that doubling the speed will quadruple the energy content is accurate, but to double the speed means that the energy input has to increase by a factor of four. (To punch twice as fast means that four times the energy has to be imparted into the movement.) For a sporting analogy look at baseball and the pitching of a fast ball: Most reasonable pitchers can throw a ball at fifty mile per hour, but there are few that can achieve the one hundred mile an hour fast ball. It takes four times the effort to achieve that compared to throwing a 50 mph pitch. Four times the effort in about half the available time. [The simplified and approximate reference to 'half the available time' is because the distance (arms length) is the same in both instances yet the end speed achieved has doubled.]

Back to fighting—to get twice the speed into a punch you have to put in four times the energy and you have only about half the available time to do it. This is very difficult. This demands endless practice and attention to minute detail in the techniques applied. Here is another instance where advancement will be only by incremental improvement. Fighters are not interested in throwing a ball or trying to break some hand speed record, they are working to improve their punching power. Having twice the speed and virtually no strike mass produces virtually no force; see section 7.10. Also, as we reduce the time to complete the punch, then the opponent has less time to identify and block or evade the strike. With training it takes around two tenths of a second to punch someone and, to bring this into context, on average a person needs about three or four tenths of a second to blink.

Facts for Fighters
A trained fighter is likely to be able to punch faster than the average opponent can blink.

4.5   Elastic Collisions

Before we go much further let's just touch on one of the distinctions in the different forms of collisions: elastic and inelastic collisions—'bouncy' or 'sticky' impacts. Drop a rubber ball onto a concrete floor and it will bounce back up to almost its original height. This is an elastic type of collision. It's a similar type of collision to that seen when playing pool or snooker and the cue ball is struck with force and impacts another ball – changing the speed and trajectory of both the cue ball and the target ball. At our level of physics, dealing with the visible world, there are no totally elastic collisions—the bouncing ball never quite returns to its original height, the billiard balls always experience a degree of loss of kinetic energy to sound and heat. It can help your understanding of the effects of strikes if you start to consider if a strike is basically elastic or inelastic.

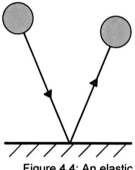

Figure 4.4: An elastic collision

4.6   Inelastic Collisions

Instead of the rubber ball, drop a lump of wet putty onto the concrete floor. There will be no bounce back, the putty will simply 'splat' onto the floor with deformation and loss of shape. This is an inelastic collision, where the colliding objects tend to stick together.

In an action type of movie you may have seen a scene where an oncoming train rams into a car that's stalled and straddling the railway tracks. As the train hits the vehicle the car it is either pushed out of the way or it deforms and crumples as it is pushed along by the locomotive. During the collision the change in velocity of the train is trivial because the mass of the car, compared to the train, is minor. The contact time can be long— because the train pushes the car along as it deforms and 'sticks' to the train, rather than 'bouncing off' on impact. This is an example of an inelastic type of collision.

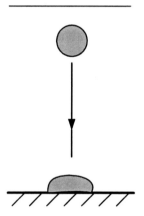

Figure 4.5: An inelastic collision

4.7 Partially Elastic or Partially Inelastic Collisions

There is a range of materials between the rubber and wet putty examples just provided: Materials such as wood or steel. These materials will 'bounce' to varying degrees or heights. The associated collisions can be more towards elastic than inelastic or vice versa. There is a broad band of partially elastic or partially inelastic characteristics.

These properties can be extremely important. In sports such as tennis, baseball or basketball the elastic characteristics of the ball have to be kept within stringent control limits. The 'co-efficient of restitution' (COR) of a baseball is around 0.54 which means that its rebound speed is 54% of its striking speed on a hard surface. The COR of a tennis ball is 0.67 and the COR of a basketball is 0.76. If nothing else note that an object with a COR of around 1 collides completely elastically, while an object with a COR of 0 will collide in-elastically, effectively "sticking" to the object it hits and not bouncing away at all. This concept will emerge again later, particularly where Chapter 7 deals with the calculation of energy imparted into an object during a collision or strike.

From a fighter's perspective, for now at least, the point can perhaps be best seen by an example: The back-fist type of strike can be undertaken in two distinct ways—

- Firstly, as a snapping action, with the fist retracted as fast as it went out to strike the target. An impulse, or snap, type of strike.

- Secondly, as a 'through the target' type of action where the motion of the fist is deliberately continued, trying to strike and 'follow' through or push the target (say the head) through an arc. There is no snap back here—the fist follows a circular path and takes everything with it.

The above action is shown schematically in chapter 6, figures 6.1 to 6.3. In the first, snapping, example the strike contact time is short, as the fist penetrates and snaps (or even 'bounces') back. In the second example the fist deliberately 'sticks' to the target, elongating the contact time, imparting energy for a much longer period. The first action tends towards being (mainly) elastic and the second action is (mainly) inelastic.

Allow me to explain a little further, by illustration: A snapping back-fist strike action has comparatively little effective mass. It is limited to the mass of the fist and a proportion of the arm, since it is hinged and there is almost no 'body weight' behind it. It will almost 'bounce off' when striking a heavier and robust target. Imagine, for example, a snapping action back-fist being aimed at the nose, but the opponent drops his head and takes the strike on the roof of his skull. The fist can be pictured as bouncing off such a hard and massive object. This 'bouncing off' is akin to an elastic type of collision. If the same strike was to hit the vulnerable point on the opponents' temple then, if executed correctly, the shear speed of the strike will have an effect—the impact can do damage and cause pain. If the strike were to hit the opponents' nose then the energy content and short contact time can be more than sufficient to cause breakage. When breakage occurs the strike usually has inelastic or partially inelastic characteristics because as the fist goes into the target, for that fraction of a second, the weapon and target are in full contact.

As stated, an alternative method of delivering a back fist strike is to follow through rather than retract the fist. Here you can image the fighter striking the side of the face and perhaps trying to damage the jaw or cause a knockout.

The article *The Physics of Karate*, by Feld et al (1979) reported on the study of the action of the bones of the hand during a hammer fist strike on concrete. With photographs spaced a millisecond apart (0.001 seconds or 1/1000th of a second) the fist shows clear depression and distortion, concluding that the fist cannot be considered to act as a solid object. For the extremely short period that the concrete block is bending and starting to break, the block and hand remain in contact and move together – as an inelastic collision. The contact time of the hammer fist strike referenced, in breaking a concrete block, was measured as 5 milliseconds (0.005 seconds). Further consideration and insight into the dynamics of breaking boards is provided later in this book.

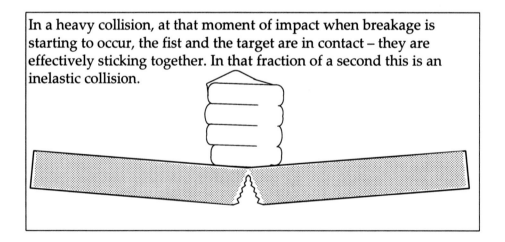

In a heavy collision, at that moment of impact when breakage is starting to occur, the fist and the target are in contact – they are effectively sticking together. In that fraction of a second this is an inelastic collision.

4.8   Summary

The implications of the principles associated with momentum and energy are of interest to fighters for they help to explain what happens when two objects collide. Two moving objects can have the same mommentum but vastly different energy levels. A lighter faster object can have more energy than a slower but more massive one yet the product of mass and velocity in both cases is the same. For example, if one such object is of half the mass of the other but twice the speed then its energy level is twice as high, despite the fact that their momentum levels are the same.

If we keep the mass the same and double the speed then:

- The momentum will have doubled—because we have twice the speed
- The energy will have increased fourfold
- Quadrupling the energy of an object provides four times the pentration potential—this increases the pain felt and damage done by such a strike.

On the other hand, if we double the mass but leave the speed unaltered then:

- The momentum has doubled—because we have twice the mass
- The kinetic energy has doubled—because we have twice the mass
- The penetration potential has doubled—because twice the energy exists.

Collisions can be elastic (bouncy) or inelastic (sticky), or somewhere in-between. A thust action technique tends to be more inelastic; with an extended contact time it's prolonged impact can be used to take a joint beyond its limit of flexibility. A snap action technique tends to be more of an ellastic colisions with an impact that is precisely targetted, having a short contact time and less penetration.

Punch a large cushion with a bare knuckle fist travelling at 10 m/s and there is no pain; great penetration and a long contact inelastic collision but no pain. Punch a stone wall in the same way and it's a totally different proposition. The pain felt will be severe, there will be virtually no penetration (of the wall at least), the contact time will be short and the collision is mainly elastic - as the fist virtually bounces off the stone surface. And the forces? In the first strike the peak force is low (no pain), in the second case the peak force will be so high that the person will be lucky to escape without broken bones of the hand.

"The true science of martial arts means practicing them in such a way that they will be useful at any time, and to teach them in such a way that they will be useful in all things."

Miyamoto Musashi
The Book of Five Rings

CHAPTER 5: EXAMINATION OF A STRIKING FORCE

5.1   Introduction

The study of the martial arts often concentrates on force. We talk about the force of a technique, the force of the opposition or the force of opposing armies. An understanding of the technical meaning of the word 'force' is most useful and Chapters 2 and 3 defined and discussed the term 'force' from a technical perspective. The forces of nature form the very foundation of our universe and although forces at the sub-atomic scale remain mysterious our biomechanics operate at the macro scale and from a fighting perspective we can restrict ourselves to the types of forces we experience daily. When striking, a fighter is interested in the forces involved when two objects collide. Those two objects could be a fist and a face.

Prior to collision any two objects, perhaps in their resting state, may have no influence on each other—just as a bat and ball can lie passive within the same baseball kit bag with neither affecting the other. However, the forces that each experience when brought into violent contact depends on the collision mechanics and the very nature of each of the two objects. The previous chapters have looked at how much energy a fist or foot may carry and how that relates to the force it can deliver. This section introduces the relationship between forces and the contact time or distance over which a punch or kick is brought to a stop by the target it hits. We have already seen that the action of a force that is causing deceleration and stoppage is described by Newton's second law. Sir Isaac's first law tells us that a body continues without change unless a force acts upon it and the third law gives us the insight that 'to every action there is a reaction'. This chapter describes the interactions between colliding objects of different masses, with the objective of providing insight into what makes a technique effective.

5.2   The Theory - Impact Force and Impact Time

Start with an everyday experience: Think of driving at 40 mph with your dog, Rover, on the passenger seat and a stop light ahead. You apply the brakes and over a distance of a hundred yards bring the car to a smooth easy stop. Nothing unusual, Rover's happy and puts his head back out of the window. Different scenario: same car, same dog, same speed but this time you have to do an emergency stop, slamming on the brakes as hard as you can and coming to a full stop in a fraction of the distance previously enjoyed. You may be pleased that you didn't collide with the idiot who pulled out in front of you but Rover is really upset. Dogs don't wear seatbelts and he didn't enjoy being bounced off the dashboard and ending up rolling on the floor—luckily only his pride is hurt.

What are the differences between these two scenarios? In both instances the vehicle speed and mass are the same, so the momentum and kinetic energy was the same, but Rover bears painful testimony to the fact that the peak forces felt were not the same—with hard braking the force was enough to throw him off his seat and put him in fear of going through the windscreen. The difference is the degree of deceleration or the reduced time taken to bring the car to a stop; that is the shorter distance covered by the vehicle in slowing down from 40mph to zero.

Stopping a moving object in a short distance can cause damage

Punch someone in the chest and he will feel an impact. If the person hit could process signals fast enough he may be able to detect the strike, feel the force and then recognize that the impact has died away, perhaps leaving behind the pain and residual feeling of being struck. We know from the previous chapters that the overall force experienced is dependent upon the speed and the 'weight' of the punch but that's not all that determines the peak or maximum force caused by the collision. The forces involved when an object strikes a target are also dependent upon the characteristics of the object that is struck—plus the form and hardness of the missile itself. Put simply, the force experienced by the target is dependent upon the 'give' in that target. Section 4.8 describes the difference between hitting a stonewall and a cushion; that the peak forces experienced from the cushion will be much lower.

Hit something that is soft and the cushioning absorbs the blow, reducing the peak force and spreading the impact over a longer time. Hit something that's hard and the force level rises very rapidly and then decays away quickly; the impact has a short contact time and a high peak force.

There is a difference in the forces experienced by the bones of the skull when struck, compared with the same blow landing on an opponent's stomach. Intuitively we know this and the technical basis to explaining these differences will relate to the time and distance experienced: The hardness of the target influences the *time* taken to disperse the energy of the striking projectile (e.g. foot or fist) over the *distance* of penetration. The shorter the time the higher the peak force.

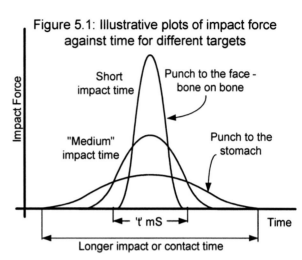

Figure 5.1: Illustrative plots of impact force against time for different targets

Hence, when striking an opponent recognize that not all targets have the same characteristics. The head is mainly bone, a hard target. Punch the face with an ungloved fist and it is basically bone striking bone. Speed of strike is therefore of dominant importance. Unless the target is obese, the ribs of most people have little padding to offer protection. So this is another hard bony target and ribs are slender and fairly easy to break. However the ribs use flexible ligaments and cartilage for skeletal connection and thereby have a limited capacity to deflect or absorb the forces and extend the contact time.

The abdomen of the average individual is very different—this is not a hard bony target. Being basically composed of skin, fat, muscle and fibrous tissue the abdomen is much softer with a comparatively longer path of penetration. An increased contact time must be expected with a strike to the stomach, particularly if the target person is large and even more penetration is needed. Hence the contact time and impact force 'shape' is not constant for all targets. Not every strike should be the same. Hitting the stomach of a 'robust', overweight, individual is not the same as striking the head of the same man.

Don't train as though all targets are equal.

A Fighter's Insight

A sharp punch to the face, with limited penetration, may be enough to break an opponent's nose and convince him that he really doesn't want to fight. The same strike to the stomach may have no noticeable effect; more penetration is needed.

Not all strikes are equal—what you hit influences the force felt.

[And a strike to the nose can result in a lot of blood – nowadays a fighter should try to avoid this if possible.]

As an alternative perspective, imagine throwing a ball against a brick wall. Throw it straight and horizontal. Watch it rebound straight and horizontal and know that the speed of the ball has decreased. The collision has not been perfectly elastic, hence the drop in speed, and a force has been needed to turn the ball around. If the ball is relatively rigid, like a baseball or a cricket ball, then the collision time will be short and the peak force will be large. If the ball is more yielding, like a tennis ball, then the collision time will be longer and the peak force will be lower. This illustrates the differences in force–time curves that can be expected, as shown in figures 5.1 and 5.2. In each instance the force starts out at zero, rises to a maxmum during impact and then falls to zero as the ball leaves the wall.

If I drop a glass bottle onto a concrete path it will probably break. The surface is hard so the impact time duration will be short causing the peak force to be sufficient to cause breakage. If I drop the same bottle from the same height onto a bed or cushion then it is likely that the bottle will remain intact. The striking kinetic energy in both instances is the same, for the bottle mass and impact velocities will be unchanged, but in the latter case the cushioning of the bed prolongs the contact time, lowering the peak forces. In these types of circumstances, whatever average force and contact time is involved, the change in momentum is unaltered; the object still has the same mass and is still reduced from its collision speed to zero speed. When an impact stops a moving object, the change of momentum for that object is a fixed quantity but the time taken for the full impact can make a huge difference to the forces experienced.

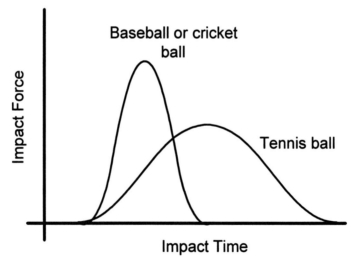

Figure 5.2: Difference in Force Impact
Between a Baseball and a Tennis Ball

5.3 The Theory - How Do We Calculate the Impulse Force?

When two objects collide, such as a bat and ball or fist and face, they exert forces on each other. What follows below shows that the change in momentum of the colliding body is equal to the impact exerted on the body, and that the contact time of the collision affects the level of force. This statement about the contact time is important and will be developed further.

In this theoretical section we can start with Newton's 'Force equals mass times acceleration' or F = ma

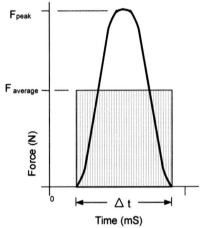

Figure 5.3: A graph of impact force against time

This leads to: $F_{average} = m \times a_{average}$ *Equation (5.1)*

Acceleration equals the rate of change in velocity; if we represent the change in velocity as Δv and the related change in time as Δt, then acceleration equals Δv divided by Δt and hence:

$$Force = mass \frac{\Delta v}{\Delta t}$$ *Equation (5.2)*

Therefore $Force\ \Delta t = mass\Delta v$ *Equation (5.3)*

Where $Force\Delta t = the\ force\ impulse$

And $mass\Delta v = the\ change\ in\ momentum$

This indicates that the impulse of force on a colliding body is equal to the change in momentum of that body (provided the mass is constant).

As an illustration: As a baseball hits a bat a force impulse is applied to that ball. The bat hitting the ball applies a force for a short period of time and this time variable is important. The contact time duration has a significant influence on the average and peak force.

Momentum is equal to mass times velocity. Impulse of force is equal to change in momentum or mass times the change in velocity; which equation 5.2 showed is equal to the product of average force and change in time.

$$F_{impulse} = mass\Delta v = F_{average}\Delta t$$ *Equation (5.4)*

The above equation shows that for an unchanged force impulse, or "$mass\Delta v$", if the contact time (Δt) decreases then the average force ($F_{average}$) has to increase - and vice versa.

5.4   The Theory - Changing the Contact Time of a Punch

Let's apply the theory and do a few sums and see what the mathematics suggest about the forces involved with a punch. Assume that an attacker hits with a punch that on impact has a velocity of 7 meters per second and carries with it a mass of 4 kilograms. Using the above numbers and equation (5.2) we can determine the force as follows.

$$Force \ _{average} = ma \ _{average} = mass \ \frac{\Delta v}{\Delta t}$$

If Δv is assumed to be a linear change in velocity—which is 7 m/s to 0 m/s (or $\Delta v = 7$) and Δt is the time duration over which the velocity changes, or contact time, and is 0.01 seconds (10 milliseconds) then the calculation becomes:

$$F = mass \ \frac{\Delta v}{\Delta t} = 4 \times \frac{7}{0.01} = 2800 \ \text{Newtons (~630 lbs force)}$$

You can calculate that with a velocity of 7 meter per second an object coming to a stop in 0.01 seconds will cover a distance of 0.035 meters or about 1.4 inches, assuming a linear deceleration. This is the contact or penetration distance. If the defender was able to ride the punch and extend that contact distance to about 4 inches or 0.1 meter then you can calculate the new *force* experienced. Intuitively it may be seen that increasing the contact distance by a factor of 3 will therefore reduce the force threefold – from 2800 N to 933 Newtons, or about 210 lbs force. This can be confirmed by either (a) first calculating the energy using the kinetic energy equation (2.4) - knowing that *Force equals energy / distance* and that the distance is now 0.1 meter, or (b) convert the new distance into a new contact time (of 0.03 seconds) and repeat the original calculation: $F = mass \ \dfrac{\Delta v}{\Delta t} = 4 \times \dfrac{7}{0.03} = 933 \ \text{Newtons (~210 lbs force)}$

The basic point is that there is a big difference between being hit with 210 pounds force compared to 630 lbs force, and it's the contact time interval that is making this difference. If a heavyweight of 210lbs should stand on your hand for a second it's likely that pain will be the only consequence with no permanent damage, but place a 630lb weight on a hand for a fraction of a second and the result will probably entail at least one visit to the hospital. What is being stated here is that if the speed or mass increases then the force increases but if the contact time increases then the force decreases. As fighters when we are being struck in the face we naturally lean back and away from the punch, trying to increase the contact time in order to reduce the force felt. When a fighter rides a punch the force felt is reduced but experienced for longer. This is a far better proposition; the body can tolerate this much better. The graph labeled figure 5.1 shows how the force level varies with contact time and quotes the kind of bodily targets that will give different contact times

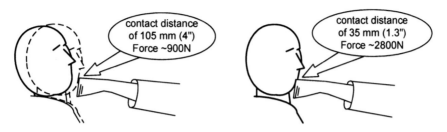

Leaning back and riding the punch - extending the contact time and
distance to reduce the force felt.

The relationships between force, momentum, mass, velocity, energy, time and distance feature throughout this book. The above has concentrated upon impact force and its relationship with change in momentum, which involves time and the impact distance of collision. It did not explicitly discuss the energy of the moving object involved in the collision. However, we have previously shown that the product of force and distance is work and that work is equivalent to energy, and so Energy = Force x Distance.

This equation indicates that in an impact where a moving object is brought to rest, the target that is struck must do enough work to take away the kinetic energy of the colliding object. Translating, if I punch into a target without pull back or reaching a limit due to the length of my arm, then the target has to bring that punch to a stop. The more energy I punch with the more it takes to stop the punch. Stopping my punch involves a high force over a short distance— or a lower force over a longer distance. It is that simple, as understood by Rover the dog in section 5.2.

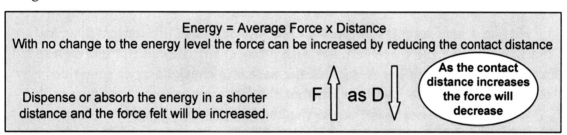

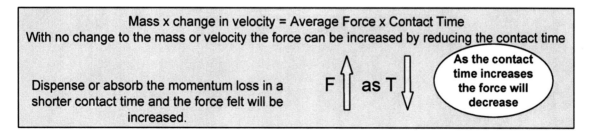

You may have been involved in a sparring session where you were hit with a punch to the face that was seen coming but you were unable to block it, alternatively you may have been hit without spotting the incoming blow. The latter hurts more. In fact, in real circumstances, without control on the part of the attacker, this is when you get really hurt. If you see the strike coming then the body will instinctively try to turn away from the incoming blow—thereby preventing the strike from hitting 'square', and so reducing the peak force. The body will also try and 'ride' the blow, lean away or 'go with the flow', staying in contact with the punch but trying to follow its path or intended trajectory. It's preferable to ride out that path, rather than be tense and stand firm in an effort to stop the trajectory—don't try 'taking' the blow on the chin in a rigid manner.

Those that have played cricket may recognize another natural example of this practice. Catching a high-speed cricket ball can be painful, particularly to an unprotected hand; for the fielders in a cricket match do not wear gloves (unlike those playing baseball). A fielder soon learns to catch a high-speed ball with a 'loose' arm that follows the path of the ball as it is being caught. This can increase the contact time considerably and reduce the forces (and pain) accordingly. A ball 'caught' with a stiff hand and arm can break a bone.

The above comment on the unseen blow being so damaging can serve as a reminder to be aware on the streets. A verbal argument with the person directly opposite can be brought to a painful close by some unexpected attacker striking you from your blind side.

A Fighter's Insight

Hitting a hard target, such as the head, will decrease the contact time and thereby increase the force felt. Hit such a target with a solid fist and high speed and a bone is liable to break, such as the nose or a cheek bone; or something may dislocate, such as the jaw. But note that the fist experiences these forces also – and something in the hand can be damaged.

(Open hand techniques have a place and purpose.)

Example 1: A baseball traveling at 50 mph

In this first example, a baseball is traveling at 50 miles per hour (22.4 meters per second) and is brought to a stop within about 4 inches or exactly 0.1 meter. A baseball weighs about 0.14 kg, 5 ounces, or 0.31 pounds. We know that kinetic energy = (½) mv², hence the energy of the ball is calculated as 36 Joules. And we know from equation *(2.2)* that work, or energy equals force times distance, hence:

$$Force \times Distance = \frac{1}{2}mv^2$$

$$Force = \frac{1}{2}mv^2/distance$$

$$Force = \frac{1}{2}0.14(22.4)^2/0.1$$

$= 360\ Newtons = 80\ lbs\ force\ approx.$

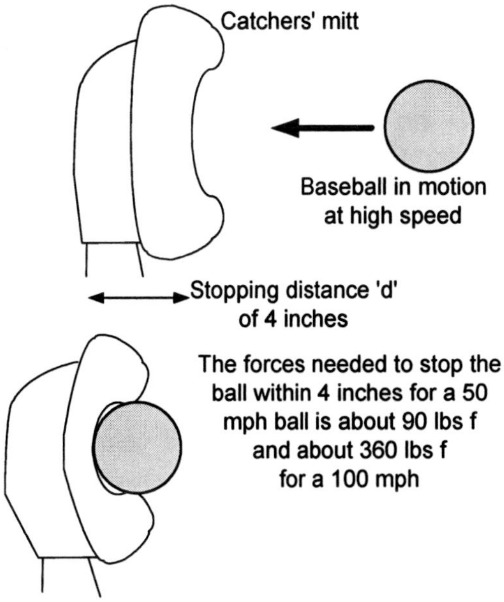

If the stopping distance was only one inch then the force would increase fourfold, to around 320 pounds force.

Catchers' mitt

Baseball in motion at high speed

Stopping distance 'd' of 4 inches

The forces needed to stop the ball within 4 inches for a 50 mph ball is about 90 lbs f and about 360 lbs f for a 100 mph

Figure 5.4: The force needed to stop a fast baseball.

Example 2: A baseball traveling at 100 mph

This time the same baseball is traveling at 100 mph (44.7 meters per second) and is again brought to a stop within about 4 inches or exactly 0.1 meter. Since the velocity has doubled we know that the kinetic energy is four times greater than before and therefore calculated as *144 Joules*. Since the force equals the energy divided by the distance, if the distance is unchanged at 0.1 meters then the force = (144/0.01) = *1,440 Newtons* or ~320 pounds force, *four times the previous calculated value.*

Does this sound familiar? Double the speed and the force increases fourfold and furthering the distance 'traveled' by these forces, prolonging the impact time, can go some way to reducing the increased forces of fast moving objects. If this super-fast ball was given twice the distance to be stopped and the hand moved back when catching the ball by about 8 inches, then the force would be half or 720 Newtons; which is somewhat better, though still twice the value of a 50 mph pitch stopped over 4 inches.

A Fighter's Insight

If struck, try to stay loose and 'go with the blow'.

5.5   Bounce or Penetration: Are the Bullets Rubber or Steel?

To develop the previous examples and somewhat academic content of this chapter let's move on to a technical illustration of the possible effect of the hardness of the striking missile. Imagine firing a steel (or aluminum) bullet and a rubber bullet at a block of wood. Both bullets are the same size, shape and mass and both travel at the same speed before striking the target. If it helps to come to terms with the fact that the bullets are the same size and mass think of the metal shells as being hollow and the rubber bullet as solid. The rubber bullet bounces off the target, the steel bullet penetrates. The steel penetrates because of its hardness and shape retention on impact; the rubber can more easily deform, reassert itself and rebound off the wooden surface. What are the different forces and effects involved? In both instances the mass and velocities are the same, so the momentum and kinetic energy of each of the two bullets is the same.

Since the rubber bullet bounces off the target the surface impulse experienced by the block of wood is greater, because it has to first stop the bullet and then 'turn it around'. The surface impact contact time is longer than it would be if the bullet had penetrated. [The contact duration time, or Δt, shown in figure 5.3 and equation 5.3 is higher.] This rebound effect can make this surface impulse almost twice as great (depending on the elasticity) and so the momentum imparted on the block can be up to almost twice that of the steel bullet case. This means that the likelihood of the block being knocked down or turned over is higher.

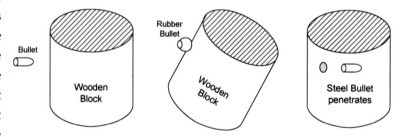

Figure 5.5: A steel bullet may penetrate, where a rubber bullet would bounce off.

When the steel bullet penetrates into the block there is a consequential transfer or surrender of kinetic energy. The energy that the steel bullet puts into the block is the energy of heat, damage and deformation. The rubber bullet when it bounces back has velocity in the rebound since it still has some kinetic energy that was not given over to the wooden block.

The steel bullet penetrates and thereby puts all its remaining kinetic energy into the block. It may even continue right through the block causing an entry wound, internal damage and an exit wound; on exit it carries with it any unused kinetic energy that has not been absorbed by the 'victim'.

The rebounding strike imparts more momentum but less energy:

> It is more likely to knock the block over.

The penetrating strike imparts more energy but less momentum:

> It is more likely to inflict internal damage.

The implications are obvious: a strike from a rubber bullet can really hurt; a strike from a steel bullet can really kill.

A Fighter's Insight

Understand the difference between the effects described. Are you firing bullets of rubber or steel?

There are occasions when you need to be rubber rather than steel—where the strike, or push, is intended to knock a person over.

There may also be a time for devastating effectiveness—when the strike needs to penetrate the enemy and impart enough energy to cause breakage or internal damage.

Note that in the law enforcement and military fields the term 'rubber bullet' has a specific meaning. As used in crowd dispersal and riot control, non-metal projectiles are fired at fairly high speed with the knowledge that if such a projectile strikes a person the likely outcome is not fatal. Usually the impact will knock a person over with such force that the individual will be temporarily incapacitated and will carry the deep bruise or hematoma for several days. If such a strike is at close range however, or to a vulnerable area, then the injury can be very serious and potentially non-recoverable.

A video ('Jackass') demonstration is available of a 20 gram bag, projected at a speed of 250 feet per second (170 mph or 76 m/s) striking the unprotected stomach of a young adult male volunteer. The bag bursts on impact and the person literally keels over and is completely incapacitated, rolling around in nauseous agony. The bruising to the stomach, at a point a few inches below the navel, is severe and is present in vivid color several days later.

5.6   Delivery of a Punch – the Practice

Where is all this leading? How does the theory and calculations help? What I am trying to provide are insights that will help martial artists to work out how best to achieve results. Let's try an example—what's the best way to deliver a punch? From the previous work this should be fairly clear (and the following is not meant to be an exhaustive study):

(i)   We want the punch to be fast.

The striking hand velocity should be as high as possible. If the punch is a left jab, for example, *relaxing the body will help*—particularly the left side upper body, shoulder, elbow and wrist. You do *not* want muscles to be tightened before release of the jab, you *do* want to lower the resistance of joints or tendons or ligaments to the movement. When appropriate, try and use some of the opponents' speed or momentum against him. Try to catch him on the way in and moving towards your strike, this adds his available velocity into the equation.

(ii)   We want 'weight' behind the strike

To create a larger mass in the equations quoted earlier, we want to hit with more than just the weight of the hand. Moving your bodyweight, your center of gravity, into the strike *simultaneous* with the strike landing will create a larger striking mass. 'Landing' at the moment of impact, or just after, will effectively increase the mass. Think of a stepping punch and the front foot hitting the floor at the same time as the fist lands, rather than landing and then striking. That can also work for a standing jab or cross strike; it is not restricted to a stepping punch action. With a jab, for example, try dropping the weight onto the front foot to coincide with the impact of the hand; 'stamping down' into the target, trying to shift the body's center of gravity towards and into the opponent at the point of impact. With a cross or reverse punch the core of the body (not just the punching hand and arm) should be moving toward the opponent, with the feeling of going into the target at impact.

Figure 5.6: With a reverse punch move the core of the body into the target.

In each case the creation of high 'effective mass' and acceleration starts from the floor; the stance and leg actions are of importance and the strike often starts from the back foot: Pushing 'upward and inward' into the strike, from the floor, getting everything going in the right order and manner. The importance of hip rotation and forward movement is discussed again in later chapters.

iii)   We want to optimize the contact time

A punch to a hard, bony object should be a sharp strike not a protracted affair. You want fast and complete release of the power of the strike into the target, with that target making the fist decelerate very rapidly, causing the strike area to be 'penetrated' and deformed. Remember that to achieve a knockout blow to the head you are trying to accelerate the brain inside the skull. An over rapid impulse like movement of the brain will cause the switch-off that we know as unconsciousness. When a boxer is trying to achieve this he has to go for a degree of 'elongated penetration', because his gloved hand is padded. Padding extends the contact time and reduces the peak impact force compared to the same strike as bare-fist punch. In trying to achieve a knock out, know that certain strike points and trajectories or 'angles of attack' are more effective than others. Certain blows, such as a hook to the point of the jaw, tend to amplify the effect on the brain. A punch to an area of the opponent that is **not** hard or bony will probably warrant a more protracted strike, with a longer contact time. This idea is developed later, when considering the difference between a snapping and thrusting type of action. Think about contact time when next in front of a punch bag: See the difference between a fast sharp strike and a long thrusting action. Look at the indentations made on the bag and think about the penetration achieved

(iv)   We want to hit square

For maximum penetration or effect the trajectory of the strike at impact wants to be perpendicular to the surface of the target. We don't want to lose energy with a 'glancing' blow, with force being deflected away. Nor do we want the opponent to 'ride' the punch— increasing contact time and dispersing the force; which is why pinning your target against a wall or one of your own limbs before striking increases its effectiveness. Most of this will be well known; intuitively understood and learned through instruction.

5.7   Striking Hard

If you stood in front of a heavy bag and decided to hit it hard you would not consider using a spear thrust strike, where the ends of the fingers are jammed into the target. However if you were in real close quarter combat and the throat or fleshy area under the jaw presented itself then this spear strike may be the technique to use.

We know intuitively that some hand positions are stronger or 'harder' than others. The term harder is used in the sense that some hand positions have less compliance, less 'give', than others. Parts of the body are also harder than others—the skull is harder than the throat; we would attack the skull with a fist rather than the end of a straight finger.

If you want to penetrate a hard target you need to use a hard or resilient weapon or missile. The ancient bowmen of Europe and the Native American Indians independently learnt to put bone or flint arrow heads onto wooden arrow shafts to make them more deadly.

If a rubber ball hits an object such as a wall it will tend to bounce off. The wall is hard and that means that the ball will bounce off with most of its original energy, at a similar speed to what it had before the collision. Alternatively, if the ball hits a soft cushion or putty like material and penetrates, rather than rebounds, then the deformation energy is high. The energy has been used to cause permanent deformation of the target or missile, *or both*. For damage you want your missile (fist or foot) to be harder than the target. In short, when hitting and trying to penetrate into something or someone you need the strike to be powerful and solid. Any weak spot in the structure of the strike will be found and some of the available striking energy will be lost through that weakness, rather than delivered to the target. For every action there is an opposite reaction; for maximum penetration you want the missile to be harder than the target.

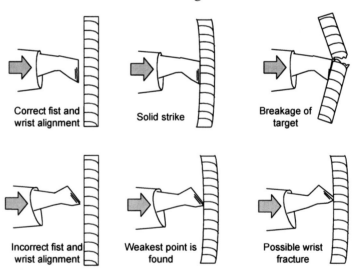

Fig 5.7: Wooden board breaking with a hand strike. For breakage you want the missile to be harder, more solid, than the target

5.8   Striking Efficiently

Chapter 2 defined momentum and pointed out that a massive object at low speed can have the same amount of momentum as a small object at high speed. When two objects collide the total amount of momentum just before the collision will equal the total amount just after the collision: Each object will typically have a different momentum after the collision but the total momentum just after the clash will be the same as it was just before.

It was once fairly common to see the so-called "executive toy" of a cradle of identical hanging steel balls on the desks of mangers with nothing better to do than to encourage creative distraction. (This toy was named 'Newton's Cradle'.) With a four ball set if you let one ball fall then the ball at the other end would fly off in response to the strike. The two center balls remained almost still and the incoming ball would virtually stop dead on impact, as all of its kinetic energy and momentum is transferred to the outgoing ball via the middle two. [The reason why two balls could not fly off in response to this single incoming ball, each with half the speed of the incomer, is because although that would conserve momentum it would not conserve kinetic energy.] If you allowed two balls to be raised and released then when these balls hit the other two they would be stopped 'dead' but the other two would move and be elevated to virtually the same height as the first two had. [Again, this two ball strike could not produce a one ball projectile with twice the speed because of the need to conserve both momentum and energy.]

Using the image of the executive toy let's mentally play with three different illustrations. In the first a small ball strikes a larger, heavier ball, in the second case a heavy ball strikes a smaller one and in the third the balls have equal size, equal mass. Figures 5.8 to 5.10 show these three particular cases of elastic collisions and it is worthwhile considering these illustrations from a fighter's perspective.

A Fighter's Insight

Matching the weight of the strike with the weight of the target will help maximize the transfer of momentum and transfer of energy into the target:

Strike too heavy and you will tend to overbalance or over-commit and follow through even though the target has been moved away.

Strike a heavy object (such as the body of an opponent) too lightly and you will effectively 'bounce off', with little penetration of that target.

Are you able to choose - to hit 'Heavy' or hit 'Fast'?

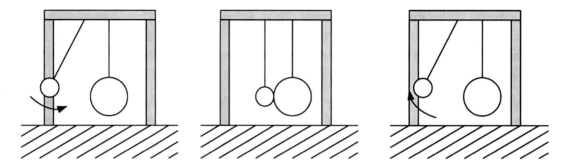

Figure 5.8: A small object strikes a massive one - the result is that the incoming ball recoils back in the opposite direction & the massive ball is hardly affected.

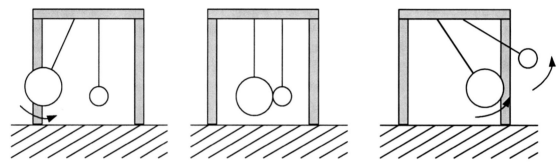

Figure 5.9: A massive object strikes a smaller one - both now move on, with the smaller ball having a much higher speed than the larger one

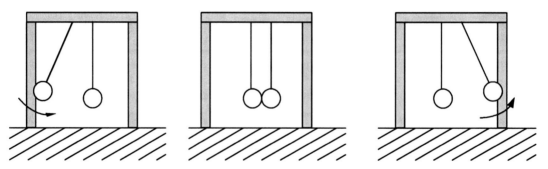

Figure 5.10: Elastic collisions of equal mass - complete exchange of momentum and energy

Analysis:

Too Light: Figure 5.8 shows how, if we strike with too little mass, then unless the speed is extremely high the target can be virtually unaffected. A person on a motorbike traveling at 70 miles per hour wears goggles to protect the eyes but is unaffected by insects hitting the face—despite the fact that they are striking at about three times the speed that we can punch. The weight of the insect is insufficient to have a noticeable effect. Even at 30 meters per second with a mass of less than one gram the kinetic energy is only a fraction of a joule. A rifle bullet on the other hand has a velocity of around 2000 miles per hour or about 900 meters per second. The muzzle energy of a 9mm Luger is approximately 500 joules while that of a .44 Magnum is over 1000 joules. Those that specialize in guns know of the differences made by the caliber of the weapon, the weight of the bullet and the corresponding stopping power. It isn't just about shooting and hitting a person, it's often a matter of stopping that person from continuing the attack and reaching or shooting the defender. The analogy with firearms is very limited but if you are attacking the body and trying or stop an assailant then you need to 'hit heavy' – or find a vulnerable area. The trunk of a human body carries almost half the total weight of a person.

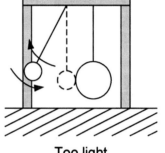

Too light

Too Heavy: Figure 5.9 shows how, if we strike with too much mass, then the target is overwhelmed and we are prone to 'carry through' and follow the target, perhaps even to the floor. We are still expending energy even after the target has been impacted and is now out of range and we may be off balance and losing control. This is a difficult topic and concept but as an illustration imagine someone about to break a two inch thick white oak board as he has done a hundred times before. The board is held by an assistant but unbeknown to the puncher the oak has been replaced by a reduced thickness board of white pine; a more fragile wood. The puncher thinks that he has to punch as hard as he has previously, deliver as much energy as he has done before, and punches accordingly. The board breaks far easier than expected, the punch goes straight through the board and the striker almost falls into his assistant.

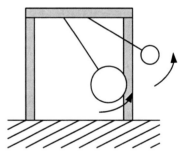

Too heavy

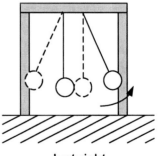

Just right

Occasionally instructors will indicate that a 'lighter' strike is all that is needed against certain targets. Many of us have witnessed instances when true experts or lucky strikes have knocked out a person with what appears to be no more than a 'tap'. However, if physically threatened by a thug that could be carrying a concealed weapon it may not be the right time to think about applying a 'lighter' touch. Training and practice will develop the ability of hitting fast and hard without suffering from over extension and loss of balance. Also, unless there is more than one attacker, being over extended to positively ensure that the attacker is finished can be acceptable. If there is more than one attacker however it could be a different story.

Equal Mass: Figure 5.10 shows that for a complete exchange of momentum and energy the mass of the incoming or striking object should be the same as the target. Think on this for a moment. It is extremely rare that we strike a target that is identical to the object we are using as the weapon. We never punch a fist. When did you last deliberately kick a foot? With the exception of a head butt the striking weapon *alone* usually has less mass than the target. Think of how effective a head butt is and reflect on how the weapon and target are 'matched'. The weight of a head is about 7% of the total body mass: To match that weight with a hand strike would need to have an effective mass that is more than the collective weight of the hand (0.5%) and forearm (1.5%) and upper arm (3%).

Hence we are taught not to strike with the weapon mass alone, we have to put weight (or mass) behind the weapon, making it heavier, making it effectively more massive.

Fighting Insights
Think about matching the mass of your striking weapon to that of the target.

If only a low striking mass is available then select a 'soft' target and go for speed. Striking with too little mass may leave the target virtually undisturbed. Although often an effective fighting tool, too much striking mass can cause 'over-travel'. Aiming for a balanced match of striking mass to target mass can be completely efficient and effective, transferring all energy and momentum to the target. However, faced with a thug on a dark night perhaps a defender can be forgiven for countering with as much speed and mass as she can muster.

5.9   Vulnerable / Vital Points

When considering the effectiveness of a strike it is obvious that the nature of the target is important. All martial artists will, sooner or later, start to become (re)familiarized with vital or vulnerable points. I say re-familiarized because frankly many of the sensitive areas or pressure points are already well known. If you want to test that just sit for awhile and discover how many sensitive points you can find on your own face, hands and arms etc. You don't need an external instructor—just prod and probe yourself to find the weak and strong points.

One of Funakoshi's 20 Principles is "Get to know yourself first, then others". This may not be what he had in mind but it is useful to know your own anatomically delicate regions (the eyes are obviously vulnerable, the spot behind each ear is well known, the softness under the chin is easy to locate; and so on). Understand, on yourself, where strikes can lead to numbness of a limb or even temporary paralysis (the so called 'dead leg' or less common 'dead arm'). Moving on, you may want to get someone who knows what they are doing to teach and demonstrate a choke hold of the carotid restraint kind—where compression of the carotid arteries (rather than the airway) causes temporary loss of consciousness.

Having done all that, think of how your existing training can be applied on these vulnerable points. For example, consider the throat as a target and the hand techniques that can be used to strike it effectively; such techniques may be single or double handed, with a range of hand positions. It is said that every block can be used as a strike—perhaps the double handed 'x block' can be applied to the throat?

Singular vulnerable spots or pressure points are generally small in area and need a precise strike or grip; hence the emphasis should be towards (a) the accuracy of the strike and then (b) the speed of the strike. There is (usually) a lower priority towards the need for a 'heavy' blow with enhanced bodyweight behind the strike when hitting a vulnerable area. There is often a trade-off between speed and accuracy. For a very precise strike the speed may need to be slightly reduced. With a strike to a vulnerable area this reduced speed is a worthwhile trade for being exactly on target

There are many less obvious vital points, just as there are spots that can be triggered to become more sensitive by first striking another body point—leading to a sequential combination that culminates in the opponent being incapacitated—but all that is another story completely and a region where the use of an expert instructor is essential because a book is simply not enough.

5.10 Summary

The penetration achieved by a weapon when it strikes a target is proportional to the energy the weapon has at impact; the more energy the more penetration. Penetration is also a function of the hardness of both the weapon and the target. A hard missile against a soft target results in maximum penetrative effects. That's a good reason to hit with the knuckles of a tight fist. If the strike bounced off rather than penetrated the target then the momentum exchange may result in the target being 'pushed away' or even over, but the internal (penetrative) damage will be minimal.

Hit a hard target with speed and focus the strike inside the target, dispense the energy of the strike into the target and get out; the shorter the time taken to exchange energy the higher the peak forces(s). If the distance over which a strike is stopped is increased then the force felt is proportionally decreased. A bony target, such as a rib, has a short contact distance (and contact time) over which the force can be experienced—for it can only deflect so far without fracture.

There is an inherent difference between striking a hard object such as bone and striking a spongier, more compliant, material such as muscle, fat and tissue. One fundamental difference in striking hard rather than soft targets is that the contact time duration reduces and this shortening of the collision duration increases the peak force experienced. Fighters can choose to punch the head in a slightly different way than the stomach, concentrating more on speed rather than effective strike mass. Focus the power into a single strike that is fast and penetrative rather than a slow, protracted, pushing action.

Matching the weight of the strike with the weight of the target will help optimize the transfer of momentum *and* the transfer of energy into the target. Strike too heavy and you can over-commit and be off balance as the target is forced away. Strike a heavy object too lightly and you will effectively 'bounce off', with little penetration of that target. A head butt is one of the rare occasions where the weights of the missile and target are, naturally, approximately matched.

To become skillful in striking vulnerable points requires expert instruction, spending time to understand anatomy and knowing your own personal weak spots helps indicate where an opponent may be vulnerable.

If you need to do damage then use a solid high-speed strike and achieve target penetration within a short contact time. *Concentrate power into a strike that is fast and penetrative—not slow and protracted.*

Strike—don't push

CHAPTER 6: THE MECHANICS OF KICKS

6.1   Introduction

The previous chapter discussed and developed the distinctions between strikes that have long or short contact times and differing degrees of penetration. In doing so it tended to concentrate on punches. The laws of physics apply equally to kicks and it's worthwhile spending time looking at the differences between snap and thrust kicks. After all, a snap kick has a different action and shorter contact time than a thrust kick, doesn't it?

Beginners to the martial arts often struggle with the side-kicks, particularly the side snap kick. This struggle may last for the better part of twelve months of training, during which time the student is unable to display the necessary distinction between the side snap and side thrust kick. Further, there will typically be insufficient understanding of the mechanics and objectives of each of these two specific actions. The front kick and roundhouse kick are usually more easily appreciated and assimilated by the newcomer, yet even the intermediate practitioner can occasionally become confused over some of the more subtle *effective* differences between a side kick's snap and thrust actions. This chapter therefore reviews the fundamental biomechanical differences between these types of kicks. In doing so we can recall the observations made in the previous chapter that there is a distinct difference between strikes with long or short contact times and there are targets where more penetration is needed.

While looking into the mechanics of kicks, we can also examine the differences between high and low kicks from a physical perspective. That knowledge can then be applied to real circumstances and conclusions may be drawn about the pros and cons of kicking high or low, particularly on the street, in real and dangerous circumstances.

6.2   Snap Action Techniques and Pivoted Arc Movements

To prepare for an examination of the snap and thrust types of kicking action consider first the back-fist type of strike, shown schematically as figures 6.1 to 6.3. In the first instance imagine the strike to be a snapping action where the fist is retracted immediately after it hits the target and travels back to its starting point by following the same path as the outward journey. In this technique the elbow joint is acting as a hinge, and the forearm and fist 'swings' or rotates around that pivot point. The same as a trap door that springs open and then shut.

Given the nature of this hinged joint and snap-back action it is difficult to put weight behind the strike. The rotation of the hips and shoulders can be used to increase the speed of the strike—and its return—but unlike the thrusting action of a straight line punch the hinged joint rotational path and snap-back prevents significant mass being applied. The body is not in line with, or behind, the path of the striking action, as it is with a straight punch or a thrust kick. Shifting the center of gravity towards the target is only of limited use. There is little point in trying to use other upper body muscles through the impact of the strike because those related body masses cannot get behind the striking line. The key is relaxation, speed and accuracy. The elbow does not need to 'lock-out' since this is a snapping action. This is a high speed, short contact duration strike to a vulnerable point such as the temple.

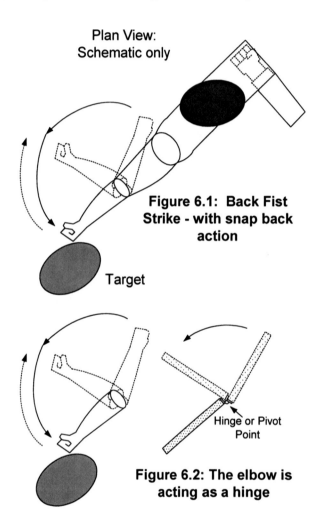

Plan View:
Schematic only

Figure 6.1: Back Fist Strike - with snap back action

Target

Hinge or Pivot Point

Figure 6.2: The elbow is acting as a hinge

6.3 Back-Fist Strike With Follow Through

The back-fist strike just described can be modified. The snap back action can be deliberately replaced with a follow through action. The idea now is to stay in contact with the target much longer and go 'through' the opponent. To allow that to happen the body leads the motion of the fist and forearm and the fist no longer 'snaps-back' but stays out and acts in a stiffened manner with arm and shoulder muscles becoming tense. It is self evident that the arm cannot hinge beyond the limit of the elbow joint, so if a straight arm is to provide further motion then to do so requires movement through a leading drive of the upper body.

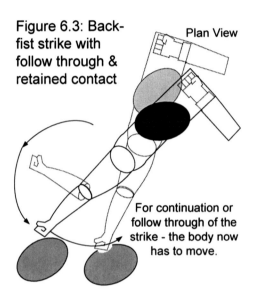

Figure 6.3: Back-fist strike with follow through & retained contact

Plan View

For continuation or follow through of the strike - the body now has to move.

The attacker now has more opportunity to use body momentum to drive into the target. We are applying a force for longer; following the initial impact of the collision with a sweeping action. This is no longer a cobra-like strike to the temple; this is more like the application of a baseball bat. Occasionally you will see fighters use a spinning body action with this kind of back-fist strike, which is powerful but difficult to control. This spinning technique can be useful when an opponent has maneuvered behind you.

6.4 Other Strikes With a Snap Back Action

There are other hand strikes that follow similar principles to those just described, where the elbow acts as a pivot point and is not normally locked-out at the point of impact. Many open hand strikes (e.g. knife or ridge hand) are delivered with an arc or rotational pathway and thereby could be first thought of as a snapping action. A knife-hand strike with a downward path, perhaps targeting the collar bone, is often delivered with the elbow bent but on contact the striking arm can be tightly connected to the body. This helps an attacker to drive some of their body weight into the blow and 'through' the target. Fighters should avoid the trap of trying to place each technique into a specific classification such as snap or thrust. Martial artists are far too ingenious to be so constrained and some strikes may be thought of as a 'cross' between two particular types of technique. Fighting at the higher level is not just 'black and white'; there are endless 'shades of grey'.

Moving to kicks, think first of a roundhouse kick where the hinge action of the knee is similar to the joint action of the elbow in the back-fist strike described previously. This type of kick can therefore be considered in a similar manner to a back-fist strike. A round kick can be delivered with a snapping action, in the way that a kick to the head is typically delivered in a Karate or Taekwondo competition. It can also be delivered with the foot or shin driving into or through the target, in the way that Muay Thai fighters typically use a low roundhouse kick to drive their shin into the opponent's outer thigh. This is not a whiplash type of snap-back action.

A reverse roundhouse kick can be of a snap-back action where the heel of the foot hits the back of the head or neck with the knee bent and then snaps back as the leg momentarily straightens. Alternatively this kick can deployed in a straight legged manner, with the leg and foot curving through the air as a 'solid' arc; aiming to destroy anything in its path. The former can have the precision of a laser guided missile, the later the brutality of a baseball bat swing

---

A Fighter's Insight

A back-fist strike can be delivered like a whiplash type of collision (fast in, fast out, minimal contact time) - or it can be delivered as you would use a baseball bat (driven through the target with a longer contact time).

A round house type of kick can be considered in a similar manner to the back-fist strike. It can be delivered as a snapping action or it can be delivered in a follow through manner with a long contact time—just as a Muay Thai fighter may attack an opponent's upper leg with a round kick.

Talking of Baseball (as a digression)

Think about a few facts and figures: A baseball weighs 5 to 5.25 ounces (150 grams), has a diameter of ~2.9 inches (7.4 centimeters) and a coefficient of restitution (COR) of between 0.51 and 0.58. This means that if a baseball is dropped onto a hard surface then the rebound speed would be just over 50 per cent of its striking speed. (The COR, or 'hardness' of a tennis ball is about 0.67 and the COR of a basketball is around 0.76, but a bouncy table tennis ball is around 0.94).

To hit a home run the velocity of the baseball after impact with the bat must be 100 mph [or 45 meters per second (m/s)] or more, at an upward angle of around 30 degrees to the horizontal. Assuming the air density is 0.07 pounds per cubic foot (1.14 kg / cubic meter) then the distance traveled before hitting the ground would be about 360 feet. Given that the pitch of a fast ball can be around 90 mph [or 40 m/s], ask one simple question: How does a batter manage to swing that bat so fast and furious that it will reverse the fast ball speed from over 40 m/s in one direction to over 45 m/s in the opposite direction; given that the ball would only bounce off a stationary hard object with little more than half its original speed?

The answer, predominately, is technique. Watch a good batter swing away and observe the hip action. The preparation and follow-through hip action, taking the force from the floor through the upper body, provides one of the best sporting demonstrations of the principles being taught throughout the world of the martial arts. (Look at the copy of a photograph of a batter at the end of his swing, ignore the fact that the front knee is almost straight but compare the hip action to a right handed reverse punch.) The hip action leads the way, from a baseball bat pull back position the hips rotate to meet the ball and the hands and bat follow—similar in principle to a golf swing. If the hips are restrained then so is the result. This has been tested, with batters fairing badly if they have their hips held and restricted by someone while they swing and hit a pitched ball.

6.5 The Front Snap Kick

The basic front kick is often taught as having two modes of action:

- o A completely snapping type of action.
- o A thrusting type of front kick action.

The student can therefore be forgiven for thinking that the front snap kick is restrained to these two types of action. An instructor will explain to the advanced student that techniques are broken down and categorized in order to learn the correct basics, but in practice such distinctions become blurred and academic rather than strictly practical. A combination of these two distinct actions can be used with great effect. In fact at the advanced level a fighter starts to 'merge' many different kicking actions, for example a round house kick type of action can be 'combined' with the straight front kick technique to create a diagonal kick.

It's important that a fighter understands the many ways that a front kick can be deployed; that when standing in front of a heavy bag and considering a front kick fighters should realize that they have options. They have choices over the target to be struck, such as the height to be aimed at, the intended contact time and desired impact penetration. A fighter can choose to kick the underside of the bag, upwards, as you would use a kick to the groin; or choose a kick to the center of the bag (i.e. in the stomach area) with either a snap-back or a thrusting action. A snap action can be seen to leave a dent in the bag whilst a thrusting action can also forcefully move the bag away. The snap action can be visualized as a quick and hard kick to the ribs or belly; the thrust kick may be aiming to 'go through' a hip joint or trying to stop an in-rushing attacker. The point is that these are at least two different basic front kicks: Imagine one as a quick snap kick to the opponent's solar plexus, designed to completely wind him but without lasting injury, the other is to kick the attacker through a wall. There is the range between these extremes—the gray areas between black and white; the half snap, half thrust examples of kicks. Let's dig a little deeper by dealing first with a couple of different trajectories of the front snap kick.

6.5.1 The Front Snap Kick - Upwards

Strike the underside of a heavy bag with a fast, upwards, front snap kick and the whole bag can be seen to 'jerk' or jump upwards. Watch the top of the bag as you kick the bottom and you'll see the upper level move as a manifestation of the impact wave delivered through the bag. Imagine the damage sustained by any vulnerable target struck by such a kick. Notice that the contact time is very short and that the bag appears to jump upwards almost immediately as the bottom is struck; there is no noticeable delay even with a long heavy bag.

This ability to shock such a heavy object is probably not, in the main, due to the mass of the striking foot and lower-leg component but from its speed and trajectory, derived from the strength of the powerful upper and lower leg muscles—trained to explode into action. Unlike a thrusting kick the action of this technique, with the position of the kicking limb and the bent knee, prevents the addition of significant body weight behind the kicking foot. The emphasis here is on a fast snapping action, with the practitioner lifting the knee high, kicking in the forward and upward direction and then pulling back the kicking leg as fast as it was delivered. When the foot meets the target, towards the end of the kick's high velocity travel, the foot is immediately retracted. The body and hips are positioned and in motion to add weight behind the kick but the emphasis is on speed, not 'follow-through'. There is no desire to prolong the contact with the opponent. Again note that's a choice: a snapping, fast return, action has been selected over a technique of kicking through the target.

In its original Okinawan form the majority of karate kicks were deliberately low, aimed at a knee joint, the inside of a leg or the groin etc. In such cases the knee of the kicking leg does not lock-out and the target is struck with a slightly bent leg. The kick is always aimed to go into the target but this may not be a thrusting action. There are, of course, the lower thrusting types of kicks that follow a stamping type of action, where the knee is lifted high and the foot straightens out and downward into the target. In that instance the knee of the kicking leg may well straighten.

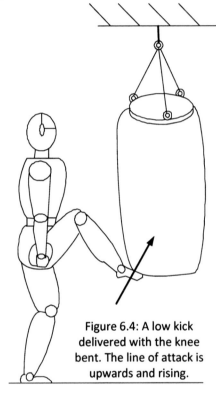

Figure 6.4: A low kick delivered with the knee bent. The line of attack is upwards and rising.

6.5.2   The Front Snap Kick – Horizontally Inwards

While still in front of a bag a fighter can think about kicking at stomach height, rather than upwards to the underside of the bag. Immediately the difference in movement can be visualized; how the knee must come up to allow the foot to be delivered into the bag. Note that the distance from the bag may change, that the fighter can be further away than when kicking the under-face of the bag. This kick may be undertaken as a snapping action with the visualization that you want to cause a dent in the face of the bag and retract quickly, rather than forcefully thrust kicking the whole bag away from you.

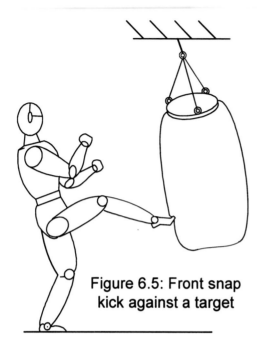

Figure 6.5: Front snap kick against a target

Shotokan Karate emphasizes the use of a front snap kick, rather than a front thrust kick. An indication of this is seen in Shotokan kata, for within the classic set of 26 kata it can be argued that there is no front thrust kick applied anywhere (and before anyone quotes Unsu as an exception ask if this is a front thrust kick or a stamping kick and, even so, it's still just one move in the 900 or so within these standard 26 kata.) As another indicator, in most karate classes when students are asked to perform a front kick they will demonstrate a front snap kick. Whereas if the class is asked to perform a side kick they may well ask which one, snap or thrust? In general the front thrust kick has fell from popularity and is now rarely practiced. Why is this? Maybe it's because the front snap kick is more useful in sport competitions, has less potential for the kicking leg to be caught and is not so easy to defend against in the usual free-style range. The front thrust kick does, however, have it use on the streets. In close quarter combat a low kick to an opponent's knee is hard to spot (and therefore react against) and a thrusting action can be devastating. If it's for real an innocent victim in fear for their life can be forgiven for not stopping to worry about damaging the knee of an attacker by kicking through the opponent.

6.6   The Front Thrust Kick

Let us now consider a thrusting type of front kick action. For the first exercise think of kicking a bag away, rather than putting as deep a dent as possible into its face. Working at very low speed it is noticeable how the body has to be behind the kick, how the hips push into the movement. Now consider increasing the speed slightly, hitting the bag harder but following through with a thrusting action. In this case, the body positioning and dynamic mechanics of the outward motion of the thrust kick is similar to the mechanics of a mid height front snap kick and at full speed there is little reduction in the outward velocity of the foot; but the final action of the kick differs. A thrusting type of action is applied at delivery, deliberately prolonging contact with the opponent and increasing the 'weight' behind the foot to impart more force for longer. Either the ball or the heel of the foot is used as the striking weapon. Note that the knee is virtually locked out at the moment of maximum penetration, allowing even more body weight to be placed behind the strike.

This thrust kick is most effective to a target at about stomach height or below. This is because the kick is thereby going directly into the target and once the knee is taken up to its maximum height then the foot is delivered in a thrusting action, straight or downward.

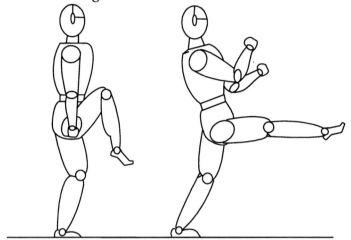

Hence the optimal target height is less than the height of the raised knee. You can always kick upwards at a higher target and push in as you connect, but a later section (6.11) will show why the horizontal kick tends to be more forceful. Here the kick is a self defense orientated thrusting and breaking action directed into the opponent's stomach, hip, leg or knee.

Figure 6.6: Front thrust kick

6.7   A Front Kick with both a Snapping & Thrusting Action

For completeness, let us consider a combination of these two distinct actions of snapping and thrusting. After training for a long period, putting work and time into the drills and spending hundreds of hours punching and kicking objects, such as a punch bag, a fighter can see that the techniques taught are endless. The distinction between a snapping and a thrusting action helps to categorize techniques and enable formal tuition, but in practice these two distinctions are fuzzy.

This is the case with a front kick, where the snapping type of action can be utilized with a degree of thrust. Think of kicking a door: If the door is of heavy solid wood and the intended action is to kick the door down then use a thrusting action. If the intent is to 'simply' kick a hole in a thin door panel then a snapping action can be deployed. If the intent is to be very targeted, perhaps at the point of the door lock, to burst the lock at the frame of the door, then a very fast kick with a deliberate but limited 'thrust' action upon contact may be the perfect approach. Now replace the image of that door (or heavy punch bag) with an opponent. Visualize this ultra-fast kick coming from the back leg and just as it connects with the opponent's stomach your hips push a degree of body weight into the target. [I can vividly remember being caught with this kind of kick in the solar plexus—it must have been over twenty years ago but can still recall how the impact felt.]

6.8   Side Kick: Snap or Thrust Differentiator

Since the snap and thrust types of side kick have such notable differences there should be less confusion than that addressed with the front kick. The side thrust kick action is a direct thrusting line, whereas the side snap kick has the foot moving through an upward arc. A developing rule of thumb can be applied by asking the question: "Is the articulated joint of interest aiming to be locked at the moment of maximum impact and penetration?" In the side thrust kick the answer is usually that the knee has either straightened or that the reaction from hitting the target prevented this. With a side snap kick the answer is probably not, only a high target could temp the leg to be fully extended in this way. Even then the force line is *not* along the line of the leg, through the knee joint and into the target; the force is transmitted through the arcing path of the kick. There is another reason for striking the target before the leg has straightened: If the knee is no longer bent then the kicking movement is coming from a leg swinging up from the hip and the high speed action of the lower leg has ended.

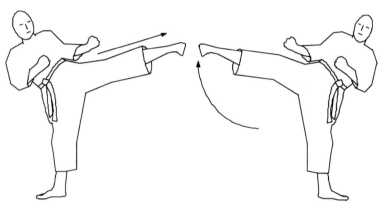

Figure 6.7: Side thrust and snap kicks - the end point may be similar but the techniques and trajectories are different.

6.9   Side Snap Kick Biomechanics

Figure 6.8 shows a simplified model of the skeletal action during a side snap kick. The leg is raised with the knee bent in this upward movement. The foot is simultaneously snapped up through the arc shown, using the hips and the upper leg muscles to drive the lower part of the kicking leg, through the knee joint connection. This is a complex movement that is a challenge to master. There is a three dimensional nature to this movement and the natural limits on the knee make it act as a restricted hinge in the plane of motion, particularly at or near the completion of a high kick. Instruction on this kick can vary. Some instructors teach that the knee should first point to the target, others emphasize that the hips should 'lead' the movement of the kick. Teaching beginners to point the knee to the target can cause them to initially confuse a side snap kick with a front snap kick that is delivered to the side. Such an error is often marked by the foot pointing upwards as the side snap kick is performed.

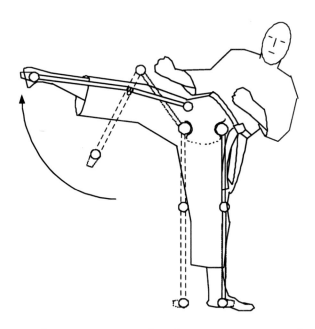

Figure 6.8: A schematic and skeletal representation of a side snap kick. The hip details are simplified for clarity.

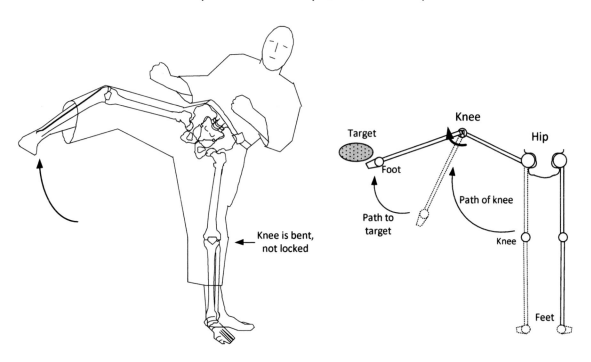

In summary, the side snap action foot movement is a three dimensional arc upwards through space. With a curving path to the target it is very different from the thrust kick straight line action where the kicking foot is extended like a piston ram type of movement from the hip to the target.

6.10 Side Thrust Kick Biomechanics

To help appreciate the biomechanical movements of a side thrust kick consider the action of forcing a piston to move along a chamber. In the model used here the connecting rod is hinged and the opening of the hinged joint is what causes the movement or thrust of the piston. The schematic shown in figure 6.9 shows this translation of motion in a simplified manner; indicating how a force action is translated or converted into linear motion. Here the action of the drive connects to a piston that is forced to follow a straight line trajectory through the constraints of the cylinder. This model is not, in itself, representative of a side thrust kick, it's not even close, but it leads to the useful visualization portrayed in figure 6.9.

With a real kick, of course, there is no restrictive chamber; we have to create our own through practice. Only by the innumerable repetitions of an accurate technique can we master the mechanism that pushes the foot through a muscularly created straight-path guide. [Note that it will need endless repetition of an accurate technique—practicing poor technique merely makes us good at kicking badly.] Figure 6.10 shows a simplified plan view of the thrust kick leg, where the hip, knee and ankle joints act and help the upper and lower leg travel from being bent to being straightened and thereby drive the foot out in a straight line, aligned with the rest of the body: Perfectly aligned, in fact, to allow the body mass to be right behind the kick. This illustration is based on the model by E. R. Serina and D. K. Lieu (1991).

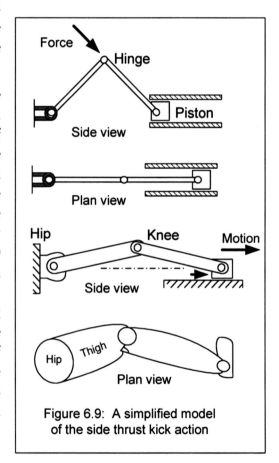

Figure 6.9: A simplified model of the side thrust kick action

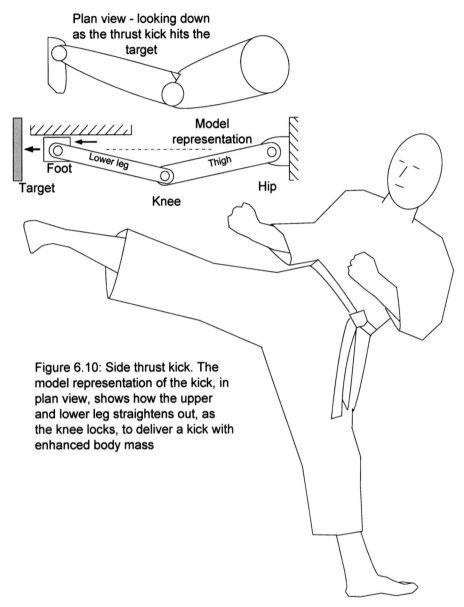

Plan view - looking down as the thrust kick hits the target

Model representation

Lower leg

Foot

Thigh

Target

Knee

Hip

Figure 6.10: Side thrust kick. The model representation of the kick, in plan view, shows how the upper and lower leg straightens out, as the knee locks, to deliver a kick with enhanced body mass

Footnote on a snapping action side thrust kick:

Starting with a classic side thrust kicking action into the target, if you then quickly retract the kick after impact this will probably mean that the kicking leg is not fully extended: a bit like a reverse punch that is immediately retracted, rather than locked out. This is a snap-action thrust kick no less. Here you have (yet another) variation on a classical theme, another indicator that the traditional strikes of the martial arts have endless permutations and adaptations.

Facts for Fighters

The side thrust kick is one of the most forceful kicks because the kick is designed to strike and penetrate with high speed and body weight behind the foot.

6.11 Kicks – High or Low: The Forces Involved

As a self-defense orientated art, techniques should be judged on their effectiveness for survival in combat. Ideally, techniques should allow for delivery in unfavorable conditions such as difficult terrain, inclement weather, icy ground or fighting while wearing restrictive attire that limits movement. Originally kicks were therefore taught to break or dislocate joints, disable knees, sweep away legs or 'go for gold'. (The Japanese term for a kick to the groin is 'kin geri'. Kin here means gold—as in gold jewels.)

In the past two decades many martial artists have been drawn towards performances where high kicks are considered most impressive. Indeed in some particular styles or competitions techniques demonstrating highly developed gymnastic abilities appear to be judged favorably and may score the same as, or higher than, those that are probably more effective. There are definite benefits in developing agility and having a wide range of techniques. Training in kicking high is useful, being able to kick the head of an opponent opens up potentially vulnerable areas, but what are the differences that need to be acknowledged between high and low kicks? What are the risks and disadvantages of high kicks that the martial artist should understand when fighting for real? What lessons can be learnt by kicking a real target, such as a punch bag or makiwara, rather than just fresh air?

6.11.1 Stability during the kick

It is fairly clear that when a kick is delivered directly into a target with only a horizontal component then the reactive force, the force pushing back, is also only in the horizontal plane. This can be seen in figures 6.11 and 6.12.

A high kick, however, is directed upward rather than just in the horizontal direction. This gives the force line two components, one horizontal (going forward) and one vertical (going upward). The angular sum of these two components provides the resultant force moving along the line of the kick, as outlined in figure 6.13. This upward vertical component has consequences; the strike can 'ride-up' the target, rather than penetrate and the upward motion can try to take weight off the kicker's supporting leg, making it more difficult to remain 'grounded' and stable

---

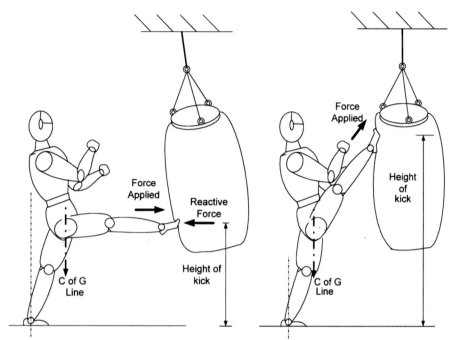

Figure 6.11: A front kick against a target - at mid and upper level.

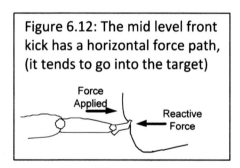

Figure 6.12: The mid level front kick has a horizontal force path, (it tends to go into the target)

Figure 6.13: A high kick has a significant vertical force component – reducing the horizontal line of penetration (it tends to slide upward)

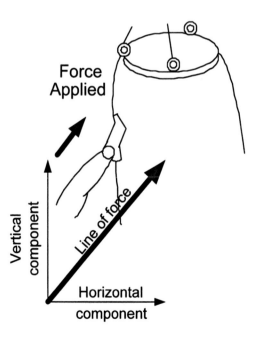

You can experiment and feel these effects. Stand opposite a wall and with a slow front kick push against the wall; firstly with a mid height kick where the leg pushes horizontally. In pushing against the wall, and feeling the wall pushing back, you will notice the forces on the heel of the supporting foot, trying to push you backwards. If you try this wearing socks and no shoes on a polished wooden floor you can easily make the supporting foot slide backwards. With the supporting leg sliding back, the tendency is for the upper body to lean forward, towards the target. Now mentally (or physically if you are flexible enough) take the kicking foot high onto the target wall and feel the difference in effects. Become aware of how 'pushing in' with the body tends to cause the kicking foot to move higher and as the foot moves higher the static stability is reduced, with the upper body now starting to want to rotate away from the target. You can begin to feel the supporting foot being un-weighted. The higher the kick, the closer the center of gravity of the body is to being under the supporting foot, rather than being further forward of this point, towards the target. This is an example of a 'turning moment', where the forces act about an axis of rotation, in this case the axis being at the contact point between the floor and the supporting foot. (Note that to see forces in action on a target just kick a helium balloon around and watch the directions of movement when it's struck.)

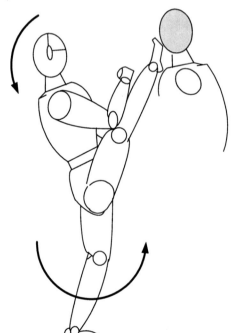

Figure. 6.14 A high front kick can cause a 'turning moment'

The 'turning moment' experienced by such a structure has a force trying to 'knock back' or more accurately rotate the kicker; in the figure 6.14 illustration this would appear as an anticlockwise rotation. This turning moment is proportional to the force applied and the height of the kick – which is the distance of the kicking foot from the ground level: The higher the kick the greater the turning moment trying to 'flip' the kicker. This can also be felt in training. Attempt to do high kicks on a polished, wet or slippery floor and you become very aware of the risk of slipping and falling on your back: During sparring it becomes easier to over extend and 'lose' the standing leg. This is another applicable point of caution for self-defense on the streets.

In summary, that impressive head high kick displayed in the training hall may not be so easy or effective in real life circumstances. Faced with a nasty surprise on the street, with no warm-up prelude or stretching, wearing restrictive clothing, perhaps with a full stomach and maybe even the effects of wine or beer on the system, it is best to keep it simple, keep any kicks low. There are always exceptions and exceptional fighters but in my view head high kicks are generally not recommended in the real life (or death) circumstances of the street. Section 6.6 dealt with front thrusting kicks and made the comment that from a force delivered perspective these kicks are most effective at about mid section height or below.

A Fighter's Insight

The higher the kick, the easier it is to over-extend and 'lose' the standing leg, to slip or be forced off balance by the very act of striking a target. All the more important therefore to have the knee of the supporting leg bent.

A mid-section (or lower) kick may well prove the best defense.

6.11.2   *Penetration of the kick*

It has already been noted that with a horizontal kick there is no vertical force component hence there is nothing that prompts the kick to slide up the target rather than penetrate into the target. The high level kick, on the other hand, has a significant vertical upward component which makes it more likely that the kick will glance off the face of the target. For kicks *below* the horizontal line the non-horizontal force components are downward, *into* the target, with obvious advantageous consequences. The kicker is more likely to penetrate into the target and there is less of a 'turning moment' that can cause the kicker to be uprooted or un-weighted. A classic front kick has been used in this section to illustrate the effect of kicking height levels. Very similar comment and analysis applies to other straight-line kicks, such as a thrust kick or straight-line back kick. A slightly different analysis applies to round or turning kicks such as the roundhouse kick or spinning back kick. The points about penetration, however, basically remain applicable to a roundhouse type of kick. At the point of impact you want the kicking foot to be at least horizontal and preferably pointing down and into the target. This is a learning point; all too often the desire for a higher kicking range causes the technique to be sacrificed and thereby result in the foot pointing upward. In a real self-defense situation a lower roundhouse kick to the opponents' ribs or knee can be more penetrating and thereby more effective. On the street a roundhouse kick to the head may be tempting because of the perceived vulnerability of the opponent and there are fighters that can deploy high kicks with high confidence, but those of us that are mere mortals should recognize that it is probably safer to kick low.

6.11.3 Summary comparison of high and low kicks:

A Practical, Streetwise, Comparison of High & Low Kicks: In Summary Form:	
The forces associated with high kicks make the kicker less stable, so a high kick on a wet surface can cause the kicker to slip.	*A low kick, below the horizontal plane, does not tend to 'un-weight' the kicker – although standing on one foot is always a risk.* *If fighting on an icy surface choose a rooted stance and try to leave the feet on the floor.*
A high kick can tend to glance off the target, rather than penetrate.	*A low kick drives inward into the target, increasing penetration.*
The higher the kick then the greater the required physical flexibility.	*No warm up is needed for kicks within the normal range of motion*
An attempt at a high kick may be made ineffectual because of clothing constraints.	*Going out to dinner in pajama-like clothing, so you can kick high in the event of an attack, is not considered cool.*
The head is a vulnerable target and a good kick to the head, that makes solid contact, can be a show-stopping end to the conflict.	*A low kick tends to keep you further away from the opponent. In the street, where an unseen weapon may be involved, this can be a life saver.*

6.12 Kicks – Training with and without a Heavy Target

Learning techniques in free space is of great value: Only by repetition with near perfect form can a technique become ingrained and of second nature. Slow, methodical and mechanical practice is needed to remove imperfections and repetition allows 'muscle memory' and instinctive behavior to be formed. [The colloquial term 'muscle memory' is misleading for muscles do not 'remember' anything. Large numbers of repetition of an action allows the neural system to learn an 'action pathway' and the related motor skills to develop. This is described more in section 13.2]

At the intermediate and advanced stage, however, there is a need to recognize that practice in free space is insufficient. Fighters must hit targets. As an illustrative example mentally imagine the performance of a thrust kick. Advanced martial artists are adept at deploying a side thrust kick in free space at great speed and being able to stop the kick at the end of its travel; then retract the foot and stand down. This practice is beneficial and it demonstrates that the kick is being locked out at full extension confirming that it is a thrusting, not a snapping, action. It should be clear, however, that when kicking in free space there is no reactive force pushing back to the kicker. Anyone that has trained regularly on a bag knows and understands this difference. Kick a heavy bag or a large target pad held strongly by a partner and you can feel the opposing force on the body, leg and supporting foot. This is exactly as predicted by one of Newton's Laws: *For every action there is an equal and opposite reaction.* Note that this is a dynamic action not a protracted, static, balancing of forces. Indeed, kick a heavy bag wrong and the bag can almost knock you over, rather than the reverse. In other words: the bag pushes back—and so will an opponent. A side thrust kick, in free space, will take on a particular form if the fighter is to be balanced at the moment of full extension and thereby able to stop the kick and remain upright.

If we were to take a photograph of a martial artist performing a side thrust kick that was controlled and balanced, such that the kick was held at the limit of its extension and motion, the image would look something like the person on the left of figure 6.15. The same martial artist performing the same kick against a heavy bag, photographed at the end of the leg extension may look something like the fighter on the right of figure 6.15. Note that these images would be literally snapshots in time; one where the balanced kick is maintained for a deliberately prolonged time and the second image portraying a dynamic kicking position that lasts for only a fraction of a second.

Static, controlled and balanced side thrust kick—where the body leans back too much

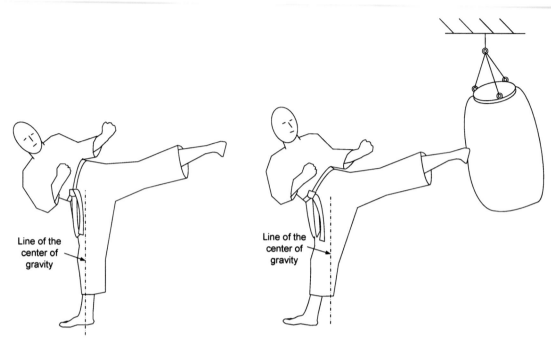

Figure 6.15: A visual image of the side thrust kick deployed and balanced in free space compared to kicking a target. In free space, to balance at the point of execution the center of gravity (C of G) must pass through the foot of the standing leg. When kicking into a bag the reactive force from the target allows the C of G to be beyond this base.

In the first case, in free space, to hold the kicking leg out in a static stance the center of gravity must be on a line that runs through the base or the standing foot: If it didn't the fighter would fall over; so to prevent this the kicker's upper body will tend to lean back, compensating for the unbalancing effect of the outstretched limb. In the second case, when the kick hits a bag, there is a returning force, pushing back against the line of the kicking leg. The kicker creates this force, it is not an inherent property of the bag, but we know that to each action there is an equal and opposite reaction. Fighters can therefore deliberately push into the kick and bag more than they could in free space. Hence, when hitting a bag the center of gravity will be further forward, towards the target. The center of gravity at the moment of impact will not be over the standing foot, it will be pushed forward and proud. *The upper body is naturally more upright when kicking the bag.* All of this movement, this deliberate forward intrusion of the center of gravity, results in a far more forceful kick. In the same way as we achieve maximum effect with a punch, we want to kick with the body not just the leg. I admit to being biased, but I've long considered the side thrust kick to be one of the jewels of the martial arts.

6.13   Classical Solution to a Dilemma:

The master text "Dynamic Karate" by M Nakayama alludes to the points made previously on balance and kicking; Chapter 3, page 71 of this book, when covering the subject of 'Balance and Center of Gravity', provides the observation that stability is important with kicks because the base is limited to the sole of the supporting foot; and that when kicking there is a shift in the center of gravity of the body. Page 149 of 'Dynamic Karate' points out that during kicking the center of gravity can fall outside the base area of the supporting foot. Therein lies the dilemma; for balance the center of gravity needs to fall within the base of that supporting foot (figure 6.16), yet during the kick the center of gravity can

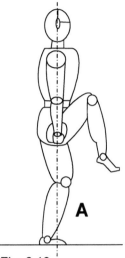

Fig. 6.16: Commencement of a front snap kick - the center of gravity falls within the area of the supporting foot

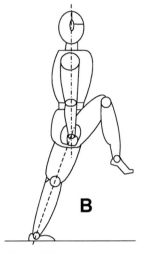

Fig. 6.17: Commencement of a front snap kick - here the center of gravity falls outside of the area of the supporting foot

shift forward. The kicking range is extended by 'reaching' out and taking the center of gravity outside of the base (figure 6.17) and the forward momentum can strengthen the kick.

The 'dilemma' basically relates to the static (remain balanced) mode compared with the dynamic (be unbalanced during movement) mode. This unbalanced state is not a new phenomenon; we walk by becoming deliberately unbalanced with each step.

When training in free space we develop our skills to help ensure that we can remain balanced and in control. When sparring or fighting we need that balance and control; we want to be able to kick and snap back in a stable position and be able to deliver another technique, perhaps another kick from the same leg, or be able to retreat or maneuver. However, at the moment of making hard (knock out or breaking) contact against a target of mass we should acknowledge the necessary total commitment, the driving extension of the center of gravity and the effect of the reactive force from the target struck. This reactive force is not present when we train in free space or spar with control and skin contact only. This is true for all strikes but is especially relevant to thrusting techniques, particularly kicks, where the penetration and contact time is deliberately extended (and we happen to be stood on one leg).

The dilemma created therefore is classic and historic. We need to train in free space, to develop our form and speed, but learning to strike without hitting something is akin to a theoretical exercise only. Similarly, we need to practice fighting to develop the skills, tactics, timing, distance and interactions with a real live opponent; but we cannot apply our techniques with full force and penetration of the target, for without protective gear this would be debilitating to our training partner: We need to learn and exercise control.

The answer, therefore, is that training should include or be supplemented by hitting targets: In the same way as a boxer spends time shadow boxing, hitting bag(s) and sparring with protective gear. All students of the martial arts should regularly spend time in front of a target because, as recommended by our previous Masters, regular practice at striking a real object is essential.

And yet:

Advanced martial artists have choices. A trained fighter can choose to kick from a balanced and stable position or allow a momentarily unstable condition to be created by the very act of lifting and using the kicking leg. As an example, in close quarter fighting a defender to an unprovoked attack may snap a low kick into the groin area from his front foot, without making any adjustment to his stance or balance. This allows the kick to be fast and delivered without preliminary movement, the front foot just coming up and out without body shift, with an acceptance of the fighter being momentarily off balance. The fighter just kicks, without warning, without a sign or 'tell'. Try it: From a forward stance, kick with the lead leg but without pulling any weight back, accepting that the kick has to be delivered in that brief moment before the foot needs to return to the ground to regain balance.

Footnote for Instructors:

You will regularly see karate or TKD students practice a front kick in free space. Sometimes the kick is delivered from the back leg and after completion is brought back to that rear foot (step-back) position. At other times, after the kick is delivered, the student will step forward. Kicking in free space is not the same as kicking an object or person. When you hit or kick something of substance such as a bag or a body then that object pushes you back, helping you to maintain balance, helping you to withdraw the kicking leg. When kicking in free space with the same energy, reach and commitment, no push back from the target is present and the student's center of gravity may be left far forward. Consequently pulling the extended leg back is difficult and to compensate, in training, the student steps forward. This training is usually supplemented with the more balanced kicking practice where the foot is withdrawn and the student can choose to step forward or back.

6.14   Summary

Kicks have the potential for being the most forceful of unarmed strikes. Snap kicks and thrust kicks are different, although some techniques can become 'blurred' and the action 'merged' into a part snap, part thrust kick. Kicks and punches are not limited to either a snap action *or* a thrust action; a kick can be delivered in a snapping action manner with varying degrees of thrust at contact.

For a thrusting action to drive body weight into the opponent the limb should be straightening and driving directly into the target; a round house kick cannot be considered as a thrust kick.

Snap action techniques are generally of lower effective striking mass than thrusting actions, although the speed is high and the contact time is short. With a thrust kick or reverse punch more body weight can be put behind the strike, compared with a snap action strike.

Side thrust kicks have a very different biomechanical movement compared with side snap kicks. The side thrust kick has a straight line action and can be very forceful; delivered with significant speed and body mass it allows a lot of energy to be imparted into the target. The contact time may be deliberately sustained. The side snap kick is very fast and will impart a 'shock' into an opponent; being particularly effective against a vulnerable target. The contact time tends to be short.

Junior martial artists need to be taught and continually reminded of the proper technique that is to be attained. Practicing poor technique merely makes us good at kicking or punching badly.

Fighters should be aware of how balance is affected when kicking and forcefully striking a target. A straight line horizontal kicking action has no upward direction component; it just goes into the target. A high kick can glance upwards off the target and it can also cause the kicker to be somewhat unbalanced, making him less stable, more prone to slip or being swept. Kicking high can carry risk, particularly in the difficult conditions that can be expected outside of the training hall. In a street fight it is usually safer to use low kicks.

Hitting an object or opponent with a heavy thrusting action, for example using a side thrust kick, will create a reactive (push back) force that is not experienced when practicing in free space. This affects balance and influences the mechanics of the movement. Practicing in free space is excellent for improving form and speed, or for the development of combinations, but it is *not* the same as hitting an object.

"*We are what we repeatedly do. Excellence, then, is not an act but a habit.*"

Aristotle

CHAPTER 7: THE STRIKING OF OBJECTS

'Do not have an idea of winning, while the idea of not losing is necessary'
Master Funakoshi

7.1   Introduction

The martial arts are made up of innumerable parts—there are many routes to the top of this mountain and no true Master has ever claimed to have reached the peak. All styles or schools that I have known have two things in common: they all teach the fundamentals and they all practice the art of fighting. Many traditional schools teach kata, forms or patterns, and often that is the means by which their particular art has been passed down through the generations. These three elements of basics, kata or forms, and fighting are not discrete and independent; each supports the other and the overlaps, iterations and reinforcements continue throughout a lifetime of study. These three parts of the martial arts curriculum involve the real or imaginary striking of objects and some may say that this is of dominant importance, for at the center of the art is effective self defense. Traditional karate, for example, has the aim of stopping an opponent with a single strike.

This chapter builds on the work covered earlier on collisions and forces to provide a review and analysis of the striking of objects. At its best the martial arts can develop the physical, psychological and spiritual aspects of a person. In this book I will not attempt to provide my views on psychological or spiritual development, for this publication is more concerned with the physical and does not address the aims of perfecting character or clearing the mind for battle.

I am a strong supporter of including the 'hands on' striking of training aids in the practice of the martial arts. Regular workouts on a punch bag or similar will improve a fighter's effectiveness. Initial instruction and regular review is recommended but a person hitting a bag receives continuous tactile feedback *from the bag*. The act of hitting the bag will show the effects achieved and hence practice will naturally tend to improve technique and coordination. (Some forms or kata have us striking our own hand with a fist or elbow, which also provides immediate feedback on our striking ability.)

It should be recognized that each of the array of training aids has different characteristics. There is a big difference between a speed ball and a heavy bag. The technique employed on a 'hard' target such as a makiwara, will not be exactly the same as that applied with a softer striking pad. (Just as there is a difference between hitting an opponent's head compared to the stomach.) There is a time for training in multiple striking combinations; for fluidity and speed, perhaps lightly striking a punch bag while attacking from a variety of angles and distances. There is a place for training in a strong, rigorous and basic manner using the same technique repetitively, perhaps against a makiwara striking post or heavy bag. There can be occasions in the life of a martial artist when the breaking of wooden boards is appropriate, perhaps because of a personal need to test and confirm the effectiveness of a technique. Fighters do know, however, that board breaking is a controlled test and although it may be a measure of an achievable striking force, on its own it is not a measure of fighting proficiency. Similarly, whilst conditioning of the hands to hit objects can be considered useful for the martial artist, always think rationally and carefully about the training that you do. With that caveat, let's now examine the usefulness and technical aspects of some of the more popular training aids.

7.2 Striking a Makiwara

A makiwara is a traditional Japanese striking target, originally made from a tapered wooden post of about seven foot length, with the first two to three feet buried and wedged in the ground, and the remaining four to five feet available for striking. The upper striking area was traditionally wrapped in straw, from where the name arose. It is used as a target for punches, open hand strikes and kicks to develop technique, strength and spirit. Makiwara can still be found in traditional training centers, frequently alongside other training aids such as punch bags. Although a makiwara face does have a little initial cushioning and the post has a degree of compliance it is a fairly hard or resilient object to strike. For me, the primary purpose of makiwara training was orientated towards helping develop correct technique, form and physical alignment. To strike such a hard object means that on a punch the wrist, elbow and shoulder need the right alignment, connection to the body and strength. Historically the practice led to the development of calluses on the hands, which occasionally were mistaken as the aim rather than the effect. There are suggestions that the regular and repeated use of a makiwara can be detrimental to the hands. I have no expertise to allow me to make a comment on this, but I strongly believe that moderation would be in order.

Figure 7.1: Makawari training

You may have heard of a makiwara being broken by exceptional punching power. This is difficult to believe unless the post has been worn and weathered over a period of years. Like any such structure a makiwara could be broken by pushing the top of the post back beyond the point where it can bend and recover. Under such circumstances I would expect the post to break almost at the bottom; just above the point where it emerges from the ground. This would be at that juncture where the continuing deflection meets the section of post that is held rigid by the wedged burial; the point of maximum change of deflection that makes stress fracture most likely. This is easy to see—when next out in the park, put your foot on a dead branch and bend it till it breaks; if the branch is of approximate uniform thickness with no weak spots the fracture will be near your foot.

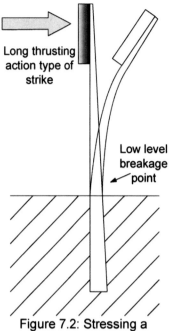

Long thrusting action type of strike

Low level breakage point

Figure 7.2: Stressing a makiwara to breaking point

You can also imagine that a very strong and long thrust kick to the makiwara could possibly have the same effect, taking the post beyond its elastic limit and causing it to crack or break. This is unlikely, since a makiwara post is designed to be resilient, with wood that is chosen to withstand the worst punishment that human assault can inflict. However, like all structures, continued heavy use will cause wear and fatigue. I am sorry to say that I have never witnessed the breaking of a makiwara, but someone who was privileged to see Master Nishiyama break two with punches noted that they splintered a few inches above the floor mounted brackets on which they were held.

An interesting point was made in an article called *Build Your Own Makiwara* that can be found on Rob Redman's '24FightingChickens' website. I recommend reading the article fully and following the link to the discussion on 'focus'. It is pointed out that, as we know from Newton's Laws, the harder you hit a makiwara the harder it hits you back. Moreover, the more you force a makiwara backwards the more it wants to reassert itself and return to its normal position (like a spring). Hence if you strike a makiwara with complete commitment, speed, mass and good form—starting from the floor, rotating the hips and hitting right through the target—then it's going to hurt. The more striking energy employed then the more it will hurt; the better you hit, the more it hurts. Since the body does not enjoy being hurt a potential sub-conscious side effect is that training with a makiwara does not naturally encourage you to continue to improve your punching technique.

Another point made within the 24FightingChickens article is that the makiwara 'stacks in reverse' in a manner opposite to the way punch bags do. When you strike a person or a heavy bag the highest force experienced is at, or near, the surface of the object and thereafter it tends to reduces as you 'punch-in'. With a makiwara however, as you penetrate the force needed is increased not lessened, so once again there is this potential sub-conscious side effect that can limit improvement; hence spirit or determination is needed. One final point is that if you strike and focus (contract muscles) on impact then you may be able to 'hold' the makiwara back at its point of deflection. An assertion made in the article is that with the contraction of supplementary muscles you will actually reduce the strike speed and therefore the force applied, hence there will be less deflection of the makiwara, hence it is easier to hold it back. It is therefore suggested that a person who strikes with their highest speed and momentum will not be able to hold the makiwara back while in a static position. Mr. Redman's website '24FightingChickens' is recommended for prompting thought and discussion about many aspects of karate and the martial arts.

To quote one Master:

"When I first started training at Takushoku University it was mandatory that we hit the makiwara 50 times per hand. Even though this does not seem like a high number, a senior student would place his hand two inches behind the board and count only the punches that made the board slap into his palm. As you can imagine, sometimes it took over 200 punches to do 50 correctly! This practice quickly forced us to fully commit to each punch without thinking about how many repetitions were ahead because only the focused techniques were counted."

Master Okazaki

7.3   Striking a Bag

Think of walking up to a punch bag and pushing it as far and as high as you can. By using a previous equation *(2.3)* we can calculate the potential energy that the lifted bag now has because it is now higher and further from the floor. The act of lifting the bag provided that energy and the heavier the bag or higher the lift then the more energy you need. This is an inelastic collision—the person pushing is in constant contact with the bag over the duration of the 'lift' and the contact time is long. Contrast that to being able to impart the same energy into a single, fast and furious strike: with a contact time that is around one tenth of one second. In such circumstances you will see the bag first indent and then move or swing away. This time the swing will be nowhere near as high as you previously pushed the bag, despite using the same amount of energy. In this instance the energy was concentrated in an explosive manner rather than spread out over a long duration.

Putting numbers to this illustration: If the effective weight of the lifted bag was 20 kilograms and we push it up by a 1 meter (around three feet) increase in height then the energy used is the product of mass, the gravity constant and height; which equals 196 joules. [Note that the bag will actually weigh more than 20 kg. but some of the load continues to be taken by the ceiling support.]

Since force equals energy/distance we know that the force involved is 196/1=196 Newtons. If that same energy had been applied across a distance of only 0.1 meter (about 4 inches) then the force would have been 196/0.1=1960 Newtons; a strike that penetrates by 0.1m has ten times the level of force as the same energy imparted over one meter. We know this from experience, it's the reason we will 'ride' a punch that we can't avoid or block.

The previous chapter (6) discussed techniques that range between the extremes of a relatively long, thrusting type of action and a very fast, snapping type of strike. A side thrust or back kick technique can have a high speed impact with correspondingly high initial impulse force. This demonstrates that the kick is a strike not just a pushing action, although it can have a high follow through action that continues to impart energy into the target, increasing the damage caused.

A bag can be used in many ways. There is a time to repeatedly test single techniques and there are times to work on combinations. With a set combination being built up in stages, practice on both left leg and right leg forward fighting stances. Such a routine may be jab ten times both sides, then jab, reverse punch ten times both sides then jab, reverse, hook punch ten times etc. Building upon each strike can

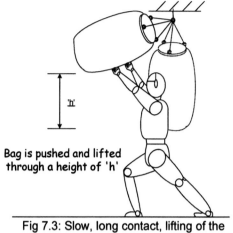

Bag is pushed and lifted through a height of 'h'

Fig 7.3: Slow, long contact, lifting of the bag

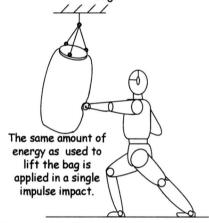

The same amount of energy as used to lift the bag is applied in a single impulse impact.

Fig 7.4: Fast, short contact, strike of the bag

create a lengthy combination that may be orientated towards punches only or a mixture of hand strikes, kicks, elbows and knees. Practice such combinations both heavy and light.

In most respects a bag is an ideal training tool. It serves as a means of testing and improving techniques and combinations, by providing immediate feedback of the efficacy of such techniques. When you strike a bag you can see, feel and hear the effect. The bag shows the brute power of an elbow strike and painfully illustrates how barefoot kicking demands correct foot and toe positioning. The bag acts as the teacher and we learn from it on both the rational and the intuitive level. (I know someone who once kicked a bag in an unfamiliar training hall only to painfully discover it to be filled with compacted sand.)

7.4   Breaking a Wooden Board

Board breaking has often been used as a test of a martial artist's progress. Breaking a substantial piece of material with one's 'bare hands' has long acted as a demonstration of ability. Once usually a private matter between fighter and instructor, frequently this is now a more open affair, as part of a grading or as a competition to see who can 'break the most'. However, as one martial arts expert put it "boards don't hit back", meaning that the test is not representative of fighting. (Remember that our physics expert stated that 'to every action there is an equal and opposite reaction', meaning that a board can hit back—as hard as you can hit it—which is enough to break bones!)

What follows are several pages devoted to providing insight and the mathematics associated with breaking boards or similar. This includes a worked example to show how to numerically check the level of difficulty in breaking boards. This gets very technical and specialized and if the topic is not of interest I suggest skipping ahead to section 7.9.

Through the consideration of material sciences it can be shown that the force needed to break a piece of wood is proportional to its modulus of rupture (its bend strength or how far it can resist deformation under load), the width of the board and the square of the thickness of the board. This simply means that a thick board is much harder to break than a thin one, that wood from a pine tree is easier to break that ash, that it's easier to break a narrow board than a wide one. As you would expect, the breakage force is inversely proportional to the length of the board. In other words a long, narrow, board is easier to break than a short and wide one of the same thickness and material. The mathematical relationship representation for this (Feld et al 1979) is:

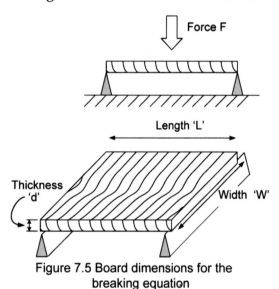

Figure 7.5 Board dimensions for the breaking equation

$$F \propto \frac{Wd^2}{L} \qquad Equation\ (7.1)$$

Where: F = Force to cause breakage,   W = Width of wood

d = Thickness or depth of board,   L = Length of the board

and ∝ is the symbol for proportionality.

The labeling of length and width is not arbitrary; it is determined by the grain of the wood and figure 7.5 illustrates these dimensions. The characteristics of the wood, such as its modulus of rupture, convert the proportionality of equation 7.1 to an absolute numeric relationship, allowing the breakage force to be calculated. A similar relationship exists with the breakage of a concrete slab, but the proportionality constants are very different, due to the differing characteristics of manmade materials compared to natural materials such as wood. The above equation can be used to help answer the question 'which is easier to break, one 2 inch thick board or two 1 inch thick boards?' This is covered in section 7.7.

Insight can be gained through the consideration of the energy imparted into a board and the deformation damage caused by a collision between the fist and the wooden board. Appendix B shows how the physics associated with the conservation of energy and momentum allows the derivation of an equation that can be used to calculate the deformation energy (ΔE) needed to break a board as it is struck by a fist or foot. This is shown below as equation 7.2.

$$\Delta E = (1 - e^2)\frac{m_w}{(m_h + m_w)}\left[\frac{1}{2}m_h(v_{h1})^2\right] \qquad \text{Equation (7.2)}$$

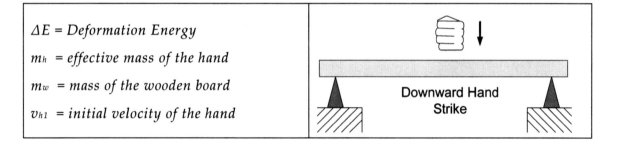

ΔE = *Deformation Energy*

m_h = *effective mass of the hand*

m_w = *mass of the wooden board*

v_{h1} = *initial velocity of the hand*

Downward Hand Strike

Examination of this equation shows that in this breaking board example the more energy the hand has the more energy transferred to the board and if the board is infused with more energy than it can handle then it will break. There is an interesting term (1-e²) introduced by this equation; a term that is described in appendix B. This factor 'e' is a function of the hardness or softness of the colliding objects. The deformation energy imparted to the board depends not only on the energy of the strike but also on the coupling and the coefficient of restitution or elasticity term 'e'.

When attempting a break the student is taught to drive through the board, not to aim for the surface but to a place beyond the far side of the board: Do not strike the board at or very near the maximum extension point of the arm, for here the striking velocity is reducing. This aspect is covered in Chapter 8.

As the fist hits the board the wood will bend. This deformation will compress the surface and upper half of the board, and stretch the lower half of the board. If the stretch is too great at the lower surface then the board will start to crack at that bottom surface. The cracks start at the bottom because wood (and concrete) is weaker under tension than compression. The crack will spread upward and the board will break if the transfer of energy is great enough, with the fist then driving through the cracking board. This transfer of energy is a force and distance product and we have previously seen that energy and work are equivalent and that work equals force times distance.

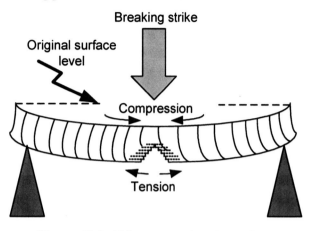

Figure 7.6: When struck a board can bend, crack and break

"If the area of the dent of the board that is struck dents a sufficient distance, it will break. Since the distance it dents depends on the energy transferred to it and the amount of energy transferred depends on the velocity of the karateka's hand: A high-speed strike is most likely to break the board."

A J Chananie; The Physics of Karate Strikes

As stated in equation (7.2) the coefficient of restitution 'e' is determined by the elasticity of the collision and is a function of the characteristics of the colliding objects. In other words it refers to the 'bounciness' of the collision and to what extent the objects involved stick together after impact (inelastic) or ricochet apart (elastic). Objects which would collide with perfect elasticity, deflecting one another totally (two impenetrable diamonds perhaps) would have a coefficient of restitution of 1, while 0 represents a totally inelastic collision (such as the collision of two marshmallows, which would simply stick together). Most objects have an 'e' value somewhere between 0 and 1. In our considerations of striking and breaking objects the collisions will mainly involve inelastic objects - and if the 'e squared' term is very small then $(1 - e^2)$ approximately equals one and equation 7.2 converts to:

$$\Delta E = \frac{m_w}{(m_h + m_w)} \left[\frac{1}{2} m_h (v_{h1})^2 \right] \quad \text{Equation (7.3)}$$

Note that the $\left[\frac{1}{2}m_h(v_{h1})^2\right]$ term is the kinetic energy of the striking weapon, and the message, again, is the importance of the strike speed. Since, for our work here only the hand (and not the wood) has an initial velocity the term v_{h1} will be replaced by v_1.

In the case of an elastic collision where, for example, a rubber ball is bounced against a target and it rebounds with a speed of about half of its impact speed then e, the coefficient of restitution would be said to be 0.5. If 'e' in the above equation were 0.5 then $(1 - e^2)$ would equal 0.75 in the deformation energy (ΔE) equation, hence there would be 25% less deformation energy imparted and hence twenty five percent more energy would be needed for the same effect (elasticity is important - swords with brittle steel will break easier). Note that if e were 1, as in a completely elastic collision, there is no loss of kinetic energy, no damage - because the term $(1 - e^2)$ equals zero. Although mainly theoretical, since the collisions we see are never completely elastic, this is useful to remember.

In a totally elastic collision there is no deformation energy; no deformation occurs.

A previous section (5.5) asked that thought be given to the difference between an object that strikes a target and bounces off, compared to one that strikes a target and penetrates. The above shows how, if the collision with the board were totally elastic, then the board could not be broken. For a board to break more kinetic energy has to be imparted into it than it can handle. If it is a completely elastic collision this cannot happen, momentum is transferred rather than energy. Think of two diamonds colliding with each other, neither causing penetration of the other, then think about the idea of striking a soft target (e.g. stomach) with a hard object (e.g. fist)—where penetration will occur and your hand is less likely to be damaged.

Facts for Fighters

For devastating effectiveness we want our strikes to penetrate the target and impart enough energy to cause damage.

In breaking a 'brittle' object such as a board this penetration is usually completely through the wood, or object broken, for the rupture starts on the side opposite to the face being struck. In breaking a single board, vigorous deflection of only half of the thickness can be sufficient to cause fracture.

If you want to break wooden boards cleanly and efficiently then best hit fast, hit centre and hit 'through'.

7.5   Board Breaking – by the Numbers

The above may appear very academic and theoretical, but it can be used to determine what you can and cannot break. That could be useful knowledge, before you stand in front of a board or slab and put yourself in danger of injury. Of course this is after you have been shown how to strike and break something by someone qualified - and then practiced. It is, after all, your hand and arm that's at risk.

First question: What energy is required to break the board?

This is not a simple question and there is no simple answer. As a starting point, if it's a wooden board that to be broken, best check on what the wood is. There is a big difference between say white pine and ash; size for size ash will withstand about twice the impact as pine without breaking. Assuming that it is white pine we then need to find out the related properties of that material, unfortunately that is not straightforward either. Most data relates to the ability of the material to withstand a standing loads, which is very important if you are about to use the wood to support a roof or bridge, but here we are dealing with an impact rather than a static load: Here we become reacquainted with the difference between strength and toughness:

- Strength: The ability of a member to sustain stress without failure.
- Toughness: The ability to withstand impact energy before breaking.

Hence we want to look for a measure of the toughness of the material; sometimes referred to as the impact strength. Impact strength is typically described as equal to the energy that can be absorbed by the specimen before breaking (kilo Joules), divided by the cross sectional area of the specimen (m²).

$$\text{Impact strength} = \frac{E}{x} \text{ kJ/ m}^2 \qquad \text{Equation (7.4)}$$

Where E = energy absorbed by the specimen (kilo Joules)
And x = cross sectional area of the specimen (m²)

A Fighter's Insight

Many in the martial arts know a similar distinction between strength and toughness: We know individuals that are very tough but not particularly strong physically; we see those that have aged and become weaker but still stand on the front line at training sessions and withstand all that is thrown at them.

There is mental toughness.

Attempt to look up this value of "E" and you may see a range being quoted, trying to take into account such factors as the type of pine, the density of the material and water content. Since it is your hand that's at risk I would suggest choosing the upper, worst case, values.

This is an important cautionary note. When looking at properties of material such as impact strength understand that there is a tendency to quote the lower values and it is rare that the numerical tolerance or uncertainty is shown. This is because a designer or architect is normally interested in protecting a structure (e.g. house or boat) against impacts and will want to know that the figures being used are pessimistic. The designer will err on the side of safety and will deliberately choose a lower breaking load figure and where necessary use extra material to ensure that the structure is sufficiently robust. However in our case we don't want to choose a lower breaking figure—we want to know the *maximum* force that's needed to break the board, because we want to be able to exceed this and 'failure to break' is a more painful option. So knowing that the figures may be on the low end it's advisable to add a margin of, say, an additional 33% to the figure provided. So, let's assume that the figure quoted for the toughness of white pine, with the grain, is approximately 2 kJ/m². We can now calculate the expected approximate energy needed to break a board.

For reasons that will soon be apparent, let's select a pine board that is 28 cm long, 15 cm wide and 1.9 cm thick (In inches, this is a board about three quarter of an inch thick, about 11 inches long and almost 6 inches wide.) This has a cross section area of 0.00285 m², hence the energy needed to break the board is 2,000 (Joules/ m²) times 0.00285 (m²) or *5.7 Joules.* The size of board chosen exactly matches the dry white pine that is referenced by Feld et al, (1983). Within this paper the authors calculated that the energy needed to break a board of that size and material would be 5.3 joules, with a tolerance or uncertainty of ± 2.8 J. This figure of 5.3 Joules is in very good agreement with our derived value of 5.7 joules. If we follow the advice of adding 33% to 5.7 we have a (safer) value of 7.6 joules, which is fairly close to the 'Feld' tolerance included figure of (5.3 + 2.8) = 8.1 joules. Hence for the *first question*: What energy is required to break the board? We have the answer of about 8 Joules.

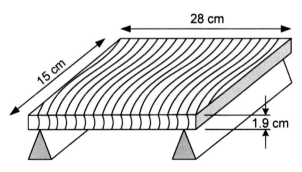

Second question: Can the person about to strike the board generate sufficient energy to cause breakage?

The starting point to this question should by now be relatively straightforward. If the person is 75 kilograms in weight and is striking down through a horizontally mounted board and can hit the target at a speed of 10 meters per second; then the kinetic energy of the strike can be determined as follows:

Assume that the strike carries the weight of the hand and the forearm only; from table 8.1 provided in section 8.10 of this book it can be seen that the hand is approximately 0.5 % and the forearm is 1.5% of total body weight giving a hand and arm mass of 2% of total body mass, or 1.5 kilograms for a 75 kg male. We know the velocity of the strike so we can turn to the kinetic energy equation as follows:

$$\text{Kinetic energy} = \frac{1}{2}mv^2 = \frac{1}{2}1.5 \times 10^2 = 75 \text{ joules}$$

So far, so good: That looks like almost ten times the energy needed. However not all of this energy goes directly into breaking the board. An earlier section gave the 'deformation energy' equation to use:

$$\Delta E = (1 - e^2)\frac{m_w}{(m_h + m_w)}\left[\frac{1}{2}m_h(v_1)^2\right] \qquad \text{Equation (7.2)}$$

ΔE = Deformation Energy m_h = effective mass of the hand

v_1 = initial velocity of the hand m_w = mass of the wood

e = coefficient of restitution

We can determine the mass of the wood, m_w, by first working out its volume as a product of length, width and thickness to give 28x15x1.9 = 798 cubic cm. If we take the density of the pine to be 0.5 g / cm³ (500 kg / m³) then the weight is the product of volume and density or 798 x 0.5 = 399g or approximately 0.4 kg. So the deformation energy available, assuming that e² is very small, can be calculated as:

$$\Delta E = \left(\frac{0.4}{1.5 + 0.4}\right) \times \left[\frac{1}{2} \times 1.5 \times (10)^2\right] = \frac{0.4}{1.9} \times 75 = 15.8 \text{ joules}$$

This is twice the energy needed to break the board— calculated as up to 8 joules. So we should feel confident enough to go ahead. Hence to the question: Can the person about to strike the board generate sufficient energy to cause breakage? The answer, for someone proficient is yes— they can generate almost 16 joules compared to the 8 joules shown to be needed for this configuration of board.

Two points to note; the mass of the strike used, as only the hand and forearm, is akin to an overhead knife strike. This makes 'dropping' the body weight into the strike more difficult than a technique such as punching down into the target; or putting more weight behind the punch when using a reverse punch. So, again, we are being conservative (or pessimistic) by not including more effective mass behind the strike. Also a speed of 10 meters per second is reasonably achieved with a downward strike, provided that the target is struck at about the mid range (arm horizontal) point and the person has had enough training and practice. The speed of a vertical downward strike roughly follows the velocity profile shown in figure 7.7, so the maximum speed is at about the halfway stage—and you should aim to strike through and beyond the board.

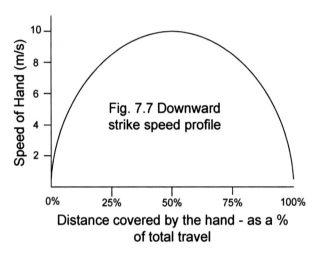

Fig. 7.7 Downward strike speed profile

Distance covered by the hand - as a % of total travel

7.6 Breaking by the Numbers — Supporting Evidence

In 1977 Haywood Blum of Drexel University, Philadelphia calculated that a standard board of No. 2 pine of dimensions 2 x 28.6 cm, x 25 cm long (nominally 1 inch by 12 inches wide by 10 inches long) would require about 64 joules of initial kinetic energy to cause fracture. [The conversion of 2 cm to 1 inch is not exact but it is repeated here directly from Professor Blum's paper. The board is described as 'nominally' 1 inch.] The footnotes to this paper point out that: *"When supported along the two edges parallel with the grain, such a board can support a static load at its center of between 444 and 1110 N (100 – 250 lb), the maximum load depending on a number of factors. This is intended to be equivalent to the strength of a human rib which the board represents."*

Since it takes less than 100 joules of initial kinetic energy to break a rib we can use equation (2.4) to indicate that a punch of velocity of 7 meters per second needs only 4 kilograms mass to cause fracture. Section 8.10 shows that the mass of the hand and full arm is about 5% of a man's total mass, hence if the person striking at 7 m/s is 80 kilograms or 176 pounds in weight then punching with only the hand and arm mass can be sufficient (5% of 80 is 4 kg). These mass and velocity figures are within the range of an experienced fighter. As discussed elsewhere, layers of cushioning tissue will always affect the force - time dynamics. Note that this figure of 64 joules is quoted as the initial kinetic energy (KE) of the striking missile, not the deformation energy imparted into the target. If the deformation energy (ΔE) needed for fracture was around the 8 joules figure derived by Feld (1983) then this is one eighth of the initial missile kinetic energy and hence $\Delta E = \frac{1}{8}(KE_{missile})$ and equation 7.2 can then be used to show that $\left[(1 - e^2)\frac{m_w}{(m_h + m_w)}\right] = \frac{1}{8}$. This shows that if 'e' is small then with a high speed strike the wood (or rib) can be fractured with a effective strike mass about seven times the mass of the target.

Question: 'Why don't the bones of the hand break when smashing concrete?'

Compared to wood or concrete, bone is an extremely strong material. Bone has a modulus of rupture that is an order of magnitude greater than concrete. Wilks et. al, in the 'Physics of Karate' paper calculated that a cylinder of bone 2cm diameter and 6cm long, simply supported at the ends, can withstand in excess of 25,000 N of force exerted at the center. However, know that the bones of the hand can be broken in a bare knuckle fight.

Question: 'Why does it hurt more when the board doesn't break?

The previous theory indicates why failing to break a board is more painful than succeeding, despite the speed and mass of the punch being the same in both instances. When you break a board the fist continues through with a significant residual velocity. When the board does not break the hand is brought to an abrupt and painful stop. The deceleration of the hand is higher and the impact force felt is higher. Blame Newton and F=ma.

7.7   Board Breaking – Degrees of Difficulty

Whilst on the subject of breaking boards let us spend a moment to think about the difference between breaking one board of two-inch thickness and two boards each of one-inch thickness. In doing so, let's assume that all boards are of the same material (say pine) and the same length and width. Section 7.4 suggested that the minimum force required to break the board is given by the equation 7.1 relationship that $F \propto \frac{Wd^2}{L}$. Hence the force needed is proportional to the board thickness (d) squared: So if a specific force is required to break a one-inch thickness of wood, then four times that force is required to break a two inch board of the same material cut to the same length and width. Hence it is easier to break a stack of two boards, each of one-inch thickness and separated from each other, rather than a single board of two-inch thickness. Indeed, this is pointing out that it is easier to break a stack of three, one inch thick, boards than it is to break a single two inch thick board.

Consider now which would be easier to break (a) three boards without spacers or (b) three boards with spacers? If it helps, ask yourself what would hurt more: (1) to have your hand under and touching the underside of a board that is to be punched and broken? Or (2), placing your hand an inch or two away from the underside of the board and feeling the impact and force as the board breaks and hits the hand, and then the punch follows through? Not that I would recommend either, and particularly not without a heavy leather glove as hand protection against cuts, shards or splinters. Alternatively note that three boards without spacers is getting close to a single three inch thick board—and we have already noted how difficult it is to break thicker boards. The answer is of course that spacers

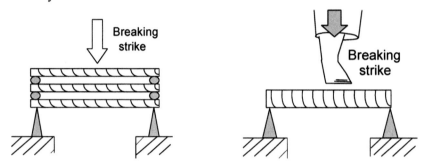

make the task possible—think on that the next time you see someone breaking several concrete slabs with their head. Not that I'm suggesting that such a task is easy—not at all.

Figure 7.8: It takes about 25% more force to break one 2 inch board than it does to break three 1 inch thick boards.

7.8   Hitting an Unsupported Object

The previous sections have discussed the act of hitting objects that are firmly supported, such as with board breaking, or have significant mass and therefore inertia, such as a heavy punch bag. Other training aids are available that concentrate on the development of speed and it's worthwhile considering the distinction. For example, imagine a wooden board that is being supported by a sponge like substance, perhaps by placing the boards between two soft target pads rather than rigid rails or bricks: Now try and break it.

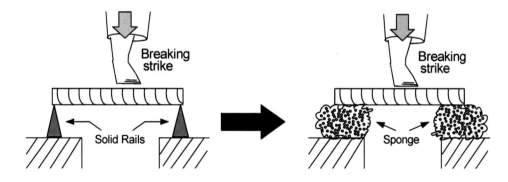

Figure 7.9: Breaking a wooden board that does not have a solid support.

It may be evident that speed, not strength, is most needed to break a board with this kind of arrangement. To help explain this observation think for a moment of pushing down on a board that is supported by two springs, compared with one that is supported between two bricks. With a board that is firmly supported placing your hand against the center of the board and pushing slowly but forcefully will quickly cause deflection and may bend the board sufficiently to cause breakage. For a board supported by soft springs a slow pushing action will continuously compress the spring, with a gradually increasing bending moment on the board that slowly increases the underside tension of the board, which is needed to tear the board apart. The pushing action could compresses the spring until it becomes virtually solid where it can then act as an unyielding support to the board, allowing further force to cause the board to bend and break. A fighter, however, is normally trying to apply a shock like impact, not a long slow push such that all compliance is removed and only then can damage occur.

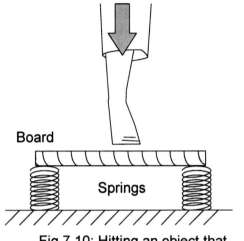

Board

Springs

Fig 7.10: Hitting an object that does not have a solid support base

In any strike there is always some degree of compliance or 'give' in the target or missile; for even if hitting a stone, the fist or foot is not solid. In this example, if the spring is a reasonable length then a normal strike to the board will not fully compressed the spring such that the board becomes supported in a solid manner. Here we are trying to impact the board and break it with high speed and relatively short striking time. To break the board in such 'springy' circumstances demands that the board is hit so fast that it hasn't got time to continue to disperse the energy along its length to the edges and thereby push down on the spring. The center of the board, when struck, has to bend and fracture **before** the deflection and forces can spread along to the edges of the board sufficiently to allow the spring to compress and absorb the energy. The board, or part of it, is effectively broken before it can move out of the way.

There are numerous exercises involving unsupported targets, including extinguishing a candle with a strike that stops just before the flame, or punching a tear in a freely hanging piece of paper. The book '*This is Karate*' by Master Masutatsu Oyama has a dedicated chapter to the topic of 'special drills', including most of those referenced here. One more test is to drop a board from one hand (held high) and strike the falling board with the other hand, with sufficient force to cause it to break—start this exercise with a thin board.

7.9   Hitting a Person

The next section shows some very practical aspects, but first let us look at the theoretical side by applying a few example figures to the equation associated with the amount of energy used in deformation damage (ΔE):

$$\Delta E = (1 - e^2) \frac{m_w}{(m_h + m_w)} \left[\frac{1}{2} m_h (v_1)^2 \right] \qquad \text{Equation (7.2)}$$

In this instance m_w represents the target on the person being struck, and m_h represents the effective mass of the strike. Assume that the velocity of the strike is 7 m/s, that the mass behind the strike is 10 kg and that the target (the head) has an effect mass of 5 kg. Assume that the square of the elastic coefficient of restitution or 'e' term is approximately zero and the calculation simplifies to:

$$\Delta E = (1 - 0) \frac{5}{(10+5)} \left[\frac{1}{2} (10) \times (7)^2 \right] = 82 \; joules$$

The 'ΔE' deformation (or damage) energy level quoted above as 82 joules can be compared to the energy of the striking weapon

$$KE = \left[\frac{1}{2} m_h (v_1)^2 \right] = \frac{1}{2} (10) \times (7)^2 = 245 \; joules$$

In this case there is factor of three difference between the incoming kinetic energy level and the deformation energy value. This is primarily because the target mass is half the striking mass, which means that the mass ratio (5/15) is one third. The kinetic energy level of 245 joules can be very approximately converted to an average force by making a couple of assumptions and using the relationships that force = energy/distance and distance = average velocity/time. Knowing that the velocity goes from 7 m/s to zero we can take the average velocity as 3.5 m/s, assuming linear deceleration for this approximation; and then we can 'guess' at a contact time of about two hundredths of a second. Hence, with a velocity of 7 meters per second, *if* the contact time was 20 milliseconds or 0.02 seconds, then the force would be around 3,500 Newtons.

In other words the force can be determined by either:

(i) Knowing that distance = average velocity x time = 3.5 x 0.02 = 0.07 meters, so the force from an energy of 245 joules equals energy / distance = 245 / 0.07 = 3,500 Newtons,

Or

(ii) Using Newton's Laws directly $F = ma = m \frac{\Delta v}{\Delta t} = 10 \times \left(\frac{7}{0.02} \right) = 3500 \; Newtons$

7.10 Hitting with Maximum Energy; Maximum Force

The equation for deformation energy (7.2) can be studied to see the effect of fixing the strike speed and varying the striking mass and then fixing the strike mass and varying the striking speed. The results of such an analysis are shown graphically as figures 7.11 and 7.12. The graph in figure 7.11 is a straight line showing that increasing the striking mass proportionality increases the energy of the strike as a 'one for one' type of effect.

The graph in figure 7.12 is not a straight line, showing that increasing the velocity of the strike has a 'squared' effect which is significantly more than a 'one for one' type of effect. In mathematical terms the relationship is quadratic and the graphical display is parabolic in nature rather than a straight line—showing, once again, that hitting faster can give us comparatively more gain in force. Note that the vertical units of these two graphs are not the same: Not at all.

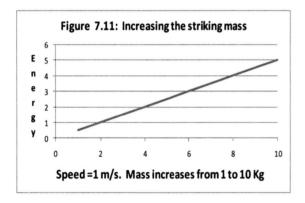

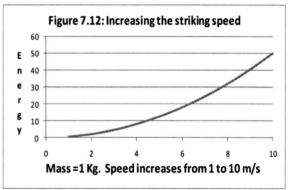

So what happens when we try to consider the best 'compromise' between the speed of a strike and the mass behind that strike? Academically, knowing that there is a tradeoff between speed and mass, we are looking for the optimal point where the speed and mass combination provides maximum energy. All else being equal (such as contact time and penetration) maximum energy will result in maximum force. We all acknowledge that a fighter needs to be both fast and strong. The lightning fast jab of a lightweight is admirable but it does not usually inflict the same degree of damage expected from the right cross of a well trained heavyweight. How do we try to look into this question of optimization between muscle mass and speed, so that a fighter can train to strike with maximum force?

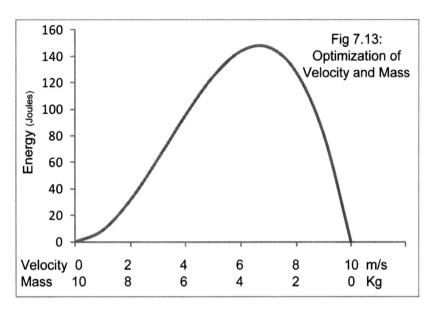

Figure 7.13 shows that if we increase the velocity of a punch from zero to 10 meters per second and simultaneously proportionally decrease the mass behind the strike, from 10 to zero kilograms, there is an optimal point where the energy level of the punch reaches a maximum. In this particular case that peak energy point is when the velocity is around 7 m/s and the mass is around 3 Kg. The actual values chosen to illustrate this concept can be adjusted – it's the concept that's important to understand. This illustration shows what happens if for every 10% increase in speed a fighter had to lose 10% of the striking mass; or by gaining 10% more mass behind his strike meant losing 10% of the striking speed. (Plotting the curve by increasing the mass while decreasing the velocity will simply produce a mirror image of figure 7.13.)

A Fighter's Insight

If a fighter, by training, has increased his striking body mass to a point where his punching speed has dropped to less than 70% of its previous value then it's likely that by continuing to train in that way his punching force will start to reduce.

To the best of my knowledge this concept has not previously been indicated graphically in the way shown here, and I have seen no published reports of studies along these lines. (That isn't to suggest there are none, but I cannot reference or credit any previous similar work.) The concept makes sense; many understand that the punching speed and body mass behind a strike are not independent variables; that a jab is typically a high speed, low mass, strike whereas the right cross tends to be a little slower but heavier. Figure 7.13 indicates that fighters that build more body mass to become more powerful may be doing so at the cost of their striking speed. Fighters and trainers should keep this aspect in mind. The above chart shows that if a fighter, by training, has increased his striking body mass to a point where the punching speed has dropped to less than 70% of its previous value then his punching force is probably now reducing. If this training is continued then from a punching respect it is likely to start to become counterproductive and may need to be tailored accordingly.

The conditioning of a fighter, rather than the technical training and practice in fighting, is intense and covers speed work, strength training, aerobic and anaerobic cardio-vascular exercise, plus stretching and flexibility sessions. The above 70:30 rule of thumb suggests that the speed work, such as shadow boxing, fast and light bag work, speed ball, plyometrics etc., should be at least of the same level and duration as the strength training of warriors that rely on their striking abilities.

Unfortunately I have found no evidence of work done elsewhere that can support, supplement or dispute the above conclusions. Caution therefore is needed; as said elsewhere a fighter should trust his instructor but he would be wise to verify the teachings.

And in practice:

Section 7.9 started by addressing a numerical and theoretical side to hitting a person; section 7.10 went on to discuss the optimization between the striking speed and mass that's contained in the energy of a punch. The practical side of striking with force is outlined throughout this book and summarized in sections 5.6 and 13.2. These outlines and summaries make reference to the following recommendations:

1. Punch or kick with high speed.

2. Punch or kick with mass behind the strike.

3. Hit the target square and aim to penetrate beneath the surface.

4. Land a punch before the fist is at the end of its arm's length.

5. Aim for an appropriate target. Accuracy is often more important than force.

6. Realize that not all targets are the same and that not all strikes are the same. The force experienced depends on the characteristics or both the missile and the target.

7. The more penetration the longer the contact time. A longer contact time can reduce the peak force level.

8. Some targets require more penetration than others.

7.11   Summary

All fighters need to practice hitting objects—punch bags, target pads or makiwara.

When hitting a hard object go for speed. To break a single board go for speed and punch through the wood. When striking a softer object—target pad or punch bag—practice elongating the contact time and penetration, allowing even more follow through type of action.

When breaking several objects or boards in a single strike, a higher degree of follow through is needed. The time taken will thereby increase, as the strike is continued to be driven through and beyond the first board to the second, third or even forth. In a breaking demonstration time is available for preparation and extended penetration. In self defense circumstances time will be at a premium and the luxury of preparation or very long contact times may not be an available option.

Boards that are spaced apart will be easier to break than boards resting on each other. Two one inch thick boards, spaced apart, are easier to break than one two inch thick board.

Do not strike a target at the end of the extension of the punching hand. As the hand approaches that final stopping point the speed reduces. Strike at about 75% of the extension limit—that's about the point of maximum speed—and punch through the target. The same principle applies to kicks.

By use of the equations in this chapter it is possible to estimate the energy needed to break wooden boards—and calculate the kinetic energy we can expect to achieve in a particular action.

Increasing the striking mass of a punch proportionality increases the energy of the strike in a 'one for one' manner, whereas increasing the velocity of the strike has a 'squared' effect on the energy level; which is significantly more than a 'one for one' type of effect.

For all fighters and all punches there is an optimal point of maximum energy, maximum force. This optimal point is the perfect combination of speed and body mass behind the punch. If, by targeted conditioning and training, a fighter has increased his striking body mass to a point where his punching speed has dropped to less than 70% of its previous value then it's likely that by continuing to train in that way his punching force will now start to reduce.

Prevent problems before they arise. Take action before things get out of hand.

Lao-tzu

Tao Te Ching

CHAPTER 8: THE POINT OF IMPACT

'First understand yourself; then understand others'
Master Funakoshi

8.1   Introduction

The previous chapters have provided a technical description of the basic scientific principles that apply to the collision of bodies and given examples of the applicability of the laws of physics to fighting techniques. This has allowed us to apply science and mathematics to help 'part the clouds' that are wrapped around the martial arts, perhaps proving an insight from the theoretical side that will supplement all that is gained from practical instruction and practice. Most of what a fighter needs to know comes through good instruction and intense training but science allows instinctive or intuitive understanding to be rationalized, verbalized and discussed. Here in this chapter we will examine the observed speed and path of a basic "karate punch"; with an eye to finding the best point at which to strike a target. This will help explain the reasons why we train the way we have been taught and allow instructors to pass on these instructions more effectively. (The term "karate punch" is meant here to indicate a reverse punch delivered from the hip with a straight line action. Neither karate nor any other martial art has a monopoly on any of the effective punches.) Also covered here is the difference between a punch and a kick, determining which is more powerful and by how much, and comparing theory to practice.

8.2   The Point at Which to Make Contact

Regardless of where the hand is when a punch is initiated, just before the movement starts it can be considered to be 'at rest'. The fighter may be in free style with the hand close to the shoulder or it may be at the hip as in basic karate training; nevertheless the initial hand velocity (v_i) is zero. If punching in free space there is a point where the fist stops; perhaps when the arm has reached full extension. When the punch has stopped it has no more speed and its final velocity (v_f) is zero. Between these two extremes of starting and ending at zero velocity the fist must have accelerated to some peak or maximum speed (v_{max}), before slowing down. We can perhaps mentally picture what's happening here—imagine the speed ramping up to a peak and then having to slow down to a stop. Picturing a hand velocity against distance traveled graph could lead to a profile that looks something like that shown in figure 8.1.

This mental exercise should show that to make contact at the very end of the reach of the striking weapon is pointless, unless you are trying to demonstrate something or frighten someone. Throw out an unrestricted punch in free space and the fist comes to a stop when the arm has reached its maximum extension. Since, at that point, there is no speed and no further forward movement then there is no forward energy to impart into an opponent. With no kinetic energy, no momentum, there can be no force of impact. And if the fist reaches a stop at the end of its travel it has to slow down *before* it gets there. We are close to asking ourselves 'at what point should I strike the opponent?' Hence we start to engage in contemplation over questions such as 'should I strike about half way through this movement, three quarters of the way or where?' Those that practice with a punch bag will have naturally learnt the answer through their training—although they may not have spent time trying to ascribe an arm extension 'percentage' figure to this point of impact.

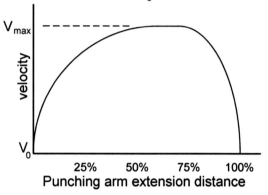

Fig. 8.1: Guess at the velocity / distance profile of a punch.

In the next section we will look at a specific profile that has been determined through high speed photography. It happens to be an examination of a basic reverse punch, as practiced in karate. This is incidental; all punches start from zero speed and end at zero speed. What's important is that we recognize that hitting something near the end of our reach is not ideal as there is almost no energy because the speed has dropped to such a low value. The punch profile in the next section has the punching hand starting from the hip, as is typical with a basic karate punch used in traditional training. In combat fighters of almost any style have their hands raised in a relaxed guard position and do not normally pull a hand back towards the hip before striking, nor do they normally retract the other arm during such a strike since it leaves too much of the upper torso open to counter attack. So please, do not get confused about the forthcoming profile or read into this section more than is intended. The point being made is simple and universal; aim to hit the target at the most effective point in the trajectory of the strike. Too early or too late is not most effective. You are looking for the point of maximum energy, which will be the same as or close to the point of maximum speed. The following section uses a scientifically determined velocity profile to indicate the point of maximum speed of a particular punch.

8.3   Analysis of a Karate Style Reverse Punch

The reverse punch is one of the core techniques at the very heart of karate and is a particularly forceful hand strike. As an illustration of this, note that a significant number of advanced karate kata often use this punch. In this section we examine the speed of the fist as it travels the full distance of the punch, from start to finish. The data that forms the graph reproduced as figure 8.2 was derived from high-speed movie analysis by J. D. Walker (1979). In this instance the fighter reached a maximum speed of about 5.5 meters per second. Chapter 1 shows that the maximum speed for a punch can be significantly higher but even at this increased peak speed the basic shape of the curve will still look somewhat similar, with the speed reducing towards the end of the travel of the fist. Even a cursory glance at the curve shows the most basic message; with a punch, aim to strike *before* the end of the reach of your arm, before the hand comes to a natural stop.

The appendices of Master Nakayama's book "Dynamic Karate" record an experimental analysis of a straight punch, as well as a lunge punch, and contain the following insights:

Regarding a lunge or stepping punch: *Setting the time required for the entire movement at 100, twenty examples of the twenty three experiments made indicated that the maximum speed was recorded at a point between 70 and 80."*

Regarding a straight punch: *"Checking the acceleration of T's fist (second-dan) when throwing a straight punch, it was noted that a great acceleration occurred immediately after the movement started, followed by a deceleration; then a second great acceleration took place when the arm was extended, followed by another deceleration."* Note that this describes a straight punch without being explicit about its detail. The above observations have similarities to the insight shown by the curve in figure 8.2. The maximum speed occurs at just around 70 percent of full extension and the acceleration is in two distinct parts: J. D. Walker's data shows a noticeable reduction in speed between the 35 to 45% (distance) percent mark. The work by Feld et al (1979) produced a different velocity against distance graph, showing a peak punching speed of approximately 7.5 meters per second being achieved closer to 85% of arms length, but this may have been a different striking action.

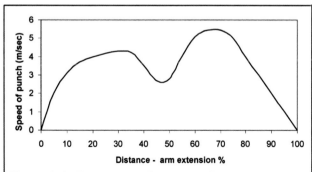

Figure 8.2: The speed of a punch, from the hip, plotted against the extension of the punching arm

This all shows several points of significance:

o With a punch, strike the opponent at about 70 to 75 percent of the arms length.

o If your arm length, to a closed fist, is around 65 cm (~ 25 inches) and you are punching with the fist starting at the shoulder to hip line, then aim to strike the target at a distance of about 50 cm (~ 19 inches) or about 6 inches before full extension

o Punch through the target, don't aim at the surface.

o When punching from the hip, the speed achieved at around the thirty percent mark is only about twenty percent less than the maximum. If your peak speed is 8 meters per second then a strike with only a third of full extension could still be around 6 meters per second.

o About half the maximum speed can be achieved after only ten percent movement. [But remember that energy is proportional to the speed squared, so half the speed carries only one quarter of the energy of a full speed strike.]

This study prompts a few questions to consider. For example, think about the effect of the length of arm: a longer arm can reach further but needs longer time to reach the opponent.

• If all else is equal, will the fist have more energy due to the extended distance traveled?

• What does this mean to the practice of 'shoulder extension' towards the end of the punch?

Another point to consider is that since the strike is at about 75% extension the fist will not by then have rotated to the normal finish position exhibited in free-space training, so:

Why twist the fist?

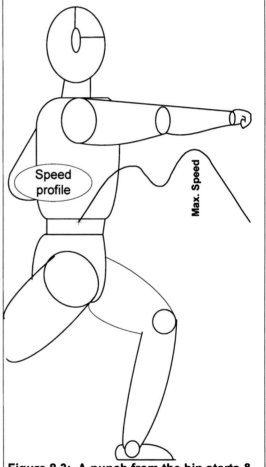

Figure 8.3: A punch from the hip starts & ends with zero speed - the maximum velocity is at about 70 to 75 % of travel

Similarly if, when practicing in free space, we are taught to apply focus or muscular tension at the full extension punch completion point:

- Do we need to adapt and apply this focus at the reduced striking point when actually hitting a target?

The answers to most of these questions can be found through training and by the striking of punch bags; however this book addresses these questions to try to help provide additional insights.

Facts for Fighters

Strike the opponent when the punching arm has reached

about three quarters of its full extension; the point of maximum speed.

Aim or focus to strike inside the opponent.

8.4   The Focal Point

The previous section asks: *". . . if, when practicing in free space, we are taught to apply focus or muscular tension at the full extension punch completion point: Do we need to adapt and apply this focus at the reduced striking point when hitting a target?"*

My brief answer is no. It's a personal view. I know of no comparative studies from which to review results and draw conclusions but nevertheless the "no" is given here as a considered opinion. I understand the concept of tension being applied at, or just before, the full extension point when practiced in free space in a traditional manner and acknowledge certain potential training benefits. However, we should note that in free space, without a solid target being hit, the punching hand's full extension point is beyond the (imagined) 75% of travel point of impact. In my view, fighters should not try to apply increased focus or muscular tension just *before* striking the target. If necessary please read that last sentence again because it is so easy to misunderstand the statement just made.

As described previously, a fighter aiming for a strong strike should start relaxed, gain force from the floor, let the legs and hips explode movement into the torso and punching arm, apply the right order of muscles for the technique and push the center of gravity towards the strike. However, the fighter should not try to contract or tense additional muscles *before* impact. It's understandable that a fighter may try to apply additional muscles *just after* impact to help increase penetration; particularly with a thrusting action technique.

Evidence suggests that ideally the moment of impact of a punch should be around 75% of the arms extension point; it is not at the 'full extension' point where the speed of the punch has passed its peak. My guess is that trying to contract *at* impact will attempt to slow the technique. A fighter should aim beyond the point of impact, allow the 'focus' to drive the strike forward through full penetration, enhancing the amount of weight behind the strike and strengthening the bodily framework to cope with reactive forces. Clearly for any movement to occur the driving muscles must be triggered to contract, but we should not try to contract supplementary or additional muscles *just before* impact to make the body momentarily more rigid *at* impact. Practice with a heavy bag and judge for yourself.

8.5 Focus and the Principle of Maximal Contraction.

As a reminder, this chapter discusses the achievement of the maximum force from a strike and thereby continues to be orientated towards the effectiveness of a technique when applied for real. Like most books the content of this one reflects the views and opinions of the author and for me the martial arts have never been akin to an aerobic exercise. However we all must acknowledge and respect the fact that for many who go to class their motivation and priorities are different – they may be 'just' going to class and don't see this as major part of their lifestyle. It could be that the self-defense aspect is becoming a primary motivator for the minority only; that achieving fully effective technique is only of the utmost importance to a minority in the class. The majority of adults that train do not see a likely prospect of being placed in harm's way and having to fight their way out (at least not with their bare hands). Some such individuals can enjoy the thrill of competing for its own sake, without worrying over any associated limitations that could become counterproductive in a real fight. A good instructor will look after these aspects and ensure that a black belt from their school has the right stuff. The instructor will insist that effective technique has to be learned, even if it isn't considered to be essential by the student. After all, we don't question a modern day champion in archery on the current need for a bow and arrow.

OK, reminder completed – back to basics. To be effective a strike has to be delivered with energy. A punch or kick needs both mass and speed. In the traditional sense the martial arts are for the purpose of self defense and in the extreme this is a matter of life or death. Although the ultimate aim of Karate is to perfect character it has traditionally tried to teach a person to be able to disable, or at least dissuade, an attacker with a single strike. Other fighting arts also look for the ability to knockout an opponent with strikes that carry mass, speed and deadly efficiency. A strike that has speed but no mass will not disable—it may not even dissuade.

This book has repeatedly discussed the composition of an effective strike and described how impact speed and mass can be attained. At the risk of entering into yet another area of controversy, let's start this section by looking at non-contact sparring competitions. When competitors are judged on points scored only and disqualified for contact then those competitors have to acquire additional skills. Specifically, they have to be able to execute strikes that would cause great damage when applied properly but exercise such good control as to ensure that the opponent is not hurt when the controlled strike is delivered on target in a competition. In addition to this, these people are in the competition to win so they want to score points and not be scored against. This is a difficult challenge and demands a rare set of attributes. It is worth acknowledging the number of martial artists who have competed over the decades with an amazing standard of form, spirit and control, developed by hard work and practice. The mark of a skillful martial artist is to be able to use a technique and be able to choose to either penetrate the target or stop within one inch of contact without loss of technique, form, timing or spirit.

We are touching upon concepts that relate to a distinct difference between scoring points in a non-contact sports competition and an act of a true martial or 'war' like nature. It is easy to appreciate that, if not corrected, in a non-contact competition the speed of the technique can start to completely dominate. When in non-contact point-scoring mode competitors are not trying to knock the opponent out, even though they may be trying to use a technique that could have resulted in a knock-out blow. Consequently, the attacker may not necessarily be intent on putting much body weight behind the strike or shifting their center of gravity forward and into the target—the scoring attacker may not be shifting their weight forward at all, preferring instead to stay back to make it easier to revert to a defensive mode.

Stricevic et al (1989) in Modern Karate point out that if the speed of a technique is more important than its actual slaying power then this can lead to the technique being executed with a sub-maximum level of muscle contractions, using only the muscles needed to support a fast technique. This reference goes on to point out that contrary to a sub-maximal level of muscle contraction, the application of a larger number of muscle fibers will enable the rest of the body to provide increased support to the technique. Such support may relate to the strength and stability of the stance, which could be particularly important if the opponent is moving in.

The above can be taken to a further extreme and prompt the consideration of the potential side effects of non-contact point scoring competitions. If such matches are poorly judged and the combatants inadequately coached then competitors can be tempted to deliver strikes with virtually no energy available on impact. It is essential to understand the distinction between a strike having no available energy and one that is controlled such that the energy is there but deliberately held in check and not *delivered* because it is 'no contact' or controlled sparring. It is not unknown, in a non-contact competition, to see a hand strike that if it hit the opponent it would be barely noticeable; not because its raw power has been controlled and contained but because it carried no weight or little impact speed. Previous work within this book has shown that a punch that is at the end of its trajectory and about to change direction from forward to back will be at near zero fist velocity. If you are momentarily 'struck' by something with near zero velocity then the force will also be near zero—previous equations have shown this mathematically and through our experiences we may have already noticed this. Yet in a poorly judged competition such a strike can look good and score, even though it's at maximum extension and not really reaching the target.

This, to me, is one of the potential problematic areas of over concentrating on non-contact sport orientated competitive sparring. Practicing for light or non-contact sparring to the virtual exclusion of the traditional, force and focus, sides of the complete art can leave a gap in practice, knowledge and understanding. This could be a dangerous exclusion and most instructors fix this gap by showing how sport orientated techniques can be used for real and then use one step sparring or similar to demonstrate and instill the lesson. Sparring with controlled risk allows students to become familiar and comfortable with facing an opponent and allows them to absorb the associated body movements and infinite range of interactions. Where competitions have rules that exclude certain targets then non-competition training should cover these exclusions. There are certain styles that, in competition, do not allow hand strikes to the head and this gap has to be filled, for in the street the head is a favorite target. Almost all competitions prohibit strikes to the groin and this gap also has to be filled, for in the street the groin is another favored target. Finally, understandably and appropriately, no MMA competitions allow strikes to the eyes.

Summary: Speed is of the essence in a non-contact competition but supplementary muscles associated with the destruction of an opponent do not always need to be employed. Exclusive non-contact competition orientated training could result in a mistaken drive to achieve speed at all costs and punches incorrectly delivered with (almost) the arms only; with minimal hip or torso rotation. When the technique does need to be destructive then speed, mass and penetration is needed and more of the core muscles have to be employed. If defending for real against an onrushing opponent a fighter may need to use a large amount of muscle, enabling the body structure to be more supportive to the strike. It takes slightly longer to completely execute a technique in this manner as the major abdominal muscles are contracted, for these big core muscles are slower than the smaller, extremity, muscles; hence certain schools or masters have taught that the body core is engaged first, followed by the extremities.

Focus: The above helps to note the distinction between wanting to score a point and wanting to knock an opponent out and makes reference to the use of supplementary muscles. In classic Karate many old school students have been taught to be able to punch such that at, or just before, the point of full extension they can tense the *latissimus dorsi*, the widest and most powerful muscles of the back, pulling the shoulder down and gaining better connection between the arm and the torso; to tense the stomach, buttocks and thighs—pushing down and connecting with the earth. In short, there should be no weak spot or 'leakage path' from the striking point (the first two knuckles) all the way through to the floor. The above principles are first taught in a natural stance without stepping forward. The hard part is then to apply it in a truly dynamic manner, with the muscle groups being coordinated in a synchronized sequence (such as a stepping punch that is timed to be completed with synchronization of breath, strike and focus).

This is one way of instilling the concept of 'kime'. In karate at least the term often becomes synonymous with 'focus' or focused energy and (to me) this focus relates to the synchronization of physical technique with mental intent and the breath, in order to deliver the maximum energy into the target; with the objective of destruction or incapacitation of an opponent. [I would expect most karateka to have their own definition, often saying essentially the same thing but in a different way.] Master Nakayama (in the Best Karate series) refers to kime along the lines of: *"The essence of karate technique is kime. The meaning of kime is an explosive attack to the target using the appropriate technique and power in the shortest time possible."*

Throughout this book differing principles and concepts are developed including:

- The use of body rotation where the twisting of the trunk of the fighter gives added speed and mass to a punch

- The use of body rotation for added speed and mass plus a shift forward in the center of gravity to add more effective mass to the strike

- All of the above, with optimal penetration and choice of target area

The principle of vibration is not discussed or taught as much as it once was but it involves engaging the trunk and intense tensioning of the stomach at the instant of the strike; providing a stronger structure to the technique, sometimes used in a confined movement or shortened stance. For a fuller treatment, also covering the shoulder extension or 'principle of expansion' mentioned in section 8.3, I recommend the "Modern Karate" book by Milorad Stricevic and colleagues.

All martial artists have to hit things, such as punch bags or target mitts, since doing so allows a fighter to feel how a technique has to have 'weight'. There is a difference between surface contact and heavy contact. The core muscles used and the lead from the floor all start to have meaning when trying to put a dent in a heavy bag; but there is a big difference between the muscles used to start the technique and the application of extra contraction at the completion of the punch. It is easy to understand how using these concepts of tensing the supplementary muscles can be so valuable to a beginner or intermediate student. It helps instill the need to hit with all that we have and not just the hand or arm. It helps to reinforce the concept of 'one chance' or the ideal of finishing the encounter with only one strike. It discourages any practice of strikes that are 'empty' or without 'weight'. It aids in the instruction of perfect technique—from the floor on which the fighter stands to the fist that delivers the strike. This can also lead to the concept of focus and synchronization of the technique, breath and intent. Developing from the basics, instructors also need to show students how a fight is dynamic and help them to become relaxed, fluid fighters that can deliver fast and powerful strikes that are capable of disabling an opponent - and combinations for the times when a single strike is not going to be enough.

8.6   Close Quarter Combat

Combat is usually engaged at varying distances. An unarmed street fight can typically include:

- o   Opportunity for one good kick
- o   A couple of punches
- o   Knees, elbows and head
- o   Grapple, throw, fall or be dragged down
- o   Floor work
- o   Finished!

Despite the fact that many of us want to stay within our 'zone of expertise' a rounded fighter will practice in all aspects and areas of combat, including close-quarter battle zones (often the colloquial range of knees, elbows, grabs and holds). For insight into close quarter combat and punching, look again at the graph in figure 8.2 that shows punching speed against the distance traveled for a reverse punch from the hip.

This plot of punching speed against distance can be cut short to only cover the distance to a target that is placed at the extension point of the arm where the punch has achieved maximum velocity. Or in other words a plot to a target that's hit when the punch is at its fastest. Using a mass of 'unity' we can convert the speed values to energy values and plot a 'normalized' graph as energy rather than speed. The energy level is calculated using the kinetic energy equation, taking the square of the velocity as proportional to energy. This resultant graph shows that if punching from the hip, you can expect the striking energy to drop to about 60% of the maximum when the distance to the strike is reduced by half. If the distance is only 25%, or one quarter, then the normalized energy will reduce

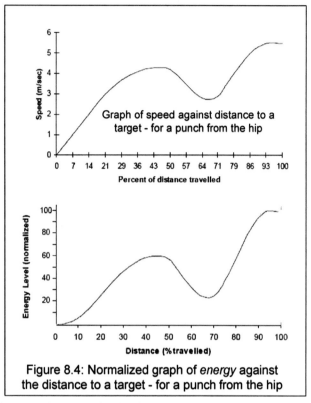

Figure 8.4: Normalized graph of *energy* against the distance to a target - for a punch from the hip

to about 40% of the original maximum. This can be seen by looking at the derived graph in figure 8.4 and reading the % energy level at 25% of the distance from the hip to a target. That answer, of course, assumes that the action employed with this reduced distance strike is the same as at the start of a full reverse punch. In practice that will *not* be the case, the change in focus brings about a change in technique; which is developed in a very specific manner. Remember that with training, significant speed and effective mass can be brought behind a close quarter strike.

Figure 8.4 shows an exaggerated drop in energy level at the 60 to 70% level, caused by the square law; remember that this is a plot of a strike to the target, not to full extension and do not spend too much time on the numerical detail—it is only one plot from one person and it is only a representation of a punch from the hip. Other punches will look different and this is only being used to illustrate the point that if a punch has to start from, and end at, zero speed then the fist must accelerate to reach a peak speed before naturally slowing down to a stop.

The drive to achieve more and more with less and less is at the very heart of the martial arts. The fighting arts developed so that the smaller in stature or strength can conquer the large and that physically (comparatively) disadvantaged people can protect themselves. This is achieved by understanding and applying the innumerable (small) incremental improvements that, together, make all the difference. There is no 'single' magic technique or secret—just years of instruction, training and dedication.

A Fighter's Insight

If in a street fight and at close range—don't forget the elbows!

Don't forget the head butt—strike with your 'hairline' to the opponent's face.

Don't forget the knees.

Don't just use the hands as closed fists.

Finding a vulnerable point can finish the conflict instantly.

Finish a close quarter conflict quickly before you get seriously hurt.

Watch out for a weapon.

8.7   Short Range Technique Effectiveness

Many martial arts schools tend to concentrate on long and mid range techniques, rather than the up close and personal side of combat. Yet traditional kata or forms contain innumerable techniques, moves and combinations that are intended for close quarter combat, making use of elbow, knee, grabs, holds and throws. The sparring practice of a striking art (rather than a grappling art) at close range is awkward and free-style close-quarter-combat sparring demands good control.

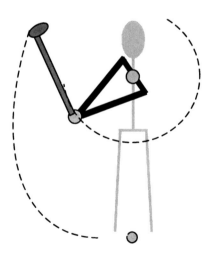

Golf club 'rotational' path

To scientifically appreciate the difference that range makes imagine a golfer driving the ball from the starting tee. Golfers will rotate their body during the swing and try to achieve their greatest speed at the point where the golf club is to hit the ball. The sketch shows the inner rotational path made by the golfers' outstretched hands during this action and the lower line shows the arc of the club as it follows the path of the golfer's arms and hands. The club-head moves significantly faster because it follows the larger circle during the same time period as the shorter arms. (Try driving a golf ball using a club that's only six inches long.) The golf ball speed from an expert golfer can reach over 160 mph. Mathematics show that the club head is travelling faster than the hands that swing the club.

That's reasonable, we have known since childhood that the fastest place on a carousel or park roundabout is at the outer edge. What isn't so obvious is displayed by the ice skater that brings her arms together, by her side or crossed over her chest, in order to go into a very fast spin. The science behind this is that by bringing in the arms the moment of inertia of the body decreases (reduction in radius) and therefore the angular velocity must increase, in order to conserve the angular momentum of the body.

Think about the above and you may come to the conclusion that you can spin the body faster with the arms closer to the body (like the ice skaters demonstrate). This should start to explain why, when facing a punch bag, it is relatively easy to 'explode' into the bag with a round elbow strike. All elbow strikes are potentially very harmful but the simple round-striking action is clearly devastating. The short distance to the body and tight reinforced

structure of the bent arm with fist against chest/shoulder and the transfer of body power (rotating mass) into the target through a hard small striking area (the point of the elbow) all make this so potentially lethal. In short, the elbow is an ideal close quarter striking tool. Of course, the elbow is not moving as fast as an extending arm and hand can achieve with the same body action but it gets to the target fast and has a strong connection to the body.

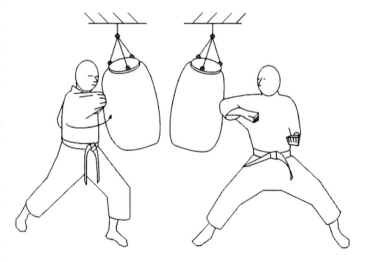

Roundhouse and straight elbow strikes

The above specifically refers to the use of the elbow in a roundhouse manner. The elbow can, of course, follow virtually any trajectory: round, straight, up, down, diagonally, forward or reverse, front or back. Indeed, although I am not an advocate of turning the back to an opponent, I could make an exception for the backward roundhouse elbow strike—

particularly if attacked from behind or blocking and evading an opponent prompts the back spin.

Depending upon your up-bringing you may be familiar with the common street-fighting technique which is about as close quarter as you can get, namely head-butting. Chapter 5 mentions how effective this can be. Other close quarter combat weapons are well known and understood: Knee strikes are commonly practiced and applied, as are hook punches and low level snap kicks. Grappling, holds and throws are beyond the scope of this book but their effectiveness rely on the physical principles associated with levers, leverage and mechanical advantage: This is outlined in section 10.16.

8.8   Impulse or Surge Energy

On the subject of close-quarter-combat (CQC), the more advanced martial artists know of the 'one-inch' punch concept, with frequent references to Kung Fu practitioners in general and Bruce Lee in particular. This is a concept that is not limited to the Kung Fu type of style of Chinese origin. In a number of the schools of the martial arts the "3-inch-punch" or "power-punch" is part of the curriculum. Subject most advanced martial artists to a modest test: place a telephone directory at the chest or stomach of a strong student then ask a black belt to place the tips of the fingers against the book and, without any retraction of the hand, punch as hard as possible.

The strike is done by 'collapsing' the fingers and trying to 'surge' all the power of the body into the punch. The forceful success rate of such a test with an experienced fighter is striking; even if they have never tried this before success is often seen at the first attempt. An advanced martial artist should, through teaching and practice, find a way of delivering power with very little range of motion. Achieving such effectiveness is, by the incremental mastery of detail, a concept at the very heart of a martial art.

Most reasonably strong and fit individuals can deliver a
punch with a degree of force but in doing so they will
typically take time and space to 'wind-up' and then deliver
a long path punch, such as a right-cross, hook or a round,
swinging punch ('hay-maker' type). They may lean heavily
into the blow to naturally put weight behind the punch. A
skilled martial artist will train and perform differently.
With good instruction and diligent practice the application
distance will reduce, without a corresponding proportional
reduction in force.

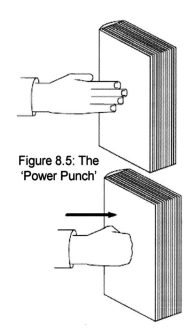

Figure 8.5: The
'Power Punch'

Close quarter techniques are made effective by a series of
attributes, including but not limited to:

o   Applying an impulse or surge action—as though
    the whole body is suddenly 'jerked' into the strike.

o   Breathing: the impulse of breathe as the stomach
    (not just the lungs) is brought into action

o   Fast twitch muscles creating 'instant' acceleration of the striking fist

o   Use of the center or core of the body (the tanden)

o   Stance: the connection to the floor, and the force brought from the floor.

All of the above being used to produce an explosive action—with focus.

So how powerful is the Power-Punch?

The reverse or cross punch is generally considered to be the most forceful punch used
against an opponent and the evidence presented in chapter one supports that viewpoint.

Serious fighters try to get a similar level of force with less distance traveled; starting from
basics, progressing to free style, punching from the upper guard position and developing to
what is sometimes referred to as the 'power-punch'. For clarity, in the text that follows in
this section the term 'power-punch' should be considered as a strike from about 3 inches.
Studies by J. Gulledge and J. Dapena (2008) to compare the reverse and power punches in
oriental martial arts indicate that advanced martial artists can expect to deliver half the force
of their reverse punch with a power punch. Figure 8.6 shows the type of force/time graphs
indicated by this study as a comparative representation of reverse and power punches.

The experimental forces determined, as a mean (or average) of the 12 advanced martial artist subjects studied, were 1450 Newtons (N) for the reverse punch and 790N for the power-punch. The maximum achieved by any single subject was 1830N for the reverse and 1020N for the power-punch. The mean knuckle velocities were 6.7 m/s and 4.2 m/s for reverse and power-punch respectively with a fastest participant reverse punch impact velocity of 7.7 m/s. The report notes that these velocities are relatively low compared to other studies and for reasons that are unclear the force figures are relatively modest in relation to the reverse punch numbers determined in previous studies. The authors correctly point out that force comparisons between different studies are difficult due to variations in the type and thickness of

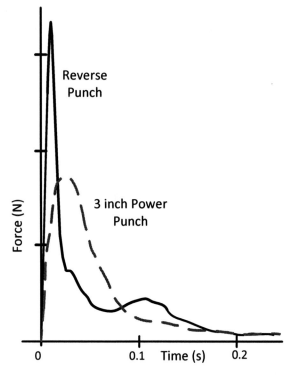

Fig. 8.6: Impulse curve comparison

padding and the interface or connection characteristics between the fist and the force plate. However, the comparison between reverse and power punching within this study should be reasonable: Since they share the same measurement system the ratio of forces of these two types of punches is probably valid, even if the absolute values of each are systematically low. It is this facet that provides a degree of confidence to the statement that a trained fighter can expect to power-punch an opponent with about half the force of their reverse punch.

In this study the typical contact time to reach peak forces was 11 milliseconds (0.011 seconds) for a reverse punch and 16 milliseconds for a power punch. Study of figure 8.6 indicates that the power punch is somewhat more 'push-like' that the reverse punch – an observation also made by the report authors.

Facts for Fighters
Aim to achieve the energy level of your best reverse punch within a 3 inch strike range. With practice you may achieve half the energy, half the force.

8.9   The Velocity Profile of a Kick

Section 8.3 describes the speed against distance relationship for a basic, karate type of reverse punch with the hand starting from the hip. The velocity profile, showing the speed of the punch as it traveled to the full extension of the arm, was portrayed as figure 8.2. This profile was shortened, as shown in figure 8.4, to illustrate the speed of the punch as it travels to the target (rather than to the arm's full extension). The velocity profile of a kick depends on the type of kick; the differing foot trajectories and knee and hip joint movements will affect the velocity/distance profile. It is easy to understand this degree of difference between a front kick and a side thrust kick because the kicking actions are so different. The consequential speeds and effective mass transfers are also dissimilar. As noted previously, one of the fastest measured foot velocities attained is with the round house type of kick at a speed of around 16 meters per second.

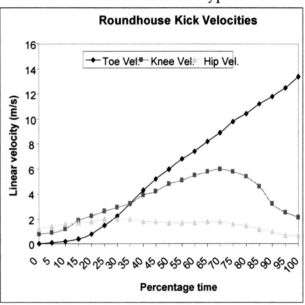

Figure 8.7: The velocity of the hip, knee and toe during a roundhouse kick

Chapter 1 provides a significant amount of experimentally derived results and highlights some of the data obtained by J. Pearson (1997). This includes a plot of the average toe velocity from a number of roundhouse kicks. This plot is reproduced here as figure 8.7. A fascinating point shown is that from the moment the foot starts to move, to the strike and completion of the technique, the foot keeps on getting faster and faster. This happens almost *linearly*. The acceleration is virtually constant. Such is the efficiency that can be achieved by someone properly trained.

8.10   Differences in Force Between a Punch and a Kick

To answer a question such as what is the difference between the forces available from a kick compared to a punch we can first look at experimental data. The 'Fight Science' reference in Chapter 1 points out that one expert delivered a punch of 4079 Newtons (N) and a spinning back kick of 6992 N, meaning that he can kick with 70% more force than he can punch. Another expert in the same study delivered a punch of 3630 N and a side thrust kick of 4550 N, meaning that he can kick with 25% more force than he can punch. To consider the question from a theoretical perspective we can return to one of our first concepts; the kinetic energy contained in each technique is described by equation (2.4) that $KE = (1/2)mv^2$

Now we need to work out how much energy can be expected in a punch and a kick; from the same person. To do this let us use some data that's available from a previously referenced punching test. Section 1.4.4 points out that heavyweight boxer, Frank Bruno, was tested in controlled conditions by Atha et al (1985) and it was found that he was capable of achieving a peak force of 4096 Newtons, attained within 14 milliseconds of contact with a punch having an impact velocity of 8.9 m/s.

Using Newtons Law that $F=ma$ and knowing that the acceleration 'a' is equal to the change in velocity with time or; $a = \dfrac{\Delta v}{\Delta t}$, we can derive $F = m\dfrac{\Delta v}{\Delta t}$ and therefore $m = F\dfrac{\Delta t}{\Delta v}$.

Consequently, if the hand velocity has dropped to zero in the first 14 milliseconds, we could determine that the effective mass behind the strike was approximately 6.4 kilograms (14lbs). Hence the kinetic energy would be calculated as 255 joules, using the equation that $KE = (1/2)mv^2$. However, at the point of maximum force the punch velocity will not have dropped to zero, for the fist will continue and penetrate slightly further. This is indicated in the force-time graphs of figures 5.3 or 8.6. Hence, in the absence of more hard data, we have to make an estimate of either the full penetration distance or the velocity of the fist at the point of maximum force. It's a good guess that the speed of the punch at that point would have dropped to less than half its impact velocity so it's reasonable to suggest that the speed after 14 milliseconds is around 25% of the initial impact speed.

Therefore Δv is 8.9 – (8.9 x 0.25) = 6.675, the calculated effective mass becomes 8.6 kg (just under 19 lbs) and the kinetic energy is thereby increased to **340** joules.

If Frank had been trained to deliver a *front snap* kick with a speed of 10m/s and an effective mass equivalent to the weight of the foot and calf we can determine what energy content of the kick could be expected. The foot and calf carry about 5% of the body weight; Frank was a heavy weight so his weight would be in excess of 200 lbs (90 Kg). If we assume 100kg (220 pounds) then the foot and calf mass is 5 kg (11lbs) and the kinetic energy is 250 joules, almost 75 % of the 340 joule punching energy level. For a *side thrust* kick calculation, let's assume that

Table 8.1: Typical approximations for % of total body mass for various body parts	
	%
Head	7
Trunk	45
Upper Arm	3
Forearm	1.5
Hand	0.5
Thigh	14
Calf	4
Foot	1

he was trained to deliver the kick at a speed of 10 m/s and the kick carried somewhere between a quarter to a half the mass of the thigh, plus the calf and foot mass. Hence the range of the effective mass becomes between (3.5+5) = 8.5 % to (7+5) = 12% of the total body mass: or between 8.5kg to 12kg effective mass. This results in an energy level of **425 to 600** joules or about 25% to 76% more energy than the punching energy of 340 joules. This result aligns with the Fight Science range of 25% increase in force with a side thrust kick and with a back kick up to 75% increase in force. Remember that to determine the force that arises from an energy level we need to take into account the contact time. A kick will usually have longer contact time than a punch, which will tend to reduce the peak force level.

For the even more academic: If we did not have real test data we would have to estimate the energy of the reverse punch, just as we did with the kick. We would pick a reasonable punch velocity such as 9 m/s and recognize that the fighter may strike with the mass of the hand, forearm and upper arm, which is 5% of body weight and for our heavyweight this is 5 kg mass. This gives an energy level of about 200 joules. With training this effective mass can increase to around 7.5 kg and the speed improve to ~ 10 m/s. This gives an upper energy level of 375 joules, which is comparable to the 340 joule number previously determined.

As a slightly alternative approach, if both the kick and the punch carried the same body weight and the punch velocity was 10m/s and the kicking velocity was 12 m/s then the difference is the ratio of the squares of these velocities; i.e. $12^2/10^2 \simeq 44\%$ greater. If the speed of the kicking foot and the punching hand is the same, at the point of contact, then the energy difference only depends upon the masses involved. If the mass involved is *only* the mass of the striking limb, that is the hand/arm or the foot/leg, then it should be clear that the kick has more power. The emerging insight is that the theory is suggesting a person can deliver a kick that carries about 50% more energy than a good punch from that same individual. There are those that are good at punching but not kicking - and vice versa - so these ratios will vary greatly from individual to individual.

The performance and effectiveness in kicking is generally related to the grade and experience of the student—a beginner can become fairly proficient in punching easier and faster than with kicking. Implicit in the above calculations is the assumption that the fighter has become proficient enough to be coordinated and able to impart 'weight' behind fast kicks or punches.

Facts for Fighters

In theory at least, a good kick can have 50% more energy content than a good punch from the same individual.

8.11   Summary

A basic reverse punch should hit and penetrate the opponent when the punching arm has reached around seventy-five percent of its full extension. Aim or focus to strike inside the opponent, beyond the target surface: Do not aim to impact at the end of the travel of the weapon for at that point the speed will be lower than the maximum. Do not aim at the surface of the target—aim to penetrate.

It takes time to accelerate to a very high striking speed. Retraction or 'pull-back' of the fist before throwing a punch gives more distance to allow a higher speed to be reached—but when fighting such pull-back is usually an unaffordable luxury and unnecessary signal of intent. Close quarter combat does not have the long reach striking distances and a fighter can benefit here from the development of synchronized hip and body mechanics.

With a traditional punch we should teach students how to apply focus or tension approaching the full extension completion point, not at the impact point. At impact, rather than full extension, we should strike with maximum speed, aided by being relaxed rather than tense, with a center of gravity moving into the target and the strike driving through the opponent with a focused or 'hardening' attitude—all in a small fraction of a second.

The velocity profile of a punch can be very non-linear; in a classical reverse punch the fist accelerates from the hip and then the speed reduces before further acceleration reoccurs. An expert can, however, perform a roundhouse kick with almost complete linear acceleration of the foot; from the floor to the target it keeps on getting faster.

Expert fighters can develop their three inch punch to be about as half as forceful as their full reverse punch.

Non-contact competition and associated specialized coaching should be complemented by more traditional training and the striking of punch bags or similar.

Both by theoretical derivation and by looking at the available experimental evidence it can be shown that a kick can contain significantly more energy than a punch. All other parameters being equal (such as contact time and target characteristics) this means that the kick will be more forceful. Individuals should be able to develop their kicking abilities to be twenty-five to fifty percent more powerful than the best of their punches.

CHAPTER 9: ROTATIONAL EFFECTS

'The art of mind is more important than the art of technique'
Master Funakoshi

9.1   Introduction

The relationships developed and used so far have been mainly restricted to linear motion. The kinetic energy equation, for example, has been used for straight line paths and forces, such as those associated with the collision of billiard balls, the 'head-on' crashing of cars or straight line impact kicks and punches. Yet the principles of the conservation of energy and momentum apply anywhere; they are not restricted to non rotational actions. The martial arts are also not constrained to linear movements and this book would be incomplete without at least a brief exploration into the physics associated with circular or rotational movement. Remember that this book is intended to serve as a reference. Parts of this chapter are fairly academic and can be scanned rather than read in detail, returning to its content if a subsequent interest prompts a desire to dig deeper.

9.2   Rotational Forces, Inertia and Angular Velocity

Fighters use rotational movements; they do not restrict themselves to purely linear actions. Bodies that rotate contain energy—we know this from driving a car or touching a spinning bicycle wheel. It is evident that this energy can be translated to a force and cause damage just as a drill is designed to penetrate wood, metal or stone and a circular saw cuts through thick timber.

Most of us are familiar with the fact that the speed of spinning machinery can be measured in revolutions per minute (rpm), and if something is spinning at 60 rpm then it does one full revolution every second. If the object happens to be round and is 320 mm (about one foot) in diameter then we can calculate that the circumference is about 1 meter. If this object is a wheel rolling along a surface at 60 rpm then in one second it will have moved forward one meter and it therefore has a linear velocity of 1 meter per second (or 3.3 feet/second). A rolling wheel of circumference of two meters traveling at 60 rpm would have a linear velocity of 2 meters per second.

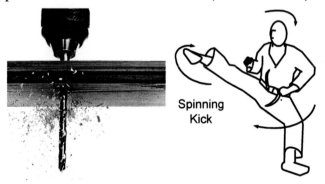

Spinning Kick

Figure 9.1: A spinning body has energy from its rotation

Another way of quoting rotational speed is in angular terms. If a wheel is revolving once every second then since there are 360 degrees in a circle we know that it travels through 360⁰ in one second. This is a somewhat clumsy mathematical method and scientists actually use a measure called a radian. To explain a radian let's imagine the wheel or flat cylinder to be a pie. If I cut out a piece of the pie so that the length of the outer, curved, edge of pie was the same length as the other straight edges then the angle of the slice would be 57.3 degrees. This is one radian - the angle of a segment of a circle where the curved edge length is equal to the radius of the circle; see figure 9.2. A complete circle has 360 degrees and 360 divided by 57.3 shows that there are almost 6.3 radians in a circle. The exact number of radians in a circle equals twice the value of "pi", or 2π (or 2 x 3.14 or 6.28). Hence if something is traveling at a speed of 1 revolution per second it is also moving at about 6.3 radians per second. This information has been included only to help the reader understand numerically some of the material described; the units associated with rotational kinetic energy include radians just because it's an easier way of dealing with rotational velocity.

Know that as you read through the following pages and see symbols and expressions that may be new and unfamiliar the fundamental principles still apply. There is a direct analogy between rotational forces or effects and linear ones, with equivalence in

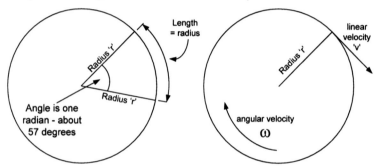

Figure 9.2 A schematic of a rotational body, with angular and linear velocity.

these relationships. The next section shows that rotational kinetic energy is proportional to the product of inertia and angular velocity squared, which is directly analogous to what has been described previously; that 'linear' kinetic energy is proportional to the product of its mass and velocity squared. This means that all of our insights remain applicable—such as double the 'speed' (or revolutions per minute) and the energy is quadrupled, double the effective mass or inertia and the energy has doubled.

Moment of Inertia

The energy associated with the rotation of a body such as shown in figure 9.2 follows a similar equation to the standard (linear) kinetic energy of equation 2.4:

$$\text{Kinetic energy} \quad KE = \tfrac{1}{2}mv^2 \qquad \textit{Equation (2.4)}$$

In this case the linear velocity 'v' is replaced by the rotational or angular velocity ω and the mass is replaced by the moment of inertia 'I'. Therefore the rotational kinetic energy relationship is

$$KE = \frac{1}{2}I\omega^2 \qquad \textit{Equation (9.1)}$$

The angular velocity of revolution ω is measured in radians per second.

Don't be too concerned about this concept of 'moment of inertia'. Previously we quoted one of Newton's laws as force equals the product of mass and acceleration. This means that a body of mass resists the force that wants to cause it to accelerate. The greater the mass then the greater the force needed for a particular acceleration—pushing a bike is easier than pushing a car. For rotational movement, an object's moment of inertia is equivalent to the object's mass; the heavier or bigger the wheel then the greater its moment of inertia (think of how a flywheel is used in rotating machines). The next section shows how to calculate the moment of inertia for a couple of common shapes. We do not need to understand the details but it helps to know that the principles established with linear motion apply in the rotational world. The table below shows how the equations we have seen previously convert into rotational equivalents.

Quantity	Linear World	Rotational World
Force	F = force	τ = torque
Acceleration	a = acceleration	α = angular acceleration
Mass	m = mass	I = moment of inertia
Momentum	ρ = momentum	L = angular momentum
Velocity	v = velocity	ω = angular velocity
Distance	d = distance	θ = angular distance
Newton's Second Law	F = ma	$\tau = I\alpha$
Momentum	ρ = mv	L = Iω
Kinetic energy	$KE = \frac{1}{2}mv^2$	$KE = \frac{1}{2}I\omega^2$
Work (Force x Distance)	W = Fd	W = $\tau\,\theta$

As stated, the moment of inertia (*I*) of a rotating object is analogous to its mass; while linear acceleration, momentum, velocity and distance become angular acceleration, angular momentum, angular velocity and angular distance. The force associated with rotation is termed torque.

Moment of Inertia, Mass, Size and Shape

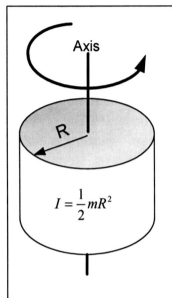

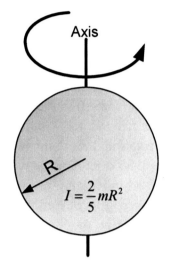

For a solid cylinder the moment of inertia is expressed by the equation: $$I = \frac{1}{2}mR^2$$ Where m is the actual mass of the body and R is the radius	For a solid sphere the moment of inertia is expressed by the equation: $$I = \frac{2}{5}mR^2$$ Where m is the actual mass of the body and R is the radius

9.3   The Effects of the Rotation of the Body

The above introduction to the energy, work and force equations associated with a rotating body allows consideration of the spinning movements that may be involved in strikes or defensive techniques. In many styles of the martial arts fighters are continuously taught to push from the floor and use a hip twisting action to help develop speed and deliver power. This rotational motion of the upper and lower body creates energy that can significantly increase the effect of a strike or block. The use of the hips is essential to help a fighter to derive power from the floor and through the body.

As we look at body rotation and the twisting of the hips it can help to visualize the image of the small, central, spinal column (back bone) connecting the hips to the upper body, through the skeleton, tendons and muscles. A small circular movement of the center thereby causes a much larger and faster movement at the outer edge of the hips and shoulders. The increase in speed is actually caused by the difference in radius of the spinal column compared to the hips or shoulders. Hence a fighter can imagine triggering that large peripheral movement by simply 'twitching' the inner connecting column. This image of a small movement producing a larger motion was often explained in seminars given by Master Nishiyama and the illustration shown on the left of figure 9.3 is based upon a drawing shown in Master Nakayama's book entitled 'Dynamic Karate'.

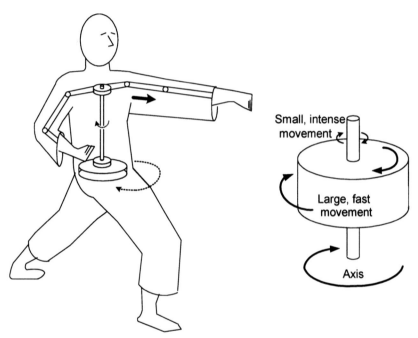

Figure 9.3: Classic simplified schematic of the reverse punch upper body mechanics - to illustrate the idea of using a small internal movement to create a larger and faster peripheral motion

We can use the earlier equations to estimate the moment of inertia of the upper torso and thereby make an approximate estimate of the kinetic energy of a body rotating through for a reverse or cross punch of velocity of 9 meters per second. (This is deliberately being simplified by taking the hips and stomach to be cylindrical and round rather than elliptical in cross section.) If the mass involved in the rotation is 30 kg and we liken the body to a solid cylinder with a torso radius of say 16.5cm (6.5 inches) then the moment of inertia can be calculated. The chosen diameter of only 13 inches may appear to be small but it does provide a circumference of around 41 inches—which is a reasonable chest measurement. A waist measurement which is less than the hips and chest is normal because we are more of an 'hour-glass' shape than cylindrical, and most fit and healthy people are elliptical rather than 'round', but this model calculation is a just a simplification.

$$(Inertia)\ I = \frac{1}{2}mR^2 \qquad\qquad \text{[Equation 9.2]}$$

$$= 0.5 \times 30 \times (0.165)^2\ =\ 0.4 \text{ kg m}^2$$

Studies by Stull and Barnham (1988) suggest that a hip velocity of about 1 meter per second is a reasonable assumption. The angular velocity is derived by knowing that it equals the linear velocity divided by the radius and is therefore determined from the equation:

$$\omega = v/r \qquad = 1\ /\ 0.165 \qquad \approx 6 \text{ radians / second.}$$

The rotational kinetic energy is given by equation 9.1:

$$KE = \frac{1}{2}I\omega^2\ =\ 0.5 \times 0.4 \times (6)^2 \qquad \approx 7 \text{ joules}$$

Seven or eight joules is a not a very high amount of energy: Similar to what could be expected with a 4 kilogram weight traveling at 2 meters / second; or a 3 kg weight dropped from 254 mm (about 10 inches). In other words twisting the hip in itself does create some kinetic energy but its real value is in driving the striking limb, such as the punching arm, and increasing the effective mass behind the strike.

9.4   A Mathematical Makeup of a Punch?

Can we theoretically break down the makeup of a punch into the various components involved and analyze these to determine the relative contributions of each of the constituent parts? If we could would that aid the debates associated with, for example the importance of opposite hand retraction (pull back) or body movements? The Shoshin Ryu Practitioner's Guide Book, edited by Brian Combo (2005), contains a chapter entitled "Understanding Power" where mathematical deliberations are used to derive an equation of deformation energy, starting with the conservations of linear momentum, angular momentum and energy. By doing so, the author calculates that with an initial bulk movement of 4 meters/second, an arm/fist velocity of 5 m/sec and initial angular rotation of 2 radians/sec, the following percentages or ratios of energy are available for delivery to the target:

44%	is from the attacker's bulk movement
20%	is from the striking fist/arm
17%	is from the retracting fist/arm
12%	is from the coupling
7%	is from the torso rotation

The Practitioner's Guide Book calculates that if the fist/arm velocity can be doubled and 10 meters per sec is attained then these ratios are approximately adjusted as follows:

23%	is from the attacker's bulk movement
41%	is from the striking fist/arm
19%	is from the retracting fist/arm
13%	is from the coupling
7%	is from the torso rotation

I cannot validate the figures derived here and remain troubled by some of the relatively high energy levels that are quoted in this reference, such as the contribution from the retracting or pull-back arm. However, the concepts applied provide an insight and the comparative (%) figures shown above are worth mulling over. For example this indicates that as the striking speed increases the bulk movement becomes less dominant. Fighters who have been on the receiving end of lightning fast strikes from a good 'lightweight' have firsthand knowledge of this phenomenon.

To my knowledge there has been little scientific experimental study on the differential effect of the practice of retracting the non-striking hand. The above table suggests that up to almost 20% of the striking energy can be derived from the practice of pull-back or opposite hand retraction. Personally I doubt that figure as a general indicator. In certain styles students are taught the importance of the opposite fist retraction but as they progress through the ranks and start sparring this practice is reduced and progressively eliminated when fighting. Watch a top notch boxer throw a really hard right hand punch and you will see the left hand basically stay in the guard position. Even when asked to throw his hardest punch to a bag a boxer will not normally pull the other hand back to the hip or shoulder. The retraction of the non-punching arm is good initial basic training because it encourages the use of the body, rather than just the striking hand and arm, but a fighter in combat does not normally drop the guard hand, not even for a moment.

There are always exceptions: There are fighters that can sometimes be so dominant, so quick and so good that they can afford to fight certain opponents with their hands casually down near their hips. There are opponents that most of us have faced that appear to be in a different class, derived from a different planet. I once faced the late Steve Cattle and on a particular move, as I attacked, he seemed to disappear—his timing was that good. I have been kicked to the head within such a close range that the only explanation I could find was that my opponent had joints that articulate differently than anyone else, as though she was related to a stick insect. There are always exceptions.

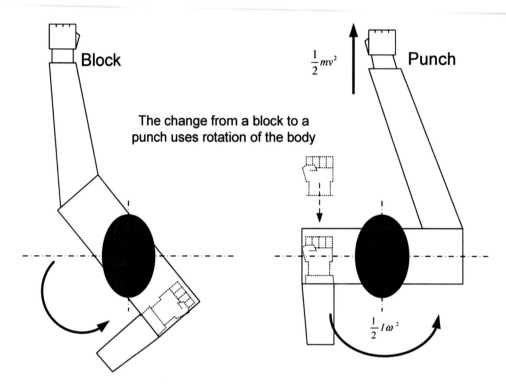

Figure 9.4: When fighting the block and punch can become one continuous movement. This can help increase the rotation of the core and increase the speed of the counterpunch.

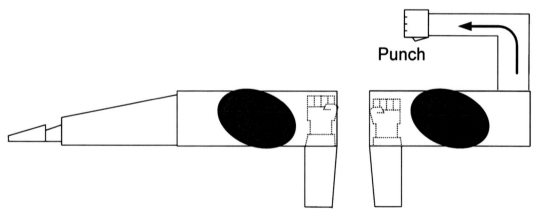

Figure 9.5: Since significant body rotation is not always available power needs to be developed by training within constraints, for example by practicing particular forms or kata.

9.5   The Rotation of the Fist When Punching

There is an energy component that has so far been neglected but should be examined for completeness. The fist, in a classical karate punch, rotates through 180 degrees in traveling from the hip to full extension— mostly in the latter part of the movement. Not all styles or schools teach this twisting action at the end of a straight punch, but this rotation must contain an energy component, so what can the laws

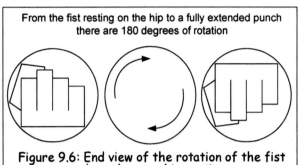

From the fist resting on the hip to a fully extended punch there are 180 degrees of rotation

Figure 9.6: End view of the rotation of the fist through a punching action

of physics tell us about it? To gain insight, let us take a look at the energy involved by using an approximation that the fist is akin to a solid cylinder, meaning that the moment of inertia is given by the equation $I = \frac{1}{2}mr^2$.

The energy associated with the rotation of a fist will be described by a similar equation to the standard (linear) kinetic energy equation, but in this case its rotational equivalent is given by:

Kinetic energy, $KE = \frac{1}{2}I\omega^2$ Equation (9.1)

Moment of inertia, $I = \frac{1}{2}mr^2$,   Equation (9.2)

Hence $KE = \frac{1}{2}\left(\frac{1}{2}mr^2\right)\omega^2 = \frac{1}{4}m(r\omega)^2$ Equation (9.3)

Where m is mass (kg), ω is the angular velocity of revolution, measured in radians per second, and r is the radius of the rotation (meters). Hence we have the equation to use, now to determine the numbers to insert:

1   Mass 'm': The mass of the hand and forearm has been shown in table 8.1 within section 8.10 of this book to be 0.5% and 1.5% (respectively) of the total body weight. With a body weight of 100kg, two percent is 2kg. That's just the weight of hand and forearm; section 8.10 used experimental data to show that a professional heavyweight boxer could punch with a mass or around 8.6kg (~15 lbs) and this figure will be used here to make sure that we are being most conservative.

2   Radius 'r': We can glance at our own fist and arm to guess that a typical radius of rotation is about 4 cm or 0.04 m. (The width of a male fist is typically just over 3 inches, hence in this simplified model the radius of the revolving cylinder is ~1.6 inch or 4 cm.)

3   **Angular velocity 'v':** There are 2π radians in a circle of 360^0, and we know that when punching the fist rotates half of one full circle, which is 180^0 or 1π (3.14) radians. Chapter 1 points out that a punch can be delivered in around 200 milliseconds or 0.2 seconds. If we watch ourselves slowly go through the technique of punching from the hip we see that the rotation, in free space and without striking a target, is roughly over the final quarter of the full movement. One quarter of 0.2 seconds is 0.05 s (using a linear approximation of distance to time). Hence we can determine the speed of rotation at that point as radians turned divided by time taken which equals 3.14/0.05 = 63 radians per second (ten revolutions per second or 600 rpm). Using a mass of 8.6kg, a velocity of 63 rads/ sec and the radius as 0.04 m we can determine the kinetic energy as follows:

$$\text{Kinetic energy} \qquad KE = \frac{1}{4}m(r\omega)^2 = \frac{1}{4}8.6 \times (0.04. \times 63)^2 \approx 14 \text{ Joules}$$

In section 8.10 we calculated that the energy of a punch from a heavyweight fighter, 'carrying' 8.6 kg of mass and striking with a speed of almost 9 m/s, was **340** Joules. In comparison with this quantity of energy from the complete punch this fist rotation energy component value of 14 joules is only about 4% of total.

There are many ways we can rerun the numbers but the percentage figure will remain comparatively low. I remain of the view that at the moment of impact, with about 75% extension of the arm, the rotation is more to instill good form and to produce a follow through or penetration intent. I have seen no comparative study designed to establish the difference in force between rotational punching actions compared with a 'straight' punch; hence the above comment is based on the calculation shown and subjective judgment. It would appear that a karate student is taught to punch from the hip with the fist turned up to establish correct hand and arm movement through the strike. Numerous biomechanical factors are involved, not least of which is keeping the elbow 'in' and close to the body — to help ensure straight-line trajectory, structural connection and efficient muscular action. This teaching is extremely important, particularly through the early years of the student's practice. The discipline of seeking efficiency of movement and effectiveness of technique is at the very heart of the martial arts. It is critically important that a student be shown, exactly, the correct movement and form of the style being studied.

Facts for Fighters

The time taken for a punch to be delivered is around 200 milliseconds. The average time taken to blink an eye is between 300 and 400 milliseconds.

You can be hit—in the blink of an eye—without seeing the strike coming!

Later the higher-ranking grades will work through a far wider range of strikes and recognize that rotation is not always applied to punches, such as in a close quarter uppercut. They will also contemplate the fact that since the impact of a real strike occurs before the end of travel of the punching arm, the final rotation is "stopped" by the target. The theory outlined above shows that this 'stoppage', this absorption into the target, can create more damage. One can easily imagine that stopping an oncoming shaft that is rotating, as well as moving forward, takes more effort. Nevertheless, with regards to a punch, my view is that this rotational mechanical (as opposed to biomechanical) difference is not that significant. In other words it's the punching technique that's important, not the absolute energy content due solely to the rotation of the fist. The rotation of the fist, as part of that technique, helps instill correct form. Correct overall form and intent is what makes the big difference, not the actual rotational energy due to a twisting fist.

> **Facts for Fighters**
> Although measured evidence is lacking, it appears that the actual energy content of the rotation of the punching hand is not significant.
> The rotation can assist with correct technique—helping to prevent the elbow from wandering away from the side of the body as the punch is delivered.

9.6   Rotation of the Fist and Arm when Blocking

The previous section points out that in the absence of measured data it is considered unlikely that the rotation of the fist, in itself, adds significantly more energy to a punch and that the main benefit of this practice is to help ensure proper technique. But what is the effect of rotation of the hand and lower arm in a blocking action?

Energy level of a downward block:

To do a quick analysis let's return to our previous typical Western male. This is a man of weight 80 kg or 176 lbs with a fist and forearm that in combination weighs about 2% of the total body weight, or 1.6 kg. Inclusion of half the weight of the upper arm with a percentage weight of 1.5% brings the total to 3.5% or 2.8 kg. For comparative purposes let's choose a generic block and simply assume that the arm moves about as fast with a block as it does with a punch. (We are only looking for proof of comparative significance, hence the use of such an approximation.) With a speed of 8 m/s the block, using the 2.8 kg mass of the arm only, carries an energy of $\frac{1}{2}mv^2 = 0.5 \times 2.8 \times 8^2 = 90$ *joules*.

Energy level of the rotating fist when applying a downward block:

Let's assume the hand rotation with the block is through about a quarter of a circle or 90⁰ (or $\pi/2$ radians), with a blocking speed that gives a travel duration of 200 milliseconds or 0.2 seconds, and the rotation occurs in the last 10% of the movement. One tenth of 0.2 is 0.02 seconds and therefore a rotational speed of $(\pi/2)/0.02 = 79$ radians per second would be calculated. Assuming that the rotational component is restricted to the forearm and fist then the effective mass of the rotating component is 1.6 kg. Hence from equation 9.3:

$$KE = \frac{1}{2}\left(\frac{1}{2}mr^2\right)\omega^2 = \frac{1}{4}m(r\omega)^2 = \frac{1}{4}(1.6) \times (0.04 \times 79)^2 = 4 \; joules$$

What do the numbers mean?

This figure of 4 joules is a potential increase of less than 5% compared to the 90 joules of blocking energy calculated earlier. With a blocking hand rotation that occurs in the final 5% of the movement, the associated (turning) energy would be recalculated with twice the angular velocity. This gives an kinetic energy of 16 joules which would raise the previous blocking level from 90 joules to 108; an increase of about 18%. This range of a 5 to 18 percent increase in blocking energy is equivalent to that achieved by increasing the blocking arm speed to 8.2 m/s at the lower end and 8.7 m/s at the higher end. An increase of 18% is worth having but it may be considered as only a modest improvement; but since we are dealing with a block this increase in energy should be considered one stage further.

Experience and common sense tells us that the force required to deflect a strike can be a fraction of the potential impact force of that striking object. A car that hits and slides along the safety barrier at the edge of a highway is being deflected from its path by that barrier. In such circumstances even though the car is heavy and traveling at high speed the barrier may show little structural damage. If the car were to hit the barrier 'face on' there would be massive damage to both the car and the barrier. As a goalkeeper I can think of innumerable occasions where I have deflected a fast moving soccer ball with the fingers of an outstretched hand—and I would have been physically incapable of stopping the ball at that stretched reach. The force needed to deflect such a ball is only a fraction of the force needed to stop it. When you deflect an incoming fist that's about a foot (30 cm) from your head you are aiming to change the path of the punch so it misses your face. You alter the angle of the trajectory through an angle that moves it about 4 inches (10 cm) from its original path over that 12 inch distance. That angle happens to be around 14 degrees, and it increases if you have to shift the punch when it's closer to your head. This ratio of 4 to 12 (or 3 to 1) indicates why the energy needed to divert an incoming missile is lower than that needed to stop it. This suggests that if it takes 90 joules to change the course of an incoming strike that has 340 joules of energy, (a ratio of 3.8 to 1), then 106 J can deflect a strike of 400 J.

The consideration of forces provides insight into what's involved with the deflection of an incoming strike by a static object (such as the motorway crash barrier) and how the strength needed to deflect the incoming object will depend on the deflection angle.

As a long term practitioner of the art of karate I know that the twisting action of a block can make a significant difference, particularly with a downward block. The twisting action helps with technique, the turning motion helps to deflect the incoming arm or leg with an action that will knock the opponent away and, with a downward block, it seems to help to 'drop' the weight into the block.

The above generally deals with blocks that are designed to deflect the incoming strike. There are times when a fighter will choose to attack the incoming strike—trying to hurt the punching or kicking limb in order to distract or dissuade the attacker.

> Science cannot currently model and explain all aspects of an art - no computer can paint a Renoir or duplicate the skills seen in the MMA.

And on a practical note:

Anyone who has trained in one of the harder styles of the martial arts knows that there are certain sessions where bruises are to be expected, if not embraced. Many have returned from a special weekend training event with forearms that act as a multi-colored witness to back-to-back sessions involving repeated blocking and sparring. Despite this punishment it is rare indeed to see or hear of a blocking arm being seriously damaged or broken. The only instance I have knowledge of a fracture involved a block against a kick where the shin caught the lower arm virtually 'straight on' or perpendicular to the bone, giving no deflecting path and resulting in a clean break. As Sensei (Dr.) Tim Hanlon (6th Dan Shotokan, Doctor of Medicine and Surgeon) once pointed out: "The action of the downward block allows the forces experienced by the ulna to be spread out over a larger surface area, thereby reducing the likelihood of serious injury to the blocking arm." The major styles teach martial artists how to block properly, reducing the chance of injury. These same styles insist on realistic attack and defense, so the impacts become part of the training.

In addition to reducing risk, the application of the turning movement also seems to help with the 'focusing' of the block. It assists with timing and techniques but more fundamentally with the spirit and attitude of the block. I know from experience that the rotation of the fist and arm in the downward block causes more 'penetration'. Experience of being on both the providing and receiving end of such a block, with and without the twist, has demonstrated the difference: a noticeable difference in degree of deflection or pain received. These experiences have not, however, been numerically measured under controlled conditions, and the above arithmetic does not suggest such a difference. It would be relatively straightforward to undertake a scientific study of the effect that rotation has on the deflecting force of a block: using repeated measurements, with a reasonable sample of subjects, blocking with and without the twisting action. Perhaps one day this and many other aspects of the art will be studied scientifically. If so, perhaps we can also measure the effect of 'dropping the weight' when applying a downward block. This was taught by Master Nishiyama and others and to me the effect felt can sometimes appear to be far more intense than should be mathematically expected.

9.7   The Effect of Distance: Round & Spinning Kicks

Equation 9.1 shows that rotational kinetic energy is proportional to the product of moment of inertia (I) and angular velocity squared. Equation 9.2 showed that the moment of inertia I is proportional to the product of the mass and the square of the radius of the revolving body. This leads to the understanding that rotational kinetic energy is proportional to mass multiplied by the radius squared times the angular velocity squared: see equation 9.3.

A wheel rotating with a radius of twice that of another wheel of the same mass and same speed of rotation has far more kinetic energy at its edge. If we think of one of our long range kicks, such as a roundhouse or spinning kick, then the radius involved (about the length of the leg) is long and the speed of the foot becomes considerable. There is significant energy contained in this kind of spinning action, as shown by equation 9.3. Being struck with the heel of a foot engaged in a jumping spinning kick provides a very tactile sense of the laws of physics. Imagine spinning a lead weight above your head, on the end of a piece of cable. As you feed out more cable the velocity of the weight increases, so does its energy level and so does the force felt if struck by this high-speed weight. When a fighter uses a rotational body move to launch a long range spinning back kick, hook kick or roundhouse kick the effect can be devastating. The heel of a spinning back kick has enough speed and mass to knockout anyone unfortunate enough to get in its path.

Spinning Kick

9.8   Summary

A body in motion has kinetic energy, regardless of whether that motion is straight or circular, and this energy can do damage when converted to an impact force. The linear relationships and equations used previously can be related to their rotational equivalents. All the insights gained through the study of the linear relationships can be applied to their circular cousins. The proportionality of kinetic energy to mass and the importance of speed and its square law all have direct bearing in the rotational analog.

The rotation of the body is shown to be important in everything we have examined. Trained fighters do not punch with just their hands and arms—they use their body to twist and move into the strike. Hooks and roundhouse types of punches require tuition and bag practice; once again the core of the body has to be employed for full effect. Control of these circular strikes is difficult, influencing their use in competitions. The swinging 'hay-maker' seen in a bar fight is used by so many because it can deliver a lot of force.

The rotation of the fist during a karate style of punch does not, in itself, carry significant extra energy. This action does, however, help the development of technique and a penetrative attitude. The calculated additional energy associated with a twisting arm block, compared to a block that does not use this swivel motion is, on its own, insufficient to explain the achievable increase in effectiveness by this means of blocking. Again this rotational action is considered to be for technique and attitude.

In close quarter hand-to-hand battles circular actions can become important and circular elbow techniques can be devastating. One of the important aims of the martial artist is to achieve more with less: Fighters want to be able to strike an opponent at very close range with a similar effect to that achieved with the luxury of distance and time. The science that we have worked through points out just how difficult this is, for with very little distance, and therefore time to accelerate to a high striking speed a fighter has to quickly 'impulse' into effectiveness. Some styles and instructors refer to this as a vibration like action; others use the one-inch punch type of test to aid development. All should picture this as an explosive action. Chapter 8 points out that with only a few inches of movement a punching energy can be achieved that is as high as 50% of the full range punch.

Practice and training may be clean, even pure. Street violence is messy.
Excellence in the Martial Arts is achieved by understanding and applying the innumerable incremental improvements that accumulate to make the difference.

"What is difficult in training will become easy in battle"

Alexander Suvorov

Train hard, fight easy

CHAPTER 10:   A WARRIOR'S STANCE

> *'Postures are for the beginner, later they are natural positions'*
> *Master Funakoshi.*

10.1   Introduction

No technical study of the martial arts would be complete without an examination of the way fighters stands or move or how their stance can be used to aid the delivery of a powerful technique or assist in evasion. This is a subject that could fill a book or be restricted to only a single page. Here we will take a middle course, neither overlooking the subject nor spending an inordinate amount of time stating the obvious.

10.2   The Basics

All standing structures rely upon their base or foundation for stability; the taller and more massive the structure the more important its base and foundations. This point is of particular importance if the structure is prone to adverse conditions that cause stress. The structure being described could be a building, such as a tower block, and the adverse conditions could be hurricane forces or earthquakes. The architect of such a structure has to contend with design requirements that combine strength and flexibility—producing a building of stability and durability yet not so rigid that it fractures and falls due to the seismic effects of a moderate earthquake.

If that tower block picture is grasped, mentally shift now to an 'alternative' structure composed of our own skeletal framework, connected together by muscle, joints, tissue and ligaments; namely 'the body'. The human body may, at one moment, try to remain still and straight despite standing on the deck of a storm-racked boat or on a rocking subway car. That same body may, at a different time, attempt rapid movement away from a rooted stance on a solid (or unstable) surface, perhaps to sprint or leap. The stances of fighters have had to be developed to cope with many conditions, differing intentions or circumstances; including:

Attack	Defense	Firm ground	Soft ground
Striking	Blocking	Single attacker	Multiple attacker
Evasion	Jamming	Body shape	Natural preferences
Stability	Mobility	Confined space	Open space

A single stance cannot be expected to cope with all of these challenges. The need to survive through a history of warfare and battle has brought about the development of innumerable fighting methods and an associated range of stances. The selection process is truly one of the survival of the fittest, with and without weapons. Techniques that work can be passed on, refined, and used again but the advocates of techniques that fail would tend to be imprisoned by invading armies, or eaten by the saber toothed tiger from which they were trying to escape.

In considering the range of stances available do not concentrate solely on an individual martial art such as Ju Jitsu, Aikido, Karate, Tae Kwon Do, Kung Fu, Judo etc. From the time that Homo-sapiens first stood upright, stances have been developed all across the planet - because armed or unarmed combat has always been a global matter of survival. It should be no surprise that everywhere you look you will find similarities in the stances taught in 'different' martial art styles. Look, for example, to European fencing, foil and saber, or in Asian swordsmanship, kendo or escrima, in kyudo or archery, even in traditional East Indian dance. Put simply, warriors from different times, backgrounds and cultures have come to similar conclusions on the best way to place the feet in combative situations. Stances have been developed independently— at different times and in different places. This is seen when watching children play at being pirates or storm troopers and observing where they naturally learn to place their feet and weight when defending or attacking with a toy sword.

The insights we gain through training, are likely a repeat of the insight of someone in, say, the Japan of Musashi (born 1584), or in Sparta at the times of the Trojan wars (circa 1200 BC). In art and science re-invention is to be expected—look carefully at the first two 'warrior' poses of yoga and ask if the name is coincidental.

The book by Master Teruyuki Okazaki and Milorad Stricevic, entitled *The Textbook of Modern Karate* lists seven 'natural' stances, ten 'fundamental' stances and derives at least nine sparring stances. These are termed 'derived' only because the sparring stances are basically developed versions of either a natural stance or a fundamental stance. Simple examples of some of these stances are as follows:

Natural Stances	Fundamental Stances	Sparring Stances
Open leg stance	Front stance	Sparring front stance
Right angle L stance	Back stance	Sparring L stance
Right angle T stance	Cat leg stance	Sparring cat leg stance
Parallel leg stance	Straddle leg stance	Sparring straddle leg stance

Each of these natural, fundamental or sparring stances serves a need in a particular set of conditions. Examination of the referenced book is recommended for those that wish to study the nature and purpose of each of these, and other, stances. However, from a technical perspective it is sufficient to appreciate the scientific principles associated with the characteristics and function of a stance. This will help in the examination and basic understanding of any stance. In the next few sections certain terms will be used that are meant to have specific meaning. It is therefore useful to define these terms and avoid the risk of ambiguity:

o **Mobility:** this is the quality or state of moving freely, an ability to change.

o **Stability:** this is the quality of being resistant to change or displacement, resilient and able to maintain equilibrium, despite applied forces.

o **Balance:** a state of equilibrium characterized by the cancellation of all forces by opposing forces.

o **Equilibrium:** a condition in which all acting influences are canceled by others, resulting in a stable, balanced, or unchanging system.

o **Center of Gravity:** the center of gravity (C of G) of a body is that point where all the parts of the body can be balanced, it is the point where support can be provided to the whole body, and it is the point within a body where gravity can be considered to act. Normally the C of G of an object, being the average location of weight, coincides with the object's center of mass.

The above definitions will be useful as we consider types of stances and the footprint of a stance. Note the similarity between balance and equilibrium—this text will tend to use the term 'balance'.

10.3   The Proportionality of a Typical Body

To allow examination of the characteristics of a range of stances, a typical human body has been theoretically constructed. The following sketch provides the dimensions of several parts of the anatomy of a typical, 75 kg, British male: namely the overall height, the height to knee, hip and shoulder and the length of reach of the arm. These dimensions are taken from the second edition of *Bodyspace: Anthropometry, Ergonomics and the Design of Work* by Stephen Pheasant (1996). This therefore provides comparative relationships and ratios between these proportions of a human.

If you happen to be 6 foot 2 inches tall and therefore consider yourself significantly different from the 5' 8" height referenced please don't be concerned, the ratios will not be that different. These anthropometric numbers are only being used to provide proportionality, so that the legs or arms are about average for the body drawn and examined. There are always exceptions to general rules, people with long arms or legs, we know this—we have even fought against them in some training hall or ring (or perhaps they only appeared to have longer limbs because we could not get as close to them as they could to us).

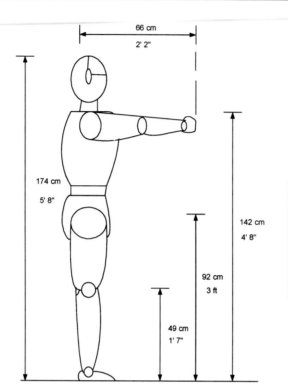

66 cm
2' 2"

174 cm
5' 8"

142 cm
4' 8"

92 cm
3 ft

49 cm
1' 7"

Other dimensions of interest:

Shoulder to elbow: 36.5 cm
Elbow to fingertip: 47.5 cm
Hand length: 19.5 cm
Hand breadth: 8.5 cm
Foot length: 26.5 cm

Center of Gravity: 55% of
height - on average:

Centimeters	Feet & Inches
174	5' 8"
142	4' 8"
92	3 ft
66	2' 2"
49	1' 7"
Kilograms	*Pounds*
75 kg	*165 lbs*

Figure 10.1: Typical Male
Body Proportions

10.4   Forward Stance and its Structural Lines

The execution of a classical reverse punch from a front stance can be examined using these typical dimensions. In figure 10.2 the back foot has been placed a distance of approximately two shoulder widths behind the front foot, with the knee of the front leg leaning over the toes of the front foot. When this form of stance is used to deliver a reverse punch then the fighter is aiming to strike with energy and a stable footing that helps create an effective technique.

Where does the force come from?

This question was addressed in section 3.3 where a sketch was used to illustrate the action and reaction principles found in Newtons Third Law. This sketch, showing a man pulling a cart or rickshaw is repeated here and added alongside is a sketch of a man pushing a wheelbarrow.

Figure 10.2: A reverse punch in
forward stance

Figure 10.3: Illustrative examples of the use of a 'forward stance'.

Using these types of examples, section 3.4 answered the question of "where does the force come from?" as follows:

"Assuming that the road is flat and smooth you basically need to overcome the backward pull from the frictional effects, particularly the friction of the wheels in contact with the ground. **And what pushes you forward? The ground does.** *As you push through the legs and feet the ground pushes back with equal force."*

What does the connection to the floor look like?

If you were to visualize the back leg straightening to push off the floor, then the musculature force being applied down the line of that back leg, through the foot to the floor would look similar to that shown in figure 10.4. This figure shows several features, including:

o The lines of force pushing down through the front and back legs.

o The reactive force as the floor pushes back.

o The breakdown of these forces, into their horizontal and vertical components.

o How the back leg has a significant horizontal component, providing a force to move forward.

o How the horizontal component of the front leg is small, because the lower part of the front leg is almost vertical.

o This shows that the force that generates forward movement when trying to sprint or step is mainly from the back leg.

o In a front stance the force that initiates the drive for a strong punch with body weight (rather than a jab) is mainly from the back leg connection to the ground.

This is a single sketch, a slow motion video of a reverse punch would show how the back leg is bent and pushing the floor prior to straightening—it's still slightly bent and in motion at the moment of impact, even if it is straight at the conclusion of the technique.

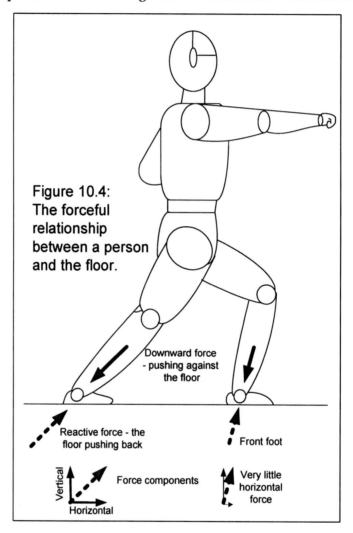

Figure 10.4:
The forceful relationship between a person and the floor.

Downward force - pushing against the floor

Reactive force - the floor pushing back

Front foot

Force components

Very little horizontal force

Vertical

Horizontal

Is this a picture taken just before or just after impact?

Be aware of the differences between the static (non-moving) and the dynamic (moving) case. There is a difference between hitting and penetrating a target that is static or tending to move away compared with dropping into a solid stance and performing a classic strike to an oncoming, in-rushing, opponent. Previous chapters have explained how to try and ensure that all energy, all the potential momentum of a strike, is imparted into an opponent.

In most of these examples, the visualization has typically been towards a static opponent or one whose attack has been blocked and, in that moment of quiescence, we are counter-attacking. Here moving our center of gravity towards the opponent at the moment of impact is of particular importance. (The image shown as figure 10.4 is only meant to portray a picture of a fighter that has completely delivered a punch to a static opponent.)

If the opponent is charging-in, trying to run you over, and you choose to strike 'head-on', without trying to evade, then being able to drop into a stable solid stance from which to hit hard and strong is clearly of benefit. In such a case, the stance and bodily structure has to contend with some very serious forces. These include the forces that *you* have to generate, from the floor, to hit and penetrate that opponent and the force needed to oppose the energy of the incoming opponent. These combined forces can expose any weakness in that stance and structure. What is wanted is for the opponent to 'buckle' from the force of a technique driven from a solid, virtually immovable, object—namely you. What is not wanted is for you to have a weak point, perhaps at the foot, ankle, knee, elbow or wrist; because such a weak point can cause failure. In a static situation, the strength of the structure (the body) arises from the natural linkages of the individual parts (e.g. bones, joints, ligaments, tendons and muscle) and their connection to the earthly foundations of that structure. The ability to resist external forces is dependent upon the framework that connects the structure to its foundations and the arrangement, strength and flexibility (or pliability) of the individual members of that framework.

> A target may be stationary, moving away or moving towards you. A technique may be delivered from a static position or one that's moving either towards or away from the target. Think about how these circumstances can affect the choice of the stance adopted and the deployment of the technique.

The importance of the connection with the floor and the lines of support emanating through that contact point should be reasonably evident from figure 10.4 and aligns with the points made in section 3.4 with respect to Newton's Third Law— *for every action there is an equal and opposite reaction.* This can be considered in two parts:

1. Pushing off the floor to gain the forceful energy that goes into a strike.

2. Hitting an oncoming opponent, penetrating with the strike, and resisting the reaction of the punch and the opponent's oncoming momentum.

A significant portion of this book has concentrated on the energy that goes into a strike. Here we examine a stance to adopt when hitting and penetrating an incoming opponent.

Figure 10.4 shows how the force forward for the punch is mainly derived and emanating through the back leg. The sketch draws imaginary connecting lines through the floor to the front and back legs. The front leg is almost at a right angle to the floor, while the back leg can push both down and away from the floor. A line drawn through the back leg to the floor is more horizontal, closer to the line with the striking trajectory than the front leg line. This allows the push off from the floor and helps with providing a solid base to resist the reaction from hitting an onrushing opponent. In fact, the longer the stance the lower the angle of this back leg connection line to the floor and hence the more able to resist any reactive forces; but we must stay within reasonable boundaries, for a stance that is too low and too long has little mobility.

Test 1: Consider this from a different viewpoint: If a martial artist is stood in a forward-stance, reverse-punch mode and their training partner pushes back on the outstretched fist then that pushing force is resisted by the structure through the connection pathways to the base and earth. If that structure or connection path is not strong enough then the weakest structural points of that person will buckle, collapse or move. To demonstrate this, take up the position of a reverse-punch delivery and allow a training partner to push against the outstretched fist and thereby show the biggest weaknesses, such as the collapse of the wrist or the buckling at the elbow. When your partner can push hard enough against the fist that your complete body has to shift back as a single unit then that shows there is no single dominant weakness in the structure. A fighter can then work at 'pushing down' further into the floor, increasing connection by muscular tension, making it more difficult to be pushed back. And so the work, and progress, continues.

Test 2: Stand in front of a very heavy bag and push it away. When trying to stop the bag as it swings towards you, you will find that you will tend to catch the bag on the way in, with outstretched arms and soft elbows, allowing the arms to bend and accept the forces as you bring the bag to a stop. Now try using straight arms with locked elbows and look at where the feet are best placed to accept the forces. Naturally you will tend to use one foot behind the other, rather than them both being on the same hip line (and stopping it while standing upright on one leg will be a challenge). Finally, try to stop the bag with a punch—this is the dynamic case and a better representation of striking an incoming attacker 'head-on'. Everyone will come away from this exercise with differing observations and sensations; for me it is often the impact felt on the bare knuckles and the forces that really want my elbow to bend. This is a tactile demonstration of how the body feels and deals with the reactive or consequential forces of hitting something. You don't need to be a physics major or expert on anatomy to figure out that the body parts closest to impact are going to feel the initial effects first and that those effects lessen as you physically move away from this impact point. Those that promote the theory that the shock waves from an impact *simply* travel down the body to the floor, and so you want a 'hard-body' that is better able to 'reflect' these forces back to an opponent, should recognize that we are not a super-hero (nor made of steel) and that there are innumerable soft connections along our bodies between the point of impact and the floor.

Test 3:   With a reverse punch, at the point of impact, the striking path is horizontal. It should therefore be easy to imagine that in the static case more strength comes from any structural support lines that are closer to the horizontal—in other words, the vast majority of support comes from the back leg rather than the front. This is easy to demonstrate. Simply make a classic reverse punch in forward stance and then push the punch against a wall. Be aware of the pressure on the hand and arm, as the wall pushes back, and notice where the supporting forces are felt. Note the connection from the fist all the way to the floor. It should be possible to feel the strain on the hip and other joints of the back leg and in particular on the ankle and back foot itself. To prove where the majority

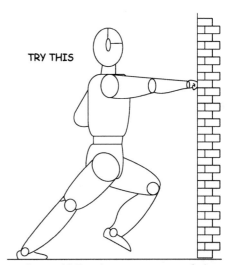

TRY THIS

Figure 10.5:   Demonstration of the support through the back leg

of support is derived, simply take the *front* foot off the floor completely. See figure 10.5. Picking up this front leg up is fairly easy because there is so little support coming from this leg. This is as indicated in figure 10.4 where the support force line drawn through this front leg is almost vertical, almost perpendicular, to the punching line. The back leg however, has a support force line at an angle of around 45 degrees and provides a strong stance and substantial supporting frame, which is capable of delivering force and resilient against a pushing action. (Good luck trying to lift the back leg.)

Something to think about: Imaginary Intersections

Figure 10.6 shows a reverse punch technique in forward stance and how a line drawn through the path of the back leg will intersect the punching arm just before the wrist, and that a line drawn through the forward leg will also intersect the arm at about that same point. Using a computer-drawing package that allows the production of scaled drawings, and a 'standard' 5 foot 8 inch person, it can be seen that the distance from shoulder to intersection of lines (at about the wrist) is approximately 57 cm, out of a total arm length, to the knuckles, of approximately 66 cm. As a percentage of total reach 57 cm is 86% of that total length of 66 cm. This percentage would reduce if the hips were turned beyond the 90

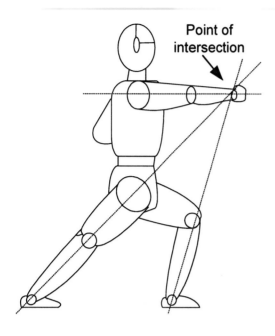

Point of intersection

Figure 10.6: The reverse punch in forward stance, showing imaginary structural supportive lines

degree point or if the punching arm shoulder is 'extended', as some senior karate instructors recommend. Doing so would probably bring the percentage position closer to the 75% impact figure that is discussed in Chapter 8. This is approximately the point of maximum speed and the point at which we should aim to strike.

A question worth thinking about is: "Is it merely coincidence that we have these lines of structural support intersecting around this striking point?" Whatever the answer, this image allows the visualization of force or support lines along the skeletal path of the lower legs. It's a demonstration that can be done in the training hall using a couple of poles or 'bo' to make the students think about structure and lines of force.

A dimensional derivation of forward stance?

For those that are thinking that this section could easily have been developed to provide a 'dimensional' description of forward stance, based perhaps on the ratios of body part dimensions, allow me to quote a Shotokan Karate expert:

"From (the) natural stance (shizentai), front stance (zenkutsudachi) can be formed by simply bending the knees, keeping the back straight, not moving the body position backwards, and sliding one leg back in a straight line maintaining the same width of stance. The position of the front knee is automatically correct if it is formed in this way. All the lengthy explanations about the exact weight distribution or the number of centimeters from the big toe to the perpendicular of the knee become superfluous."

Dr. David Hooper

JKA - Thoughts from Japan: Back to Basics, Dragon Times

10.5   Taking it to Extremes—Leaning Forward

The attributes and mechanics of the forward stance have been debated for decades. People from different styles compare stances and argue over the merits of one against the other. Cognizance is taken of the stances shown in old photographs or still seen in traditional schools. The front stance, its depth, height, mobility and application have been points of discussion for most martial artists. Over the years I have changed my stance to suit different instructors (and times) and engaged in endless conversations on stance efficiency and effectiveness. (Looking back at my very old photographs it is amusing to note just how low I initially practiced front stance.)

Figure 10.7: Exaggerated (low) front stance

Science often uses extreme cases to test or prove a point. We can think of an 'extreme' forward stance, one where the knee of the front leg is pushed far too far forward: One where the stance is so low and awkward to be virtually ineffective, providing neither stability nor mobility—something like that drawn in figure 10.7. A comparison between the stances shown in figures 10.4 and 10.7 is provided by figure 10.8. This drawing has an overlay of one stance over the other and may help to reveal several points, including:

With respect to the lowered stance:
- o   The hips have dropped and height has decreased.
- o   The reach has been extended.
- o   Mobility has decreased and it takes effort to 'rise-out' of this position.
- o   The position mimics a forward, attacking, type of movement; rather than a stable, static and sustained, structure.

Figure 10.7 was drawn in a somewhat exaggerated manner and is not meant to imitate any particular style. Nevertheless, if you examine the photographic demonstrations by Yasuhiko Suzuki in the 1994 edition of Karate-Do Nyumon by Gichin Funakoshi, a likeness with the above figure can be observed. [The stances of Master Funakoshi himself, shown within *Rentan Gishin Karate Jutsu* originally published in 1925 are much higher and have no illustrated instances where the knee of the front leg, in forward stance, extends beyond the toes.]

Although an exaggerated, transitional, stance may be used in dynamic circumstances such as sparring, repetitive basic training in that way can be physically detrimental. As this stance is adopted the forces on the patella or knee cap increase significantly as the knee moves forward beyond the toes. Training to improve muscle strength and flexibility helps prevent injury but deliberately risking long term damage is unwise. Also, in this type of exaggerated position there is a tendency for the upper body to lean forward, as indicated in figure 10.9.

The stance sketched as figure 10.9 has numerous deficiencies, weaknesses or concerns: the fighter is virtually off balance, mobility is being decreased, the back is no longer straight and the head and face are starting to be thrust forward into harm's way. Yet this elongation or extension can be desirable at times because it extends the reach – allowing the fighter to punch an opponent that is further away. Expert fighters have their own way of achieving the basic aims and intentions of the elongated reverse punch (developing a reverse punch that has an increased reach) yet retains an upright body line—one that allows the hips to twist even further into the strike and permits dynamic mobility.

Allow me to introduce you to a 'raised heel' debate.

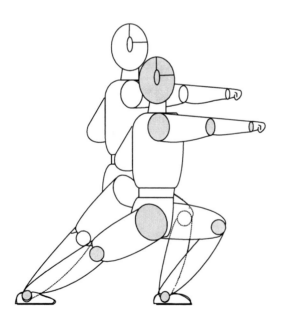

Figure 10.8: Comparison of a classical karate front stance with one that is significantly lower.

Figure 10.9: Exaggerated front stance, with a leaning upper body.

10.6   The Back Heel Debate

John Cheetham, the editor of the Shotokan Karate Magazine (SKM) and a Shotokan instructor of excellence made several observations in issue 64, August 2000, of SKM. He pointed to a typical demonstration of wood breaking where an expert was about to strike a board with a reverse punch. John noted how the person holding the wood was in a strong, firm and low forward stance, with both feet rooted to the floor, helping to ensure that when the wood is struck it is well supported. This concept is similar in principle to that described in section 10.4 of this chapter, when referring to withstanding a 'head-on' attack.

The article pointed out that when the attacker strikes through the wood his back heel is up and off the ground—contrary to the classical instruction provided previously in traditional Shotokan Karate. An illustrative sketch of this position is shown in figure 10.10. An overlay of this new 'heel raised' position with the classical one will show the extended reach (figure 10.11). Neither figure 10.10 nor 10.11 includes the extra extension from increased hip rotation, these figures display only a modest extension, fighters can reach a lot further.

This observation, of a raised back heel when board breaking, prompted a debate that ran for over nine months, through SKM issue 64 of August 2000 to issue 67 of May 2001. There were also innumerable internet sites that provided a forum for venting and vacillation. Many martial artists had a view on whether the heel should stay down or be allowed to rise (I admit to liking the comment that 'fighters do not fight flat-footed'). Unfortunately the topic was often approached with preconceived views rather than in an open and rational manner. It is, after all, difficult *not* to have a preconceived view when you have spent thousands of hours training a certain way. The principles contained within this book however should help to form an opinion based more on technical consideration.

Earlier sections of this book have explained in detail the importance of achieving high speed and putting mass (or body weight) into and behind your strike. It has also been indicated that the elongation of the strike length (arm and fist extension) can be helpful in achieving a

Figure 10.10: Reverse Punch with the back heel raised off the ground

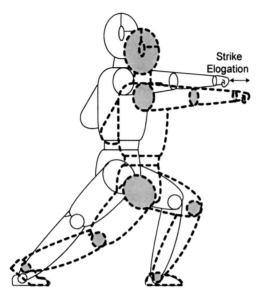

Figure 10.11 Overlay of the classic and 'heel-raised' positions

higher striking velocity. You have more time to attain a higher speed—that's one reason why amateurs will want to pull back their fist before striking. In a forward moving reverse punch, all of this can be *enhanced* by allowing the back heel to be raised. Try it. You can feel the enhanced hip rotation; the longer reach; the dynamic forward movement of the body's center of gravity as the heel is released. Of course a longer reach also means you can strike an opponent that is further away—another useful attribute. Imagine all of this in a *forward, attacking, mode against a stationary or retreating opponent. Provided the movements of the technique are coordinated, the speed and effective striking mass can be increased. The end result is that for an expert fighter in a forward attacking mode, a back heel that is raised at the moment of impact is not disadvantageous, not at all, it has some very positive advantages. Note the introduction of the word 'expert' – to ensure that the move is coordinated and correctly executed.

Let us now consider a more **defensive** or counter attacking mode with the reverse punch being applied to an inward rushing opponent, attempting to hit the opponent at exactly the right moment, perhaps without the need for a block. Here, together with fast technique, good timing and proper form, we are looking for stability. We don't want to be 'bowled' over by the incoming mass. We do want to hit straight and hard and be 'immovable', to let his speed add to the impact, to let him hit an immovable object and be stopped accordingly. Hence the common sense developed through training and the previous section on structural strength and stability show why in these circumstances a solid, resilient, base is of importance. The foot should be strongly in contact with the floor. To resist a powerful push/jolt against the reverse punch fist, by an incoming object that has significant momentum, you need to draw the resisting force through the legs and body from the floor. In short, you want the back heel on the floor.

In summary, when considering this back heel debate, ask: 'are you hitting a static object, an incoming opponent or a retreating target?' As a final note, anyone who really believes that a fighter cannot get enough power with the back heel raised should spend more time sparring with a free-style champion or decent boxer.

A Fighter's Insight

Imagine that, in a real fight, the attacker moves in and you block and then counter punch—as you have practiced countless times.

You want to 'catch' the opponent moving in, don't block, wait, and then counter-attack; for a pause between the block and counter may allow the attacker to escape. Having no pause also helps to ensure that the attackers' momentum is used to your advantage, allowing the attacker to 'run into' your counter strike. Ideally the block and counter punch is almost simultaneous and coupled to the movement of your mass or center of gravity into the oncoming opponent.

As you strike the oncoming attacker you want him to be bowled over by the punch - not the reverse. If not using an evasive tactic then adopt a firm or rooted stance from which to deliver the energy into and through the attacker; using a stance that forms a solid foundation and will not buckle or break with the forces involved. *The back heel is down.*

If you side step or otherwise evade the line of the attack of the onrushing opponent then there are multiple options to choose from.

If, on the other hand, the attacker is static or defensively retreating away then you can effectively move forward and punch into and through the target, without worrying about contending with incoming momentum. *The heel can be raised.*

Test it – Footprints in the Sand

Here's a simple experiment for you, when next on the beach and bored. In bare feet walk for a while on sand damp enough to leave good footprints. Now examine these prints. Notice how they are fairly regular, with roughly about the same heel indentation as that of the ball of the foot and toes. Now jog for long enough to be in a relaxed stride. Take a look at the footprints again; the heel indentation and ball/toe depths are still about the same as each other although the overall depth of print is greater than that seen from walking. The enhanced heel depth of indentation is caused by landing on the heel and the ball/toe depth is caused by pushing off to the next step. Now sprint, as fast as you can. Look at the footprint from sprinting and notice that there is virtually no sign of heel indentations, it's all ball/toe, but the prints are deep—these are feet that are landing and pushing hard into the sand to enable each stride to be fast and strong. Conclusion: When moving forward fast the pushing action comes through the ball of the foot, not the heel. Could that be why 100 meter sprinters have starting blocks that match a raised heel, supporting more of the foot and giving more to push against? During a fight, when you move in fast to catch a static or retreating opponent the action is 'sprint-like', pushing from the floor with the ball of the foot – rather than the heel. This is the fighter's classic one-step sprint.

And while still at the beach and in investigative mode try doing a kata, form or set of basics (such as stepping punch), first forward and then moving backward, on fresh sand. Work out where the force is being applied to allow the body to move forward and backward at speed. Play with other basics and combinations, come to a few conclusions to take away with you… and then enjoy an ice-cream while thinking this over.

10.7   And the Other Extreme?

Having looked at a basic forward stance it is worth considering a position where the body is in an almost upright position: A typical, high, 'free-style' stance may be at about the mid way point in the range between standing upright and a classic forward stance. The following points should be noted, with respect to the raised stance position:

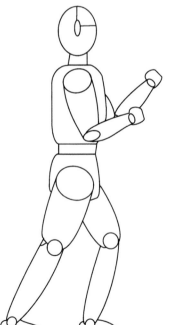

o   The hips have been raised and the height has increased.

o   Mobility has increased.

o   Stability has decreased; the center of gravity is higher.

This free-style stance is of a highly mobile nature, one that facilitates attack. Moving from an upright position to a lower forward stance drops the hips and helps to move the center of gravity into a punch. By moving the centre of gravity into the strike far more mass or body weight may be applied; thereby increasing the effect of the strike.

This stance also facilitates defense (perhaps by evasion to the side or moving into back stance). It is a stance from which you can easily kick or punch. Some schools and styles train and practice almost exclusively in this relatively high and relaxed stance, noting that it is natural and effective; boxer's naturally spar and fight in this manner. For me, there is a difference between fighting and training and there is more to training than 'just' learning to fight. Without digression into the philosophical reasons why we continue to pursue the martial way, there does appear to be health benefits to training in a

**Figure 10.12
Free Style**

wide range of stances. I believe that doing so is one of the reasons why I am still able to train seriously in my more mature years.

In traditional training we kick repetitively, introducing high stresses on the joints, particularly the knees and hips, which can cause chronic or acute medical problems. Training methods that build muscle to support these joints and help to prevent injury are of great benefit and repetitive use of reasonably low training stances will improve specific muscles around the knees and help protect the joints. Hence it is considered beneficial to learn and practice a wide range of techniques and associated body mechanics.

Facts for Fighters

High stances are fast and mobile. Fighting in a higher stance makes kicking easy.

Training in low stances helps to build protective and useful muscle mass.

10.8   The Center of Gravity of the Human Body

Not all humans are the same; in fact no two humans are the same. Hence there is no universal formula that provides an accurate pinpoint location of the center of gravity (C of G) of humans. As a starting point, there is a difference between the average C of G point for a woman compared to that of a man. A female normally has a larger pelvis than a male and this results in a slight comparative lowering of the center of gravity.

Secondly, the body type and form makes a significant difference to the center of gravity. Even if their weight and height were the same, a sumo wrestler would have a much lower C of G than that of a body-builder with his characteristically highly developed chest and shoulders. Similarly, children do not obey the same general proportionality rules as an adult. For example the developing head of a young child is, as a percentage of the size of the whole body, generally much larger than that of an adult. Nevertheless, on average, with a 'normal' body type, the center of gravity is typically located at about 55% of body height. This is typically just over an inch below the navel.

[I sometimes wonder how to classify an average body type. When in China I find myself surrounded by people that are of a healthy weight. In 2010 about 60% of the USA population was reported to be overweight, with around 25% obese. The US average has become an unhealthy standard. A fighter's 'normal' body form will be very different from that of the (western) general public.]

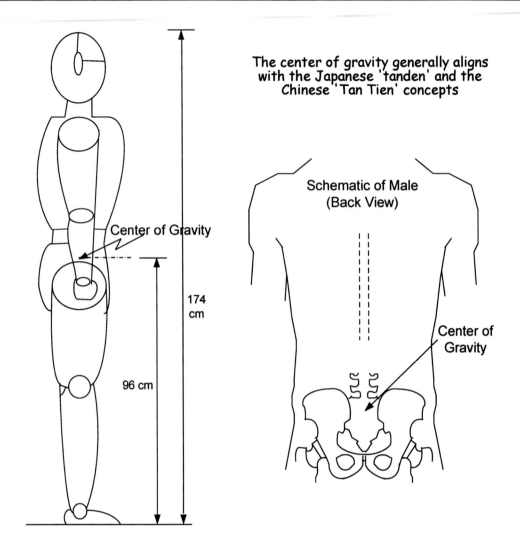

The center of gravity generally aligns with the Japanese 'tanden' and the Chinese 'Tan Tien' concepts

Schematic of Male
(Back View)

Center of Gravity

Center of Gravity

174 cm

96 cm

Fig. 10.13: The center of gravity is located at a level of of about 55% of the total height, just below the navel

Those that have been around the martial arts for a while will know of the significance of the center of gravity point that's being described. The Japanese refer to the center of the abdomen as the 'seika tanden' or 'tanden' within the 'hara'. A person of great hara, to the traditional Japanese, is a man of spirit and integrity. Within the martial arts there are references to the notion of a warrior psychologically residing within the tanden during times of conflict. Master Nishiyama spoke of this in his seminars, pointing to the marvels of the human body and system, such that we do not have to think about individual muscle movements and their control. Provided the body has been trained and the instincts have been developed, we can operate from the tanden, demand immediate and 'instinctive' response and the body will perform. As mentioned in section 9.3, a small, focused, movement at the center can instantly produce a larger movement at the physically connected extremes (for example the hips and then shoulders) with consequentially higher linear velocity.

Masters such as Nishiyama, Enoda or Kase would often relate the martial art being taught to the warrior spirit of bygone eras and by so doing explain why their particular art was so important to them. It is a matter of choice – to pursue one path rather than another - and there are always times when fighters ask themselves why they continue with the struggle. Why they are 'Seeking the Way'. This is not a subject for this book but some of the technical descriptions and equations do not fully take into account the 'inner material'. It isn't just a question of why and how fighters would repeatedly aim to move the core of the body to try and increase the efficiency and effectiveness of the outer limbs, and then how to measure the success of that training. It is also about belief in the chosen art, or instructor, and the spirit of a warrior. This isn't just an esoteric aspect, the commitment and attitude of an individual affects all they may do, including delivering a punch or kick.

10.9   Stance: Form and Function

Stances could be categorized and classified by looking at their form and function.

The *form* of a stance can be described by its physical attributes, such as:

- o   Length of stance
- o   Width of stance
- o   Center of gravity
- o   Distribution of weight

The *function* of a stance relates to the intention or purpose, including:

- o   Offense
- o   Defense
- o   Mobility
- o   Stability

Rather than try to work through all of the numerous stances and their derivatives, let us restrict our considerations to just two classic examples: the forward stance and the back stance.

(i) The Forward & Back Stance Footprints

If we add a forward stance plan view to the figure 10.4 reverse punch model it provides the 'footprint' sketch shown in figure 10.14. In this classic forward stance approximately sixty percent of the bodyweight is on the front leg, with forty percent supported through the back leg. The front foot points forward and is straight or turned inward slightly and the back-foot should generally be pointing towards the way you are going. Oftentimes a student martial artist cannot achieve this and the back foot is prone to point outward and away from the center line or line of attack.

Since the majority of the weight is on the front foot it should be no surprise that the center of gravity is forward of center, approximately following the body centerline. To gain insight, compare the footprints of forward stance and back stance, as shown in figure 10.15. A study of this comparison yields some reasonably clear observations:

Forward Stance

- The forward stance is wider than the back stance.

   o The forward stance is therefore more stable than the back stance and better able to resist a sideways force.

- The forward stance center of gravity is forward of the stance center line.

   o The forward stance therefore has more body weight on the front leg than on the back.
      ➤ This enhances forward mobility.
      ➤ This allows easy transfer of body mass into a punch or other attack.
      ➤ This allows easy kicking with the back leg.

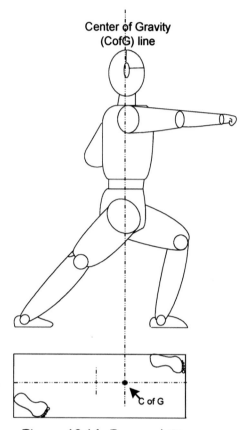

Figure 10.14: Forward Stance

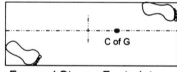

Forward Stance Footprint

Back Stance Footprint

Fig. 10.15: A comparison of forward & back stance footprints

Back Stance

- The back stance is narrow, causing a lack of stability across the heel to heel plane.

    o Consequently a fighter in back stance may be more prone to being swept, in that particular line.

- In back-stance the center of gravity of the body is behind the stance center-line.

    o The back stance has more body weight on the back leg than on the front—typically about 70% of the weight is to the back of the center line.

    ➤ This is a near perfect way of shifting into an evasive or defensive position.

    ➤ This enhances the ease of kicking with the front-leg.

10.10   Back Stance & Lines of Support

There are innumerable tests or demonstrations that can be done in the training hall with particular stances or techniques to illustrate their strengths and limitations. One such trial is to have a student adopt a back stance and see just how easy it is to push him backwards from a direct frontal line—pushing his forward hip usually does it. Look at the sketches shown in figure 10.16 and consider which stance would provide most resistance to such an action. Why would we be interested? One reason is it indicates how resilient the stance is to a reaction force from a punch performed on an incoming opponent. If the force is as shown in figure 10.16(c) and the student has a stance where the back leg is virtually under the body then the back leg cannot provide a strong line of resistance against this force. This indicates that the makeup of such a stance will not provide a strong base to deliver a counter strike, particularly against an incoming attacker. It can provide a good base to initiate such a strike but at the moment of impact the stance needs to be stronger. A good fighter can punch while stood on one leg and hurt an opponent but it would not be their ideal first choice.

The drawing of imaginary lines of support through the limbs of a stance helps indicate where the force(s) are derived via the connection paths to the floor, and figures 10.17 (a) and (b) shows that the shorter and more perpendicular stance offers far less resistance to the applied force. Try this test in the training hall. It is useful to experiment with stances and look for the strengths and weaknesses of each stance. The forward stance is able to withstand forces acting from the front to back. Push a person in forward stance from the front and see how difficult it is move their full body then push from the side and notice how the stance is so much weaker. This is even more pronounced with back stance or straddle (horse) stance where side forces cannot be resisted. However a rooted type of stance has a degree of strength in each of these four directions. Think of this as a good reason to adopt this kind of stance when fighting on wet or icy ground.

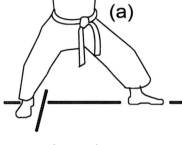

(a)

Figure 10.16 shows how shortening a back stance & placing the back leg virtually under the body will allow easier kicking from the the front foot. However, there is now less resistance in the stance to an incoming force, less stability from which to deliver a strong penetrative punch.

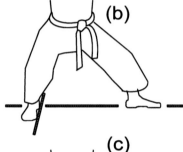

(b)

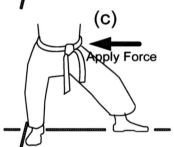

(c)

Apply Force

Figure 10.16: Shortening of a back stance.

Fighter's Insights

Forward stance is a good offensive stance from which to deliver a strong punch. Back stance is a good defensive stance from which to evade or absorb an attack and be posed to counter-attack; perhaps by converting to forward stance.
As fighters our options are not limited - we can step forward into back stance or step back into forward stance.

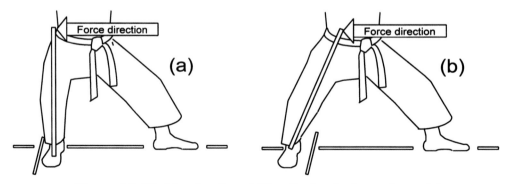

Figure 10.17: Varying the ability of a back stance to resist the reactive force from punching an opponent.

10.11 Balance and Stability

For an object to be balanced and stable its center of gravity (C of G) must lie over its supporting base. External forces and movement of the object can cause this equilibrium to be upset and affect the balance. If the external force is large enough then not only balance but also stability can be lost and the object can topple over. The stability of an object is determined by its ability to withstand displacement or external forces.

To gain insight into the point being made consider the examples of the two cone shaped pyramids shown in figure 10.18. Both pyramids are of the same height, but the diameter of their bases differs by a factor of two. The base of pyramid B is twice as wide as the base of pyramid A.

This means that pyramid B is more stable than pyramid A. It can withstand more external force without toppling over or having to shift its base position to maintain equilibrium. See the figure 10.18 illustration. Imagine a woman wearing clown shoes and think of how far forward she could lean without toppling over and then do the same mental exercise with the lady wearing stiletto heels. Lastly, remember that to make a pyramid more stable, without changing the size of the base, simply reduce the height. If you want to be more stable, whether upright grappling or walking across an icy path, drop your center of gravity by lowering your hips.

It was previously noted that if a plumb-line dropped from the center of mass of an object falls within its base area then that object will not topple over without an external force. With the conical pyramids, since they are symmetrical, we know that

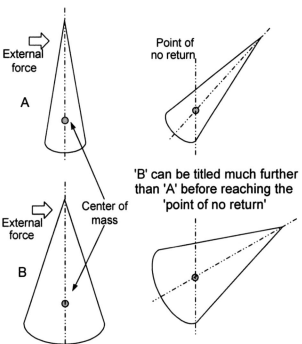

Fig. 10.18: The wider the base the greater the force needed to cause an unbalanced condition

The stability of an object is measured by the objects' ability to withstand displacement or external forces.
If you want to be more stable – when fighting or walking across an icy path – drop your center of gravity.

the center of mass lies on the initial (stable) center-line of the pyramid. We know intuitively that the wider the base the more the pyramid has to be tipped before it will fall over. The point at which an object will tip over is when the force applied has caused the object to lean or 'tip' such that a plumb-line dropped from the center of gravity shows that the C of G is at the point of moving outside the base area. This shows that pyramid B, with its wider base, can 'lean' further than pyramid A without falling over. Furthermore as you try and tip over the pyramids their center of gravity has to be raised. Work needs to done to raise this mass through that height. If on the other hand the pyramid was inverted and carefully balanced (upside down) on its tip then the slightest movement would allow gravity to pull the center of mass downward and the pyramid would fall. It is *inherently unstable* when inverted.

As children we may have seen how an object can return to its upright stable position after a punch or a push. Remember the wobbly toys that you could knock over and they always popped back up? They were weighted very low and the base surface was convex. Hence the center of mass was always within the base area and so even if you knocked them over they came back up. You can see the same kind of effect in the lower sketch of figure 10.19.

Section 10.9 pointed out that a bodybuilder with massive shoulders and slim waist would have a higher center of gravity than a pear-shaped sumo-wrestler with a larger proportion of his weight around and below the stomach. It should be apparent now which of these two is inherently more stable. Equally it is clear that to help with stability a fighter should 'lower his center': When throwing someone a typical action is for the attacking fighter to lower their hips to try and get 'under' the opponent. The relevance of all of this to the characteristics and effectiveness of a range of stances should be considered.

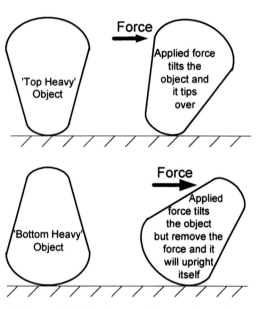

Figure 10.19: Lower the center of gravity to be more stable: More force is now need to reach the tipping point

Within the martial arts we deal with both static and dynamic stability. The static (motionless) mode may only exist for a fraction of a second, as a focused moment, but nevertheless it is static at the time. At that fractional moment the most important aspect may just be the stance adopted and the degree of contact that the feet have with the floor.

o Enhanced stability comes from a lowered center of gravity and/or a wider base

o Dynamic stability and balance work hand in hand—they are complementary

o Long and low stances are more stable but less mobile—there are trade-offs

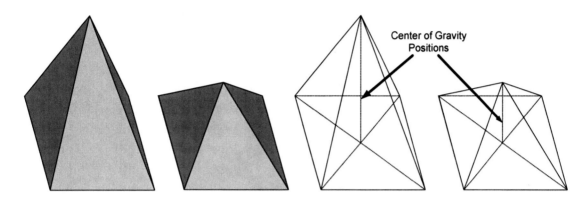

Figure 10.20: Lower the height of a pyramid and the center of gravity lowers.
It becomes harder to knock over.

Within reason, the wider and longer the stance the more stable the fighter. Pushed to the extremes however, a wider stance exposes vulnerable target areas and a stance that is too long or too low becomes virtually immobile. During close quarter combat you may deliberately choose to lower your stance, especially if you are at risk of being thrown or you wish to perform a throw. Being flexible and relaxed helps stability and balance; bent (soft) knees are recommended.

Good balance is crucial to a fighter. It can be the difference between being in control rather than being controlled and at the mercy of gravity or your opponent. We spend long hours training to maintain our core strength and develop the awareness that is needed for natural, instinctive, balance. In section 6.12 it was explained that for balance during and after the act of kicking our center of gravity line must drop through the foot of our supporting leg. Consider for a moment a typical training hall exercise: the controlled kick. This may be any kick at any speed and the challenge is to be balanced at *almost* all times. The classic side thrust kick is a good example and when performing such a kick, and pausing when the leg is fully extended, the only way to retain a balanced state is for the center of mass to be above the supporting foot. Because the fighter is holding the kick out the upper body will tend to lean back, to offset the weight of the extended leg (see figure 6.15). During the dynamic execution of a kick that's intent on hitting a target however the center of gravity will usually move towards the target. Against an opponent or target bag you would thrust your weight, your center, towards the target; such that if it were not for the object that is struck 'pushing back' then you would be off balance. Balance is not a temporary measure. We may switch from stable to mobile states but fundamentally we should stay balanced. This is a lesson for life, not just for the times that we train or fight.

> *Better learn balance Daniel-san, balance is key*
>
> *Balance good, karate good... everything good.*
>
> *From the (original) film: "The Karate Kid"*

Combat is dynamic: We cannot afford to stay static. The martial arts training is designed so that we perform or fight in an optimal manner; to be balanced, ready and capable of moving from one strike to the next, defense to attack, offense to evasion. A wide range of stances have been developed to help maintain stability in motion and the study and practice of these will provide you with more options so that at a time of need you will find the 'tool' that suits. Your instruction and training continuously puts new tools into the toolbox, and keeps the old ones sharp.

In the final analysis there is no substitute for instruction, training and practice. Books are written on such natural acts as running but after the reading is finished it becomes time to pull on the running shoes and get out and do it. Just do it. Only the miles will provide the stride, the rhythm, the balance, the breathing, the muscles, the aerobic capacity and the joy! You cannot learn the martial arts from a book, a lecture or through discussion—although each of these may be useful. Only the work in the training hall will provide the mind and body control needed to follow the way of a warrior. For how can you control an opponent if you cannot control yourself?

> *Knowing the theory helps but there is no substitute for practice.*

10.12 Stance, Sweeps and Throws

It is at the place of instruction, the training hall, where specific techniques should be taught, not in books in general and certainly not in this particular one. However, there are numerous technical aspects that have been addressed within these pages that can be of use when working out how best to sweep or throw an opponent - or help avoid being swept or thrown. The previous sections on the form and function of the individual stances and the discussion on stability can provide an insight into how to unbalance an opponent or respond should someone grab you with the intent of a throw. (As mentioned in section 1.11 *"If someone grabs you, hit 'em! Then do the fancy stuff."*)

(i)   *Unbalancing an Opponent*

Using figure 10.15 for illustration, consider the differences between a forward and back stance and their susceptibility to being swept or thrown. In the next three paragraphs the term 'sweep' refers to a technique where only the attacker's foot is being used against a defenders foot or leg, rather than using both the hands and feet to topple an opponent.

Attacking and sweeping a lead leg and foot that is in a strong forward stance is a relatively difficult proposition since the lead leg has to be moved a considerable distance before the center of gravity is outside the base of the stance. The attacker must use his own energy and momentum and sweep with his body not just the leg, in order to dislodge a weighted foot beyond the balance point. If the defender is rooted in a forward stance or similar and is determined to stay there, then the force that needs to be applied by the attacker to achieve a sweep can be of the same order as that needed to break the defender's lower leg.

Sweeping an opponent who is just about to step into a forward stance is a different proposition. With perfect timing, if you catch the opponent by sweeping the ankle of a foot that is about to land and bear weight then they will topple easily. In this instance, the opponent has already committed his weight and center of gravity and you are 'simply' redirecting that center to a position of imbalance. The difficulty is getting the timing right.

If the defender is static in a back stance then the front foot does not need to be moved as far and it is easier to take the foot beyond the line of the center of gravity. However, defenders in back stance have less weight on their front foot and may more easily evade the effect of a sweep by taking all the weight off that leg as the sweep is attempted; using this evasion as a tactical move towards a counter attack. If the attacker is total committed to such a sweep but the defender reads the move and lifts the front leg before the sweep hits this can totally unbalance the attacker. I have seen an attacker apply so much energy that missing the sweep caused him to almost fall as he turned and presented his back as an easy target.

Sweeping an opponent's lower limbs outside of his center of gravity, whilst pushing his upper body in the opposite direction, can cause an unrecoverable unbalance. A good example of this is where an attacker partially steps behind the opponent and then sweeps his opponent's legs at the same time as striking or pushing the opponent's upper body in the opposite direction. A throw that involves taking the opponent completely off the floor usually involves moving the opponents C of G outside his foundation or base area. A hip throw for example is executed by lowering your center, lifting or un-weighting the opponent and ensuring that the throw is aided by the opponent's weight acting to your advantage because their center is outside the base, making them unstable. Concepts such as these derive the classic fighter's aim—that of using an opponent's weight against him.

```
Facts for Fighters
All experienced Karateka know the 60:40, 30:70 and 50:50 weight distribution
rules for the Forward, Back and Straddle Stances.
```

(ii)   Un-weighting

When faced with a heavy opponent with a naturally low center of gravity who is basically fighting in a forward stance how can a foot sweep be accomplished? The answer may lie in insight and timing and not just in excellent technique. In an earlier Chapter (3), when discussing Newton's Third Law, a graphical plot (figure 3.5) was provided of the force experienced by the ground as a person performed a standing jump.

One point of particular interest is the fact that in preparation for the jump and just before pushing down and off the floor, the person bent their knees, lowered their body and thereby temporarily reduced the force experienced by the force plate. The display shows that this reduction was very significant, down to around one third of the force normally experienced due to body weight. Anyone that has skied on snow-covered slopes will understand how the forces beneath the skis can be momentarily reduced, to effect a turn by 'un-weighting', by momentarily bending the knees.

Similarly there are times during sparring when the weight applied or carried by a particular leg is considerably reduced. A sweep to that leg, at that exact moment, can be very effective. The simple example provided previously applies—where an attacker steps forward and you sweep their front foot and deflect it just before it hits the ground. The foot is not yet in contact with the floor and therefore easy to move causing the foot to be placed and then weighted completely outside the center of gravity balance line. This may sound easy but success in practice is another matter, demanding expert timing. A practiced fighter can also see when an opponent is constantly changing hip height (or 'bouncing') and thereby 'un-weighting' the stance; taking this into consideration can make sweeping easier. If the fight degrades to an upright grappling mode one option may be to momentarily grab the opponent, push up from the floor to un-weight him, and sweep both legs. A judo expert can do this to an unwary opponent in an instant.

Re-examine figure 3.5 to view the forces experienced as a body undertakes a standing jump. When an opponent has his weight *fully* on the floor, perhaps pushing that front foot into the ground, then he is in true contact and the floor is pushing back. The force into the floor and the force back from the floor create such a contact that a sweep is difficult. Alternatively, when a person is shifting weight the contact is weakened and the sweep is easier.

(iii)   Throws

The above sections on stability provide guidance on the laws of physics that apply when executing a throw. As always these laws don't care if the throw is labeled as Judo, Aikido or Wing Chun. To summarize:

- o   Stability is dependent upon the base area. A person stood on only one foot is easier to take to the ground that one on both feet. A person raised on their toes is easier to throw.

- o   To make something become unstable move its center of gravity line outside its base area. This is at the heart of sweeps and throws.

- o   The lower a persons' center of gravity the more stable that person is. To help prevent yourself from being thrown bend your knees and lower your stance.

- o   With two objects of the same size and shape but different weights the heavier object is more difficult to knock over. The more massive the person the harder it is to throw him.

Fighter's Insight

If someone grabs you from behind drop your weight and drop your chin.

Make it difficult for an attacker to throw you to the ground or choke you out.

10.13   Leverage

The greatest martial artists are never static or stagnant: in combat or in life. The best are always on the lookout for new ideas or different concepts, never afraid to explore, never complacent or narrow-minded. They do not fall into the trap of believing that another style or school has little to offer, knowing that some of the greatest fighters are boxers or from the style of Muay Thai. (Try telling these champions that you **must** be in a certain stance to deliver power and they may teach you a lesson in every sense of the word.)

This book is mainly devoted to strikes, not throws or locks. The physical principles of levers are used throughout the martial arts, including strikes, but the deeper discussions on leverage tend to be for techniques associated with throws and locks. Hence this section will be very superficial.

Basically, leverage allows a small force applied over a long distance to have an effect that is greater than that generated by a much larger force delivered over a shorter distance. This is a concept worthy of understanding.

These leverage principles can be derived from Newton's laws and are illustrated in figure 10.21. This shows how a 20 pound weight can be balanced with a 10 pound weight simply by adjusting the distance of the weights from the pivot point. This is a balancing-act that many parents and children have experienced on a see-saw. The diagram of a crowbar (or jimmy) shows mathematically how a very high force can be derived from a low force with leverage. This is how a classic lock or break is delivered. Bones can be fractured or joints dislocated with relatively little force if the lock is properly applied and the advantage of leverage creates a high enough force at the joint or limb.

A good examples of the application of leverage is the 'cross-arm lock'; a technique often used in one-on-one ground fighting. It can be executed in a number of ways, starting when you are astride an opponent that is on his back, or with an opponent that is being taken to the floor. The objective is to take hold of an arm (say his right arm) using both of your hands, roll or fall to his right side, throw the left leg across his neck and wedge the right foot under his right side, pushing his body up at an angle. His right elbow needs to face downward towards the floor for the arm to be

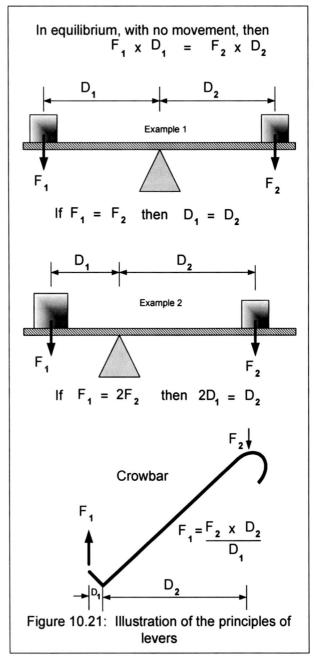

In equilibrium, with no movement, then
$$F_1 \times D_1 = F_2 \times D_2$$

D_1 D_2

Example 1

F_1 F_2

If $F_1 = F_2$ then $D_1 = D_2$

D_1 D_2

Example 2

F_1 F_2

If $F_1 = 2F_2$ then $2D_1 = D_2$

F_2

Crowbar

F_1

$$F_1 = \frac{F_2 \times D_2}{D_1}$$

D_1 D_2

Figure 10.21: Illustration of the principles of levers

properly pinned between your legs. Squeezing the knees together assists. A downward pull on the arm now creates significant force at the pivot point where the arm crosses your upper leg. In training the objective is to make your opponent 'tap-out'. Street fighters will tell you that usually a broken limb will stop an opponent from wanting to continue.

The start of the above paragraph refers to this technique being used in one-to-one combat. This is a reminder that when fighting for real think twice about going to the floor and if there do not stay too long - just in case your opponent has buddies that want to kick you in the head. In fact this particular arm lock technique can be applied as an immediate break, which can be accomplished as you take an opponent down and hit the floor (pushing your hips up to make sure).

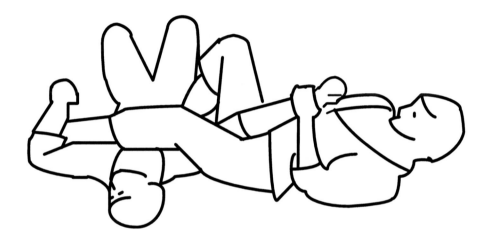

10.14   Summary

There are innumerable stances for a fighter to choose from. There is a stance or body position suited for any circumstances. In battle a warrior will not always be in an ideal stance or position but will fight on regardless. In battle a fighter will try to get the opponent(s) to a weakened position.

A solid 'forward' type of stance with a strong footing and connection to the earth is valuable when striking an incoming opponent. Martial artists often talk of how a stance has connectivity to the ground and train as though 'gripping' the floor. An onrushing opponent has an incoming momentum to contend with and facing him and striking him 'head-on' while in a weak stance probably won't allow an adequate transfer of power. Hence, even if the in-coming opponent is hit the strike may not stop him from 'running over' the defender. On the other hand, an opponent that is static and motionless has no such momentum while an opponent backing away can be considered to have negative momentum.

When striking an opponent that is static or moving away the stance adopted at the moment of impact does not need to have such a solid connection to the floor because there is no forward momentum of the target with which to contend. A solid base from which to launch the attack is more important than the connection to the ground at impact. Don't get confused with this distinction. If, at the striking point, the attack is moving into a *receding* target then there should be no argument that the back heel can be raised. In sparring and fighting there are great advantages in using techniques where the heel is raised. Recall that sprinters push forward from the floor through the ball, not the heel, of the foot.

The center of gravity (C of G) of a body is an important concept to understand. A typical human body will have a C of G point a little below and behind the navel. The lower the C of G of a body the more it is stable and more force is needed to upset it. Dropping an imaginary vertical line from the C of G of a body can indicate how much that body needs to be upset to topple to the ground. Move the C of G line outside the base area of a body (including your own) and, unless corrective forces are applied, the body will fall.

A sweep that catches an opponent when he is un-weighted requires very little force for it to be successful. An attempt to sweep an opponent who is 'rooted' in a strong stance will require significant force to be effective.

The principle of leverage is worth understanding for it demonstrates how a large localized force can be created by a much smaller one acting over a longer distance. It explains how joints can be dislocated, bones broken or opponents forced into submission.

CHAPTER 11: BARE-FIST FIGHTING VS. BOXING

'Do the kata correctly; the real fight is a different matter'
Master Funakoshi

11.1   Introduction

One of the questions often asked is along the lines of:

Is there a difference between a karate (or taekwondo) type of punch and that employed by a boxer?

First things first, boxers are amongst the finest martial artists of all time and the very best of boxers will be included as the best punchers there are in any fighting style. When the prize money at the top is measured in terms of millions of dollars then only the best will be found there. Still, the term 'best' here is simply to indicate those that win boxing matches; nothing more. Secondly, as phrased the question is actually flawed: Let's face it, when fighting, a fighter should be able to throw almost any kind of punch. There are no exclusive rights on an uppercut or hook punch and in a real situation outside the ring there is nothing to stop a boxer from using open hand techniques or grappling. It's just that each style tends to specialize in certain techniques and those practitioners will therefore tend to prefer and revert to the techniques they have practiced.

When under pressure, for example when perceived to be in life threatening circumstances, we all tend to revert to our instincts. The natural reactions or instincts of trained fighters are developed and honed through repetitive practice. At best, fear and adrenaline will help us fight better than we perform during training. At worst, through fear and panic we can freeze or only be capable of delivering a fraction of our potential.

11.2   Differentiators and Differences

With respect to the use of the hands, evidence shows that, in general, there is little to differentiate between the levels of punching ability that can be achieved by a practitioner of one fighting art compared with another, including boxing. It is known that the hand speeds of experienced boxers are in the same range as the hand speeds of experienced martial artists of an Asian style. Experimentation (Whiting et al 1988; Pieter and Pieter 1995; Stull and Barham 1988) has demonstrated that the speed of a reverse punch or 'right cross' type of strike delivered by an expert is in a range of around 10 meters per second (see section 1.7). There are always the exceptional athletes capable of breaking records and notching up higher speeds but in general experienced boxers and other martial artists tend to achieve similar hand speed. Further, with regards to force delivered, Chapter 1 shows how the punches of some of the better boxers and other kinds of martial artists have been measured and the force levels recorded for the best of each are similar.

Based on observations it is fairly simple to create a list of the basic differences between boxing and other martial arts and how this may affect punching techniques:

1. Boxers in the ring only punch, other martial artists may punch, kick, elbow, knee, sweep, throw, grapple, lock or choke.

2. Boxers wear gloves—in the ring at least, they wear fairly heavy, well-padded gloves that help prevent facial cuts to the face of an opponent.

3. Other martial artists tend to fight bare-fisted—in general any gloves or mitts used in sparring or competition are relatively lightweight, again to help prevent facial cuts to an opponent and to protect the hand of the wearer. Traditionally, such mitts allowed open hand techniques and the use of the fingers.

4. Boxers usually aim to knockout their opponent—or render them unable to continue fighting—and do so with punches only.

5. In other martial arts the knockout is only one of a larger number of tactics and these fighters are not restricted to punches only.

6. Fighters wearing gloves are less likely to break bones.

   • When forcefully striking a hard target, such as the head, with a hard object such as the knuckles, it is more likely that something will break compared to being hit with the same energy by a punch from a hand wearing a well padded glove.

   • Recall that high force per unit area (pressure) causes fracture; a bare knuckle strike has less area and therefore a higher pressure effect.

Of course, for much of the above we can find exceptions: there are innumerable instances of a boxing match being stopped because of the uncontrolled bleeding from a cut, boxers having their nose broken, or the jaw being fractured or dislocated. Yet typically, had the 'gloves come off' the injuries would have been worse. As a traditional karateka, for me controlled sparring without gloves is commonplace. Accidents happen and, like many, there have been times when I have been badly cut from a bare-knuckle strike where I knew that had the fighter been wearing gloves I would have avoided the stitches. This leads to the observation that traditional martial artists, when sparring, are usually punching with control—they are trying to 'score a point' not to knock someone's head off. Care has to be taken to avoid this becoming habitual to the extent that in a real conflict fighters are disadvantaged because they are not usually punching to truly penetrate the target. Time spent training with a punching-bag will help redress this.

11.3 The Effect of Wearing Heavy Gloves when Fighting

In terms of punching, a dominant difference between the formal and traditional side of karate or similar compared with boxing is clearly apparent and it is there to see whenever you watch a boxing match: *fighters in the boxing ring are wearing gloves.* These are not just light mitts; these are large gloves that are typically 10 ounce of weight in competition and sometimes more for sparring. These protect a fighter's fists and to a degree the opponent, because the padding means there is less chance of cuts or breaks. The high-ranking boxers are amongst the best (gloved) punchers in the world but training and fighting with the use of gloves makes a difference: bare-handed fighting is different from bouts where the competitors wear heavy, well-padded gloves (as opposed to the very lightweight mitts used to protect the hand). There are numerous consequences of wearing gloves that are relatively heavy and the extra weight is significant, for with the same speed they carry more momentum and energy than an empty hand. A 10 ounce glove may not sound very heavy but the weight of a hand of a 75 Kg (165lb) person is less than 0.5 kg or just under 17 ounces. So a 10 ounce glove is more than half of the weight of the hand it covers.

To achieve this momentum and get that much more energy in motion, takes a little more effort than it takes to achieve the same speed with bare hands. Repeatedly 'swinging' a gloved hand therefore takes more work and punching becomes more draining on the fighter. Technique will naturally adapt. To get the fist going (repeatedly), to overcome the increased inertia that comes with the use of a heavy glove, a boxer will learn to apply the body accordingly, making particular use of any available motion as a starting point. This means that the gloved fighter will typically be adept at starting with the legs, knees or hips to engage a rotational force to initiate the hand motion and then translate this to linear motion prior to the strike. The use of the word 'typically' is to recognize that there is a wide range of techniques available and the above is a generalization. Of course, other fighters are also trained to make use of the very same set of actions; the above is not meant as a differentiator.

There are other effects of wearing large gloves, such as the fact that they provide a larger available blocking area and that the padding will alter the striking characteristics of the punch, compared with a bare-fist fighter.

11.4   The Effect of Striking When Wearing Padded Gloves

If the first distinction is that gloves make the hands heavier, the second statement of the obvious is that they provide padding. When delivering a strike energy is not the only thing of importance, there are other variables that can dominate: such as how a strike will penetrate and how the consequential force is focused. The padding provided by a heavy glove disperses the impact over a larger area and reduces the peak force, compared to striking with just a knuckle or two. Pressure is directly proportional to the force applied and inversely proportional to the area over which the strike is delivered so the smaller the area the more intense the pressure, for the same force. This was explained and developed in Chapter 2, section 2.3.10, which shows that for higher pressure to be exerted the attacker must increase the force (hit harder) or decrease the area over which the force is experienced. The implications of this relationship should be obvious to the martial artist and is the basis of why karateka are encouraged to strike with only one or two knuckles when punching.

An experienced fighter is capable of delivering over 2000 Newtons or 450 pounds of force. Section 2.3.10 points out that if you were to strike and deliver this force with only one or two knuckles, each having an effective diameter of half an inch and therefore a total impact area of about 0.4 square inches, then the force per unit area is over 1100 pounds per square inch (psi). This is a pressure, or focus of force, that is sufficient to inflict serious damage on a vulnerable target. (Chapter 1 also points out that the very best (heavier) fighters can deliver far more than 2000 Newtons.) The effect of the padding of boxing gloves on the strike is to 'spread the load' and elongate the contact time of the strike. If the impacting area of the glove is given by an ellipse of one by two inches then the effective area is about 1.5 square inches and the two knuckle 'point' pressure of 1100 lbs/in^2 has dropped more than fourfold, to less than 300 psi. This is still a heavy strike but it is less likely to 'penetrate on impact', less likely to break a bone. The glove's padding will also elongate the contact time which will also reduces that peak force from the impact. This is detailed in sections 5.4 and 12.11. The usual knockout boxing blows tend to be the powerful cross or hook type of punches where the punch is carried through and beyond the opponent. This is mainly an inelastic type of collision where the strike hits the jaw with great energy and then forces the jaw to follow the line of the punch. Therefore the skull may be shaken and twisted with sufficient acceleration to cause a loss of consciousness.

Fighters have been fallen by short, sharp strikes, particularly where the point of the jaw has been found at just the right angle and strike trajectory. It is not uncommon for a strike to the jaw to cause almost instant disorientation, perhaps prompting a Boxing commentator to remark that; 'The legs have gone'.

11.5   The Boxer's Knockout (KO)

A boxing match is won by a knockout (where an opponent is unable to get up off the floor within ten seconds) or by a technical knockout (where the opponent is considered to be too injured to continue) or by a judgment/points difference at the end of a prescribed number of rounds.

To achieve a knockout and thereby end the match victoriously a boxer needs to strike the head of his opponent with enough energy and force to cause the skull to accelerate and move rapidly. Within the skull the brain (which weighs around 3 pounds or 1.4 kg) is not firmly fixed, hence if the head is jerked backwards rapidly then the brain inside may be struck first by the inner front surface of the skull and then as the head reaches the end of its travel it can also strike the opposite inner surface of the back of the skull. These acceleration and deceleration (or internal collision) actions on the brain may result in a loss of consciousness. A punch catching an opponent on the side point of the jaw can cause rotational effects as well as the lateral motions depicted earlier. In other words there are particular points and punching actions that make it more likely to knock someone out. Boxers develop punches that have a hooking or swinging action which will tend to cause the head to rotate when struck and again this can add to the likelihood of a knockout. In any event, the effect of the acceleration of the head, in a fight, can be thought of as causing a physical 'impulse' on the brain and thereby prompt 'switch-off' or unconsciousness.

In a boxing match the powerful (K.O.) type of blow is often set up by a combination that first provides a sharper more shock-like blow: for example, a jab off the front hand which is rarely a knockout but makes for a good starter so that the boxer can follow with a fast, hard, accurate and 'square' K.O. punch. 'Fast' we know about, it involves training, practice, mental attitude and relaxation during execution. Hitting 'hard' means using the body weight, not just the limb, pushing the body's centre of gravity towards the target at the moment of impact; as though the fighter is stepping down and through with his body weight. Also important is the concept of hitting 'through' your opponent, rather than striking the surface. Accurate and 'square' means that you hit the intended target with a strike trajectory that is perpendicular to the target surface, reducing the prospect of some of the force being deflected away. As noted previously, some strikes deliberately hit 'through' the head with a circular trajectory causing the head to partially swivel and thereby increase the probability of loss of consciousness. In 1993, the British Medical Association's report *'The Boxing Debate'* stated: *"A 'swinging hook' or a 'cross-counter' punch to the side of the jaw will produce a rotation of the head in a vertical plane passing down through the head and neck behind the ears. This movement is particularly damaging possibly because the neck muscles are at a mechanical disadvantage in preventing rotation in this plane"*.

Experienced fighters have a developed instinct for 'riding' a punch; hence more damage tends to be inflicted by an incoming blow that is not 'seen', perhaps because of a jab/cross type of combination. Alternatively, it may be that the opponent has been 'worn down' by previous blows and/or rounds of fighting. According to Unterharnscheidt (1975) one of the effects on a boxer made groggy by a series of blows is that there is a decrease in muscle tone or stiffness at and around the neck. This causes the head to be less well supported and can therefore move more easily, giving less resistance to the higher accelerations that cause a knockout. Scientific studies have been undertaken that relate directly to the differences experienced or caused by the wearing of gloves. With respect to the effect that punches have on the head, the work of Schwartz et al (1986) is valuable. A fundamental point within this report is that the peak acceleration experienced by the head, when punched, is significantly reduced by the use of 'heavy' boxing gloves.

In numerical terms, acceleration of the impacted head of around 90 to 100g can be experienced when the punches are delivered bare handed, with the lighter hand protectors or 6 ounce gloves. One "g" is an expression of the force experienced due to gravity. Typically on an amusement park 'thrill' ride a person experiences around 2g or slightly higher. A punching peak acceleration of 120g was recorded by Schwartz, which corresponds to the force that the head of a passenger in a low speed car accident may be subjected to if unrestrained and striking the dashboard. Sixteen-ounce boxing gloves reduced the peak accelerations to 50g or less. The 1993 British Medical Association study refers to accelerations of up to 520 meters per second per second, which is very close to this 50g figure. As a cautionary note however, understand that there is conflicting evidence over the efficacy of gloves to reduce 'knockout' blows. A three year survey of amateur boxing in Denmark (Schmidt-Olsen et al 1990), for example, showed that the voluntary use of boxing helmets and heavier gloves for boxers greater than 149 pounds in weight did not affect the frequency of matches being stopped because of knockouts or blows to the head. Also of interest to the martial artist is the finding by Schwartz et al that some lightweight hand protectors do not significantly alter the peak acceleration of the impacted head. Such protection is considered to be more for the wearer than the receiver of the strike, perhaps helping to overcome a person's tendency to hold back slightly, for fear of hand injury.

The classic type of hand pad used in traditional karate competition typically weighs only about 1.5 ounces, or about one tenth of the weight of a hand. Hence the effect on the energy or momentum of a fist wearing such a mitt is insignificant. The amount of padding offered by such a lightweight pad will help prevent cuts but little more; unless engaged in a full contact fight control has to be employed.

11.6   Punching Penetration and Contact Time

Imagine hitting a wooden board using a bare-fisted punch with *just* enough energy for the board to break when striking it with the first two knuckles. Now imagine putting on a large boxing glove and using exactly the same technique, same hand speed, same effective mass. Does the board break? No. In the gloved example the force is spread out more, the peak force is less, the pressure or force per unit area is reduced and the board does not deflect enough to cause breakage. Remember that in this imaginary experiment we are using *just* enough energy to cause breakage with the bare-knuckle strike. Return for a moment to section 5.5, which discussed the difference between rubber and steel bullets, and if this is still confusing think about being able to 'punch a hole' though something and imagine how much harder that is when wearing a boxing glove. Finally note that a blunt axe will not split a log. For the mathematician, Chapter 7 provides the equations associated with collisions and points to the effects of the hardness or softness of the objects on the deformation energy. Consideration of this equation will provide insight into why the 'new softness' of the gloved hand will make the breakage more difficult. All of this, coupled with consideration of area of a glove compared with bare knuckles and the differences in contact times, should provide food for thought.

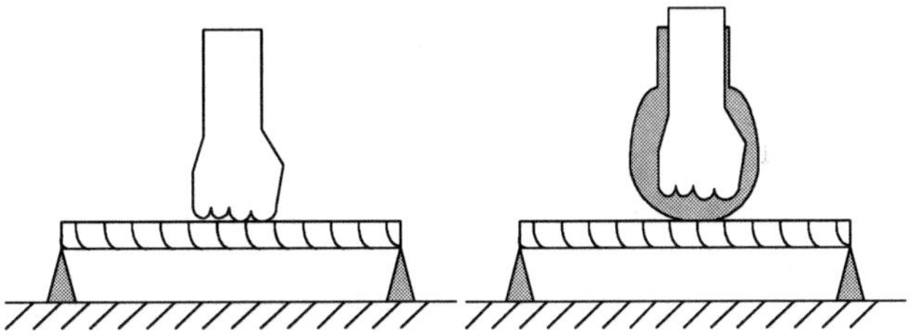

Linking the ideas in this Chapter to section 7.8, imagine trying to break a board that is free standing or hanging from the ceiling by a length of string rather than being supported against two fixed points. It therefore needs to be struck and broken by speed and impulse since a lengthy thrusting action is not possible because the board would simply be pushed away.

Figure 11.1: A bare knuckle strike uses a hard contact on a small area, A padded gloved hand is cushioned and hits a larger surface area, This reduces the peak force and increases the contact time

Breaking a freestanding board whilst wearing large padded gloves is virtually impossible since the padding allows the board to be knocked away before the full force (high energy) is applied. You have lost the effective ability to strike and penetrate in a very fast and sharp manner, with a contact time measured in milliseconds. It is importance to understand this difference between hitting with and without padding, for this is not simply related to the subtleties between one martial art and another; the same effects are seen in bare fist strikes to the body compared with those to the head.

Now move back to hitting an opponent, rather than a wooden board. An empty hand strike may not have a knockout as its primary objective; it may not even be targeted at the head.

The bare knuckle strike may be an ultra fast impulse action. It can be a 'fast in, maximum-focus, short-duration;' impact type of strike. The dominant objective can be to 'penetrate' rather than 'bowl-over': To penetrate and allow the residual kinetic energy to be absorbed by the opponent, causing damage. As discussed in chapter 5 a bone on bone strike is the collision of two hard objects and the contract time is therefore going to be short, shorter than hitting the stomach and shorter than striking the face with a well padded glove. The bone on bone peak force is going to be high and the force impact curve, described in section 5.2, will be narrow and peaky rather than flat or compressed. The contact time will be in the range of only tens of milliseconds; the energy is delivered with a high peak force over a short duration rather than a lower force level over a longer duration.

This means that certain bare-knuckle strikes can be focused, short-duration, limited-penetration strikes, rather than long looping punches with total follow through. Put crudely, against an evil attacker rather than in a sporting event, the objective may be to break the jaw or strike the throat rather than swivel the head via an elongated fist to jaw contact. The same observations can be made when considering strikes to the body except this can become a little fuzzy, since the body is generally a softer target and more contact duration time and penetration is needed, with or without gloves. Just to bring all matters back into context, this chapter started off by stating that no school or style had a monopoly on any particular type of punch. This Chapter has basically been distinguishing between bare knuckle and padded glove punches with different motives or differing circumstances. Chapter 1 points to the results from elite boxers and other expert fighters punching to deliver forces measured at around 4000 Newtons or more. That's almost as forceful as it gets.

In summary

When struck by a hard punch the effect of acceleration of the head can be to cause the brain to move or 'jerk' within the skull; to 'impulse' and stress the brain and thereby prompt unconsciousness. In the boxing ring this is an objective and to achieve this, whilst wearing large padded gloves, the boxer will follow through and maximize momentum transfer just as a tennis player or golfer would. The act of wearing heavy padded gloves will tend to change the mechanics of techniques employed thus giving a distinct difference in the boxers' punches compared with some of the classical karate or bare-knuckle strike mechanics that concentrate on high-energy focused and targeted penetration with the short contact time typical of a bone on bone strike. An energetic bare-fist strike to the head, depending on where it hits, may be more likely to cause bone breakage or bleeding than a gloved-fist strike which, with the same energy level, could be more likely to cause a knockout (depending on where it hits).

A Fighter's Insight

Imagine trying to break a free standing or unsupported board while wearing large padded gloves: the board would just swings away as the soft glove edge leads the impact, preventing penetration and breakage.

The use of heavy gloves alters the characteristics of the strike, altering the impact force experiences by the target.

The padding from the gloves and the desire to knock out an opponent can make a boxer's technique, intention and focus slightly different compared with that of bare knuckle strike.

11.7   Training Considerations

Regardless of background or style when fighters repeatedly go to work on a heavy bag they tend to converge towards some similar punching techniques. A beginner could be forgiven for observing that such techniques applied to bag work are more akin to western boxing than the form that is seen, say, in traditional Asian forms or kata. Notice, for example, that in upper-body bag work the arms do not completely straighten, even with long range punches. This is because for maximum effect with (say) a jab or cross the bag is usually hit when the arm is at about 70 to 80% of its full length. This is around the point of maximum hand speed. Chapter 8 expands on this point and uses it to explain why karateka are taught to aim and punch through the target and basic punches are deliberately taken to full arm extension and maximum focus. Of course one difference between the heavy bag work of boxers compared to others is the use of elbows and open hand techniques often deployed by Asian style fighters.

Karate and taekwondo basics and kata give you form and focus, speed and power, balance and footwork, a range of blocks, strikes and combinations. Kata is an art-form of both function and beauty. Sparring allows the development of fighting skills in a controlled and reasonably safe environment. Bag work gives direct feedback from actually hitting an object; feedback that the mind and body assimilate to improve ability and make a more effective fighter. These are complimentary practices; there is nothing here that is contradictory.

11.8   A Final Thought on the Subject?

There is more than just the distinction between gloved and openhanded punches to consider. Even a casual look at the posed stances of the old time 'bare-knuckled' fighters such as "Gentleman Jim" James J. Corbett or John Sullivan shows that before the Marquis of Queensbury rules forced the wearing of gloves, bare-fisted fighters extended their guard a greater distance from the body than do present day boxers. The introduction of gloves provided extra defensive protection that was previously not available and this complimented the earlier introduction of rules to boxing that outlawed previous hard-line practices. This changed the face and style of pugilism or boxing. The advent of widespread mixed martial arts has affected the world of the martial arts again. Evolution doesn't end.

This is of particular importance to a student of the martial arts. Prior to the mid 1800's bare-knuckle 'boxing' was effectively no-holds barred: head-butting, grappling, low blows and gouging were expected. Hence the fighters adopted a stance and guard position designed to stop the opponent from closing in and using the street fighting close quarters combat skills that are so damaging. Let this be a warning for anyone caught in a street of real and dangerous circumstances: That the direct unmodified application of the techniques of a fighting art that has evolved with rules and protective equipment may be a risky strategy, just as the attempted application of flashy, superficial techniques can be risky. This caution applies to all martial arts and artists. If you only train for fighting with protection and rules then, when the 'gloves come off' and the rules no longer apply, you can find yourself in a different world. That caution apart, boxing is unquestionably one of the best ways of becoming proficient in self-defense, it's just that on the street kicks to the groin are 'allowed' and weapons are to be expected. Finally, note that even heavyweight champions of the world have fractured the bones of their hand when engaged in a fight outside of the ring; conscious of this many fighters will employ open hand techniques to help reduce this risk.

Boxing is an exceptional martial art. Some of the greatest unarmed fighters have been developed through the instruction and practice of boxing. It is one of the best forms of self-defense but it can be improved and rounded by an appreciation of fighting without rules and the basics associated with the use of, and defense against, kicks, sweeps, throws or grappling. One of the greatest British Shotokan fighters (and kata expert) became renowned for his knockouts with kicks while serving the doors of Liverpool venues; a record that helped Black Belt magazine, in April of 2006, to rate Terry O'Neill as the best street fighter in the martial arts world. For the rest of us that could only aspire to be as talented (and have absolutely no desire to be as experienced) remember that in a street situation the hands can be either open or closed and that kicks are usually best kept low.

11.9   Summary

On average, the hand speed of an experienced boxer will not be significantly different from the hand speed of a similarly experienced fighter, of the same body type, health and condition, but from another martial art. The speed of a good reverse punch or cross will be around 10 meters per second for each expert set of fighters, although there are always exceptional athletes that can break records. Boxers can deliver punches that are as forceful as those from any other martial art and more forceful than many.

Fighting whilst wearing large padded gloves, weighing 10 ounces or more, is different from battling in a bare-knuckled manner. Hands in large gloves have more weight and when in motion therefore have more momentum than an ungloved fist at the same speed, but to achieve this same speed demands more effort from the fighter, causing more exertion.

Large padded gloves prevent small area strikes (such as a single knuckle punch) and they spread the impact load over a wider area, reducing the peak force and the penetration that would otherwise be achieved.

Lightweight mitts or hand pads make far less difference. Such a mitt, weighing from 1.5 to 3 ounces, is only a fractional increase in the weight of the punching hand, whereas a 10 ounce glove also increases the contact duration, flattening the impact force / time profile and reducing the peak force administered.

A lightweight mitt can help prevent cuts when the face is struck but a full contact strike can still cause extreme peak accelerations to the head, resulting in loss of consciousness. Lightweight gloves or mitts can make an undisciplined attacker even more dangerous, for he can lose any concerns over protecting his hands and may feel somehow 'licensed' to exhibit reduced control.

To win fights boxers want to knockout their opponents. A knockout or temporary loss of consciousness occurs when the head is impacted with enough force to cause the brain to be accelerated and stressed to such a degree that the brain effectively switches itself off. There are techniques and target points that are more likely to produce a knockout effect than others— with or without gloves.

Boxing is one of the best forms of self-defense but it can be supplemented by an appreciation of the basics associated with the use of, and defense against, kicks, sweeps, throws or grappling.

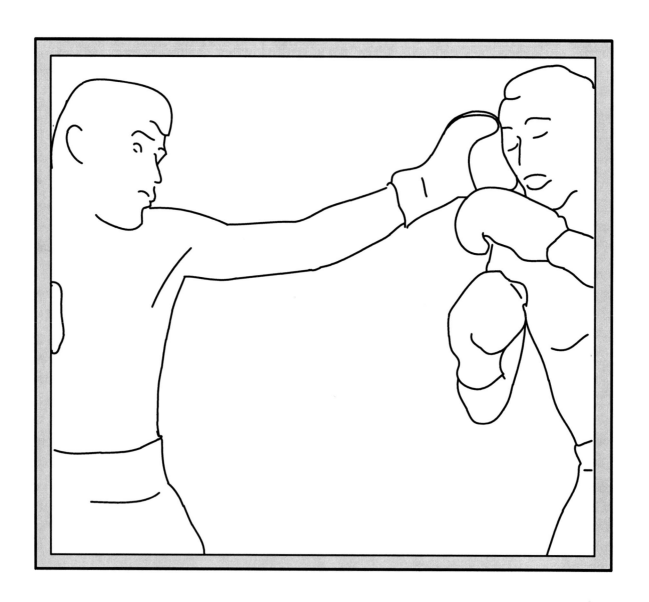

Boxers are amongst the finest fighters of our time

CHAPTER 12: THE APPLICATION OF THE SCIENCE

> *'Always be good at the application of everything you have learned'*
> *Master Funakoshi*

12.1 Introduction

There are fighters that from the very start could usually rely on their natural speed, brute strength and instincts for survival. Even without formal training these people can become formidable opponents, especially after experience gained on the streets. There are other martial artists with only average physical attributes, less natural speed, coordination or strength and maybe less courage, but through a few thousand hours of diligent training and practice they become virtually untouchable. Then there are the fighters who discovered their abundant natural talents at an early age, were fortunate enough to find the right school and instructor, and had the persistence to develop and hone their skills and enhance their experience through high level competition. Such fighters become virtually unbeatable. This book is to help all those that want to learn, those that accept that nothing of worth is gained freely and understand that learning takes time and dedication. This Chapter is to help consolidate and apply many of the principles explained previously.

12.2 Stance, Posture and Balance

Instructors of the martial arts often discuss the importance of the structure of particular stances when applying a technique. This range of available stances has evolved through human survival and the development of the martial arts; an evolution involving the survival of the fittest. Personal study of these stances and their application and limitations is useful but there is always a need for expert tuition. The traditional masters of karate or taekwondo will talk about how a stance is engaged and active; how it is built up from the floor, starting with the connection to the earth; how the various muscles are contracted to create tension through the limbs; how the stomach and breath play a part; how, in short, to make a true stance, not just a cosmetic posture.

This can be a difficult concept to understand but as an illustrative example if you think of how a bridge works it may help. A simple bridge, as shown in figure 12.1,

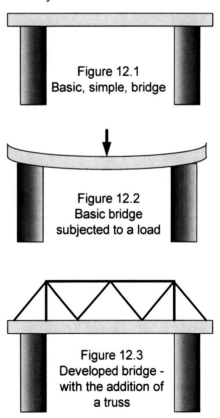

Figure 12.1
Basic, simple, bridge

Figure 12.2
Basic bridge
subjected to a load

Figure 12.3
Developed bridge -
with the addition of
a truss

may be made up of horizontal beams of wood supported by two vertical pillars or stanchions. This kind of structure is basically limited to the load that the center section can support. A force applied to the center point will cause the kind of distortion shown on figure 12.2, where the top surface of the center section of the beam is in compression and the bottom is in tension. With early wooden bridges this tension or stretching caused failure, as the wood started to tear and fracture.

The desire to support heavier loads, with minimal expensive high strength materials, led to a range of inventions and designs. One of the earliest developments was the 'truss'. Such a design is shown in figure 12.3 and it is easy to see how the suspension bridge design was developed. The members of the truss allow forces to be spread throughout the structure—as opposed to being concentrated around just one point and thereby causing high point stresses and failure.

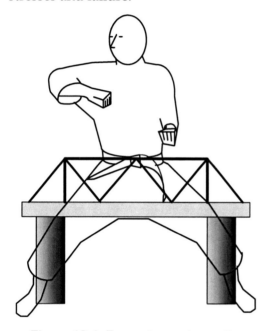

Figure 12.4: For a strong stance the right muscles need to be engaged

When the members of the truss do their job effectively they are in tension or compression. If any member is not subject to stress or strain then it is currently redundant and the other members must carry the load, leading to potential imbalance and points of weaknesses. As a load, such as a heavy truck, moves across the bridge the weight being supported by the pillars and the points of stress on the truss will change. The design of the bridge allows this transition of forces and therefore the truck can cross. Try considering this concept the next time you engage a stance. Think of where the strength of the stance is, which muscles are in tension, and how the body is strongly connected to the floor. Consider what happens as a force from an elbow strike is delivered to a target. See figure 12.4 for a visual image.

12.3   The Force from the Earth

Chapter 3 provided an overview of Newton's Laws and with reference to his third law, *"For every action there is an equal and opposite reaction"*, described how our ability to walk, run or jump comes from the earth. We push against the ground and the ground pushes back; propelling us forward or allowing us to resist a force that wants to move us backward. Every animal knows these laws naturally and instinctively. Through natural selection, evolution has provided mammals with a brain, incredible reactions, massive strength in the appropriate muscles plus organs, ligaments, tendons and a skeleton to suit. All of this allows us to quickly push against the earth so that the earth may push back; to let a tiger leap onto its prey, or give agility and speed to an antelope so that it may avoid the predator. Animals have evolved to live and not be killed. Their physiology has developed with that main purpose. Watch an agile cat, wild or domestic, to see this living poetry in motion. Recall this insight when next engaged in the study and practice of the stances and their natural applications.

"When two tigers fight one is certain to be maimed and one to die." G. Funakoshi

Continuously ask what am I trying to achieve? Where does the force to achieve this aim come from? How can I become more effective? Relearn what we once knew as a 'pure animal'.

12.4   Momentum and Movement

Chapter 2 described momentum as the product of speed and mass. Once an attacking movement has started a fighter generally wants to ensure that speed and mass is delivered into the opponent. Using a simple stepping punch as an example the idea of striking at the same instance as the step lands is to ensure that the momentum of the movement is carried into the opponent rather than squandered. If we land, become static, and then punch we have lost a significant proportion of our forward momentum to the floor beneath the landing foot. We want the moving body weight to be delivered into the strike, not lost somewhere on route. After a reasonable training period this point is appreciated and fighters become adapt at the simultaneous 'land and hit' action.

Figure 12.5:
Side thrust kick

The same principles apply to the action of kicking and it is equally important not to waste momentum. Consider for example a left foot side thrust kick where in the beginning we are taught, from side (or straddle) stance, to:

o   Step through, bringing the back (right) leg past the forward leg
o   Raise the (left) kicking knee and leg
o   Thrust out the kicking leg, twisting on the supporting foot
o   Retract that kicking leg
o   Step down with this (left) leg.

It is not necessary to provide an illustration or explanation of each of the above five stages, this was detailed by your instructor in the lessons from the early days. Suffice to say that the beginner could be forgiven for thinking that this kick is composed of at least three distinct parts: step in, kick, and step down. For the first year or so students of the martial arts tend to concentrate on the mechanics of each movement.

With practice and experience fighters translate these basic movements into a fluid, fully effective, combat strike. There are subtle differences in the way we are mechanically taught technique and the way that technique is actually applied as effective practice. All good instructors will reveal these subtleties when the student is ready to receive the lesson.

For maximum effect you want as much momentum as is practical being delivered into the target. This means that instead of the above five stages being utilized 'one after another' in a serial manner they are undertaken in a continuous overlapping manner. Such an action does not lend itself to the literal description of a methodical break down of movements— for how do you break down the action of a wave crashing on the shore? With practice and understanding, the above stages become something more akin to:

- Step the back leg up to and past the forward leg and at the instant this foot reaches the floor (and without loss of momentum) raise the kicking knee and leg.

- As you are completing the step through action, thrust out the kicking leg and strike.

- After striking and penetrating the target, retract that leg and step down.

Although more dynamically accurate than the five stage description provided previously, this method statement is still a little imprecise and insufficient. Most mechanical descriptions fail to convey the 'feeling' of the move, since a step-by-step instruction cannot convey the continuous nature of the technique. Only practice can do that.

The point should however become clear: Rather than step through and then kick, essentially you kick as you step through. In the former case momentum gained from the initial step is lost to the floor and not delivered into the target. The latter method can even be developed into a skipping type of action, rather than a slower stepping action, and from there to a fully committed flying kick. Also note that the flying side-kick can be done with the kicking leg retracted whilst in flight, ready to be thrust into the target. When synchronized this adds the energy of the thrusting leg to the force from the momentum of the whole body in flight.

Naturally there are potential drawbacks or risks to these types of dynamic actions. If a fighter should jump or skip forward while athletically engaging in this kick he has less opportunity to revise his actions. The fighter has committed himself – more so than if he simply delivered a stepping kick. Approach your training and the techniques being taught with an eye on momentum. Consider how to get started quickly with minimal effort and maximum effect, and how to retain the momentum throughout the technique and put it into the target. In so doing you will see the 'why' in the classical techniques being taught. This allows the continued development of a fighter that tries to make use of any momentum gained. As an illustration the previous example basically said don't step, stop, and then kick but step and kick as one motion. Building on this, when using combinations don't just kick and then punch— allow the momentum from the kick to be added to the punch.

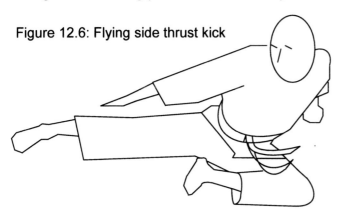

Figure 12.6: Flying side thrust kick

Once the principle of carrying momentum through each part of a technique is understood consideration is given to combinations of techniques. With the classic 'block and counter' combination allow the block to lead the counter attack as a continuous movement without loss of momentum. Ultimately there is a removal of the premise of the block and the counter being two moves, two separate techniques. There is simply the 'one strike' attitude and commitment to finish the conflict instantly.

This concept is not limited to a block and strike; it can apply to one strike being followed by another. As a combination a kick or punch can be followed by a punch or kick with the dynamic coordination of movement, breath and focus, plus the momentum gained from the first strike and the reaction from hitting the opponent to feed into the next technique. Look deeply at the application of forms or kata to see how interaction with an opponent can feed the next technique.

> **Advice from a Master**
>
> As a block is executed there is a certain power available from that technique. The delivery of a block, when done right, gains a certain power or momentum. Stoppage at that point causes loss of that available power. Do not stop—let the block lead the counter attack. This is continuation; apply it to your Kata.
>
> Personal notes from a Seminar by Master Nishiyama. Windsor, England, April 2001

[More strategically – momentum is not just about single techniques or combinations it also relates to the complete battle; just as a chess master will builds on each move and exploit each tiny tactical advantage with a relentless drive that brings victory.]

12.5   Speed and Relaxation

The concept of kinetic energy shows the importance of the speed of a technique and allows the reader to understand how speed can be a dominant factor; that if given a choice between the mass behind the strike or its speed then usually it is better to choose speed. This is important when the need arises to 'penetrate' or break a bony structure. Section 7 explains how striking mass and speed are related and need to be optimized

But where does the mastery of the art lie? One strives for perfect technique, but this is not simply about the mechanics of the movement. Physiologically, speed is achieved through excellent technique and *relaxed* initial movement. To achieve an explosive start the muscles need to be relaxed, because tension will reduce acceleration and cause slower movement. Muscle is either contracted in tension or it is relaxed (a state sometimes referred to as expansion). There are degrees of tension of course, and you can see and feel this simply by flexing and tensing a set of muscles. For example try hardening the abdominals; now increase the tension, you can feel the varying degree of tension. You may even note a relationship between the breath and the level of tension.

For any movement other than that only due to gravity, we need muscles to provide a driving force, which means that the correct muscles have to contract, or tense, to push away or pull towards. The muscles have to go from a relaxed state to a tensed condition in the right order - and at times we want that to happen as fast as possible. If some opponent is rushing in with a punch to your face you want the block and evasion to be on time, not late. So you want to start with the right muscles relaxed, for premature tension of muscle is not helpful. So relax when fighting. Note the comment that the muscles need to work in the correct order – this mental triggering of such a complex kinetic linkage is the discerning hallmark of an athlete.

Just relax! That's easy to say, but difficult to achieve in practice. Faced with an opponent that is trying to do you harm the tendency is to revert to a tense state, the exact opposite to that recommended for flight or fight. Ask yourself, is this a 'natural' tendency or have we become conditioned to behave this way? To try and answer this, look at the way that animals typically respond to a threat. When the moment comes will you be the relaxed and ready-to-strike tiger or the deer in the headlights?

Typically, after we have passed the beginner's stage of blocking in a forceful (tense) fashion we become adept at deflecting in a relaxed and sharp manner and learn to counter punch with tension applied *only* at the point of impact. It is frequently seen that practitioners *start* such a punch with tension, almost as a psychological wind up action. This is counterproductive. Such an action, or tendency, will slow the movement down and waste energy. At the moment of impact there may be a desire for a solid stance and increased body mass transfer into the target, prior to that point allow the movement to flow freely from a relaxed state and thereby increase the speed and efficiency of the striking action.

> **Relax in the face of adversity.**
> **In the face of adversity—relax!**

This is one the most important lessons that Karate has ever taught me: *to be naturally relaxed in stressful circumstances*. Like most others that have served their time and paid their dues, there have been innumerable occasions when I have been on unfamiliar territory facing an unknown opponent under pressure. None of these occasions would have been helped by becoming tense and some of my fonder recollections are when I have felt the pressure and noticed my alert but relaxed state; a calmness that has helped me cope with the circumstances and pressure. [This isn't meant to suggest that I didn't get hit; it's just a comment that being able to relax meant I got hit less often and probably less hard.]

Watch an animal defend or attack. Take a look at your pet cat or dog; when facing a threat they may initially make themselves look fierce or big. A domestic cat will hiss and arch its back with the fur standing on end to help it appear larger, more dangerous and intimidating —and this requires a degree of tension. However, watch that same animal switch into its fight or flight mode. It is impossible to see the transition. One moment the cat is standing looking fierce and then in what appears to be the same moment it has slashed a paw across the eyes of its opponent, or is now wrapped around the nose and eyes of the 'enemy' dog, or it's already a hundred meters away! If humans could respond in such an instantaneous or preternatural manner they would probably be termed superhuman or likened to cinematic vampires. (I have trained with or been taught by a few that come close to this likeness. My daughter used exactly this description when she recalled with awe the senpai at a Master Kanazawa seminar who moved 'like a vampire', she said, "He was so fast and fluid that you could see the beginning and then suddenly the end of the technique but not the movement in-between!")

12.6 Mass, Synchronization and a Problem with 'Focus'

Background:

Being raised in traditional, JKA style Shotokan, I was taught how to focus and "tense" during the delivery of a basic punch. In the old-school Shotokan karate style taught under the leadership of Master Enoeda this would be stressed at many lessons and developed in a strict manner. The term sometimes used by instructors was 'kime', a Japanese word often translated as 'focus' or focused energy. It is now less frequent to see this 'hardening' or high-tension practice, but the old-school idea is simple enough and the training method can be illustrated as follows:

Tension:

As a slow and then medium-speed standing or reverse punch was executed, the student was taught to pull the shoulder of the punching arm down by contracting the back muscles, in particular the *latissimus dorsi* of the punching side. Next, the importance of engaging the stomach muscles would be emphasized, then the buttocks, legs and the connection to the floor. The contracting abdomen and back muscles were deemed crucial in connecting the upper body to the hips and from there through the legs to the floor. All this work on the contraction of the appropriate muscles was aimed at helping the student to understand the mechanics of a basic punch and how to momentarily form a solid mass that can be driven into the target or resist an incoming opponent. The idea may be simple, but the practice is not.

Only Shotokan?

It has been indicated that Shotokan is the only karate style that formally trains students in being able to contract all their muscles for the split second moment at 'the end of the technique'. Shotokan Karate Magazine issue 78 records Master Kanazawa as stating that this practice of momentary tension was introduced to Shotokan by Master Nakayama. This may not have been an original idea however and there are indications that other martial artists of differing styles have developed their skills to a point where they chose how their breathing, movement, muscle tension and focus is harmonized. The benefits of training to punch with the aim of muscle contraction for the split second of strike completion are numerous, including the harmonizing of breath and focus, movement and muscles. Practice in this manner can help a fighter understand that the punch is not just delivered by the hand and arm. One disadvantage is that many students can become confused and start to tense *too early* and may retain the tension too long. It takes years for this required tension, this muscular set of contractions, this focus, to be applied as a synchronized 'twitch'.

Impact or completion?

Chapter 9 points out that, with a punch, a target should be struck several inches before the end of the reach of the punching hand. If the fighter's arm is about 2 foot (0.61m) in length from shoulder to fist edge then hit the target after about 75% or 1 foot 6 inches (0.46m) of travel; leaving about 6 inches (0.15m) of potential penetration to the point of completion of the technique. The reference book; Dynamic Karate, by Master Nakayama when describing the reverse punch, states that: *"If the body is not tensed at the moment of impact the consequential reaction will reduce the impact power."* The next section discusses this as a counter punch to an onrushing attacker, pointing to the need for a solid strike to counteract the attacker's momentum. When considering circumstances other than hitting an onrushing attacker in a direct (rather than evasive) manner it is difficult to understand why so much of the body should be in tension at the moment of impact.

When attacking a stationary or retreating body striking at maximum velocity is recommended. To be 'tense' *at* that striking instant will mean that the fighter would have to start contracting muscles a moment before impact. This will tend to reduce the speed of the technique and could inhibit 'follow-through'. Golfers do not try and 'tense' when they hit the driver club *through* the ball. For a home run a baseball batter wants to hit *through* the stroke; he is fast and forceful, driving with hips and legs, without contracting or tensing unnecessary muscles. Here in this book there is a clear distinction between 'impact' and 'the completion of a technique'. This is not an accidental distinction, but unfortunately the difference between the end of a technique and the point of impact is all too often overlooked.

The principle of forming a solid mass when delivering a punch may at first sight appear to match the science discussed previously—of wanting to impart significant mass into the strike, rather than punch with just the hand and arm - however the question that would then have to be asked is "how much of the new muscle mass that's now being tensed is actually moving into the target?"

In-rushing, static or retreating opponent?

Hitting with maximum effective mass going into the target is recommended. If the aim of the tensing action is to increase the mass behind the strike then we need to examine how much mass is actually going into the strike. If the target is stationary or receding away from the punch then for mass to be effective and delivered then it has to be moving forward towards and into the target, through the punching fist. I have found no comparative analysis of measured force from fighters that can deliver with and without the tensioning action described. However, after working with a heavy bag I would urge those that were trained that way to test it for themselves, because there does appear to be the prospect of confusion that could cause a loss of power. My personal (mini) tests tended to confirm fears that trying to be tense *at* impact can slow the punch down or reduce penetration and follow through. Either of these consequences can reduce the impact force felt by the target.

Again, note the differences between hitting a static or retreating opponent compared with one that is rushing in. In the latter case, you want maximum impact and a high likelihood of stopping them before they do you serious damage. You may remember this type of questioning in section 10.6 on the subject of the back heel debate'.

Training or Fighting?

There is a difference between training and the real thing. We are taught a very difficult art, with endless complexity and nuances. This teaching should be undertaken in a rigorous and disciplined manner. For me, the disciplined approach to 'tensing' or 'locking down' at the end of a technique forced me to properly consider how to synchronize everything so that I could hit something or someone with the serious intent of putting *everything* I had into the strike. It helped my training and attitude and supplemented what my instructor was fundamentally doing, which was preventing any of his students from being an actor or someone who may look the part but was actually relatively ineffective. Creating actors rather than the real thing is the worst action that any martial arts school can take, for it can cause someone in harm's way to be falsely confident of their abilities. Traditional and rigorous martial art styles are not to everyone's taste but they don't produce 'fluffy' black-belts.

In summary and to avoid any confusion, for a knockout or finishing strike my views are as follows: Do not try to be tense at or just before the moment of impact, for this means starting to contract muscles before impact and hence tending to reduce the striking speed. For a traditional 'solid mass' feel to the punch apply the necessary 'tension' or focus as a brief impulse just after the moment of impact (coupled to an exhalation of breath) and not before. Do not allow that tensioning action to stop the follow-through motion of the strike into the target. The aim is to strike into the target, not at the surface of the target. Recognize the difference between an onrushing opponent and a static or receding one.

Commitment:

This then is akin to putting everything into the punch, with body mass going into and beyond the strike and being committed to (or focused on) penetrating the target. Aim to punch beyond the target, strike fast and relaxed with body weight going to the target and at the instant of impact let everything explode into the target—using all you have: Body, breath and spirit; within a few milliseconds. This was a subject that Master Nishiyama would also reference in his final years of instruction. He would talk of how at the instant of impact everything should contract inwards towards the center of the body or 'tanden'. This, he said, allowed the internal pressure and explosive power to be transmitted into the target with a dense and focused strike.

A Fighter's Insights

There is a distinct difference between point of impact & end of technique:

- Hit and drive-in to penetrate
- Strive for the point of impact to be at the maximum velocity of the technique
- 'Focus' on completing the technique and driving mass into the target

---

12.7 Counter Attacks with Body Tension and a Firm Stance

The above goes some way to resolving the questions raised about contracting supplementary muscles when punching but it is guilty of not 'going the extra mile' and looking deeper into the case where increased body tension may be warranted. And no serious fighter should be accused of not trying to go the full distance.

Within Shotokan this practice of tension or focus was predominately related to a straight punch, particularly of the thrusting type, with a reverse or stepping punch technique, rather than a snapping type or jab. These straight or thrust punches can be practiced in an upright, forward, or natural fighting stance. Note however that there are numerous striking techniques where this ancillary tensioning is deliberately not applied, such as a back fist strike. It has been my experience that this tension is never emphasized with snap kicks - and nor should it to be. A good snap kick does not require the upper body muscles to be tensed and a relaxed action should be encouraged. To support the spine and body however, the external oblique and transverse abdominal muscles need to be naturally engaged. This concept of contraction of muscles and the 'concentration of power' appears to be basically developed for thrust punches. From my experience the main theme is in at least three parts:

- o One – to finish the confrontation. To call upon an attitude of removing the opponent with this single strike.
- o Two - to promote a firm and stable standing position so that this stable foundation allows the power derived from the floor to be transmitted through the hips to flow through the upper body and arm.
- o Three - to ensure that the strength and tension of the body will resist the incoming attacker's momentum and the reactive forces from hitting an onrushing body.

Year in and year out, fighters practice various forms of 'block and counter' where an opponent forcefully steps forward with a punch or a kick and the defender will block and counter that attack. The defender does not have to block and then counter strike in a two step manner; frequently he will simultaneously block and counter punch. The point is that to counter-attack an onrushing opponent with a punch to the body in an overpowering 'head-on' manner, the defender needs to be in a firm and stable stance and tense 'through' the strike. Otherwise the attacker's momentum will effectively 'bowl him over'.

The reference here to a 'head-on' action is to distinguish against an evasive type of defense where a defender may shift out of the line of attack and counterpunch or kick from the side or at an angle. This is a sensible tactic, for a 'head-on' counter attack is a difficult and risky task that requires commitment and near perfect technique, timing and distance. There are a number of important points in the above discussion of body tension:

- The defender is counter punching with a reverse punch to the body
- The defender is meeting the opponent 'head-on', not stepping to the side
- The onrushing target (the body) is of far greater mass than the counter striking hand and arm alone
- A punch to the body will involve a longer contact time than a punch to the face
- The defender aims to stop the attacker; trying to reverse his momentum.

Chapter 5, section 5.8, illustrates how an effective transfer of momentum will occur when the colliding bodies are of equal mass. It also outlines the characteristics of impacts that involve dissimilar striking masses. Returning to the reverse punch statement by Master Nakayama that; *"If the body is not tensed at the moment of contact, the consequent reaction will reduce impact power."* It is clear that this is considering the *reaction* on the person punching, from the attacking body that is being struck. Such a reaction is amplified if the opponent is rushing towards the striker. This is Newton's third law at play; with action and reaction, push and push back. An onrushing opponent is not going to be stopped by a jab to the body; there is too much momentum to overcome. A reverse punch with the body and hips behind the strike, from a strong stance that is connected to the floor, does have stopping power prospects—as would a well timed and executed side thrust kick. You may remember this reasoning within section 10.6 on the back heel debate where the point was made that a defender's solid stance and structure can be far more important when the attacking opponent is rushing in. This is especially important with blows to the body because catching someone square in the face as they attack naturally takes their head back and reduces their body momentum and focus. Evasion is a different action. Stepping to the side to allow the attacker to pass and expend his energy on fresh air does not demand such a stable landing position. Striking as the attacker is 'passing-by' means that this counter-strike is not trying to reverse a high level of the opponent's momentum.

Test and verify: The contents and views of section 12.6 and 12.7 should be examined by working with a reasonably heavy bag and reviewing the results seen and heard by punching in various modes with differing techniques, stances and breathing patterns. When doing so deliberately hit the bag as it is static, moving away or swinging towards you.

A Fighter's Insight
Even the teachings of a Master should be subject to a simple rule:
Trust and Verify

12.8 The Importance of the Breath

The importance of the breath is stressed throughout the martial arts—all the martial arts. The physical reasons for this are not restricted to fighting. Watch a tennis match to see and hear how the breath is synchronized with a serve or a power shot. Observe a power lifter and notice how the exhalation is synchronized with the application of effort. What is happening here? Why do tennis professionals exhale when smashing a serve or volley? Why would a personal trainer at the local gym tell us to exhale at the moment of exertion or when lifting a weight?

We can demonstrate that as we contract or tense the abdomen it pushes the breath up and out of the lower part of the lungs. Doing so engages the stomach and this can be useful in times of physical exertion. I may not need to tense the stomach or even breathe out when I am doing a light weight bicep curl, but when I want to coordinate bodily effort I will engage the stomach and the breath. It is no accident that so many sportsmen talk of the stomach as being the power-house and the air breathed being fuel for their movements. It is known that during inhalation the external intercostal muscles contract, lifting the ribs up and out; the diaphragm just below the thoracic cavity contracts, drawing it down and opening up the lungs further to receive air. During expiration (exhaling) these processes are reversed, and the natural elasticity of the lungs returns them to their normal volume. This reduction in volume expels air. In more vigorous expiration the internal intercostal muscles draw the ribs down and inward, and the wall of the abdomen contracts pushing the stomach and liver upward.

In sparring the person who, for whatever reason, cannot get their breathing coordinated with the fight is going to struggle and probably lose. Fear can ruin the natural rhythm and depth of breathe and make fighting an unbearable strain. The control of emotion and ability to find harmony within the depths of chaos; perhaps by accepting that 'today is a good day to die', all of these gifts can make all the difference—in a fight or life in general.

In the end, everything in traditional martial arts is linked to the breath and breathing. For a demonstration of this, watch and listen to a master perform a kata, but beware of the innocent mistake: don't try to imitate the sounds heard (the noisy exhalation) try instead to replicate the kata, its techniques, timing and breath. The sounds of a Master breathing through a kata are a consequence of the performance, not the aim.

Those who practice a flow style of yoga, such as Ashtanga, can feel how the flow through the sequence of positions is harmonized with the breathing. Traditionally, the postures of yoga are linked in a particular order and the sequence is executed with synchronized breath, movement and transition. Does that sound familiar?

12.9   The Body and the Hips

Repeatedly in this book it has been stressed that the hips are considered to be of critical importance in most striking techniques. Let's select a classic technique and consider the way the hips can play a role in the effective deployment of that technique. Deliberately, let us choose the reverse punch, as one of the most studied and well described movements referenced in most of the tutorial texts of Karate.

Figure 12.7: Reverse Punch

The classic text of Master Nakayama entitled 'Dynamic Karate' states that, "*This (reverse) punch begins with the rotation of the hips. The power of this hip movement is transmitted to the chest, shoulder, arm, and fist, and culminates in a strong shock on the target.*" Another classic reference, 'Karate The Art of "Empty-Hand" Fighting', by Master Hidetaka Nishiyama & Richard Brown states that the reverse punch "*gains force by making maximum use of the forward twisting motion of the hips.*" This reference to the *forward* motion of the hips is occasionally overlooked or not explained sufficiently. The Master Nakayama 'Dynamic Karate' book shows a mechanical schematic representation of the human body to allow the importance of hip rotation to be understood. This model has served generations of martial artist well; helping to ensure that the hips are used and that the rotational aspects are visualized and used.

This model has been redrawn here as figure 12.8. One difficulty often experienced is that such a model tends to indicate that the hips 'only' swivel around their center point, and many martial artists take the concept of the body rotating through an imaginary axis too literally. We are far more complex, sophisticated and agile than machines. The human body can find a way of imparting force into a target in a more sophisticated manner than a simple machine and we have to understand that any simplified model designed to help understanding is still only a simplified model. The body does not just swivel about its axis and the illustrative models used in karate or aikido should be accepted as the educational tools intended, rather than as the definitive last word. It should be clear that the old masters of the martial arts tended to know as much about human anatomy as anyone outside of the medical fraternity and never considered the spinal column to be rigid and rod like.

Although figure 12.8 indicates that the hips rotate around their center, spinal-column point, in the next two sub-sections a basic right hand reverse punch will be used to facilitate a discussion on some of the different ways the hips can be applied. This reverse punch will initially start with the right hip pulled back by about 30 degrees from the front, square, forward hip position and will finish with the hips square. Then, as a second example, the hips will be deliberately rotated further. In both instances the body will be moved forward into and behind the strike.

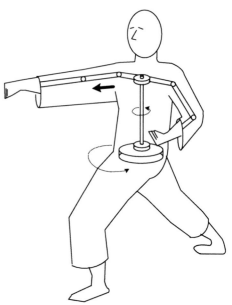

Figure 12.8: Classic simplified schematic of the reverse punch upper body mechanics

'The reverse punch gains more force by making maximum use of the *forward* twisting motion of the hips'
Master Nishiyama & Richard Brown

(a) Hip rotation and forward movement during a reverse punch:

The series of three sketches within figure 12.9 provides a simplified cut-away plan view or sectional representation of the hip action during a reverse punch, looking down and through a fighter using a right hand reverse punch technique. For clarity, all that is being shown is a sectional schematic of the hips and fist; no arms, body, legs or head.

Here the hips are shown to rotate about the central point, or spine, as usual but in this example the hip movement is not restricted to a central, pivotal, rotation only; in this analysis the hips are allowed to shift *forward*. By doing this, the center of gravity of the body can shift and push more body weight forward and into the strike, yet retain composure and posture. It has been emphasized previously how important this imparting of body weight is to increasing the force delivered. In this illustrated action, visualize the back as remaining upright and the hips being pushed forward by the legs, the fighter is not 'leaning' into the punch. Remember that the hipbones and associated joints form a complex and versatile structural arrangement, not a simple central rod and solid plate that twists on demand (see figure 12.11 for a greatly simplified schematic of the skeleton). In figure 12.9 this reverse punch is from forward stance with the feet remaining in place and gripping the floor throughout the movement, without the back heel lifting.

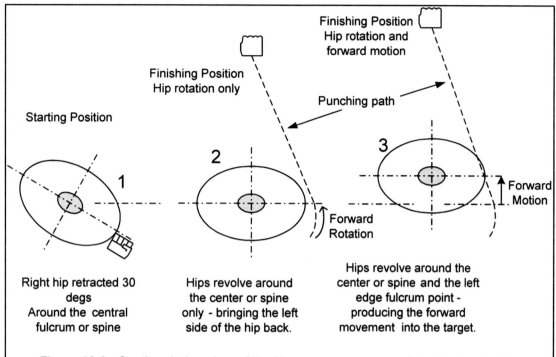

Figure 12.9: Sectional plan view of the hips as a reverse punch is deployed. Hip movement is not limited to rotation only - about the axis center point or spine: The hips also move forward pushing the center of gravity and more body mass into the punch.

In the starting position, (1) of figure 12.9, we can imagine the hips rotated back slightly, shown here as retracted through 30 degrees. Clearly that could be less or even further, such as would deliberately be the case if a left side block is performed and the right fist is poised, wound up and ready to strike. As the punch is initiated, the hips swivel quickly about their center. In the schematic drawn, this center is shown as the gray 'spinal' cross-sectional oval. When the hips approach the frontal point the fist flies from its starting or resting position; translating what started as a rotational movement into a linear movement, directed at the target. If the hips were only to rotate and stop at the 'hips square' position then this would be as illustrated in position (2) of figure 12.9. The punch line is fairly simple but if the hips only rotated about their center point then the right hip will move forward and the left hip will pull back – and we can do better than that.

To include as much body mass as is practical we want the center of gravity of the body to move forward into the strike and target. Hence the hips now move forward with rotation of the hips from the left pivot point, rather than just the center (spine). This gives a finishing position of (3) in figure 12.9, rather than (2), which may be easier to visualize by studying

figure 12.10. Here it is clear that the mass of the body has moved towards and into the target path, exactly as the previous theory has recommended. To accomplish this forward movement means pushing from the back foot, straightening the rear leg to drive the hip and fist forward. This further movement has to come from somewhere and practice will show that before delivery the back leg needs to be 'off-lock' and slightly bent. If this complete action is difficult to visualize think of two types of doors:

1. A revolving door—one that turns on its central axis, akin to the hips twisting about the axis of the spine
2. A normal house door—one that swings on the hinge connected to the frame, akin to the hips rotating **forward**, from the edge.

Figure 12.9 (3) illustrates a combination of revolving around the center *and* moving forward by revolving from the body 'edge', showing a technique finishing with the hips turned square towards the target.

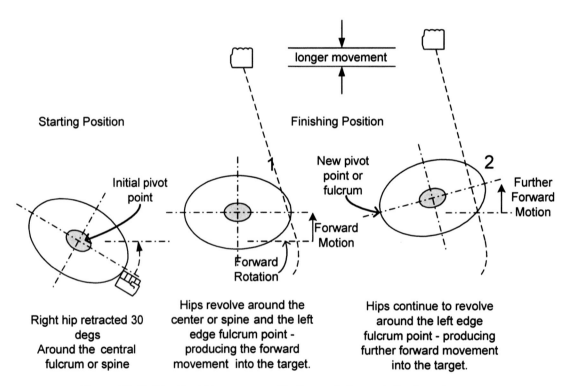

Figure 12.10: The final hip movement is forward - towards the target

(b) 'Further' hip rotation and forward movement during a reverse punch:

It is possible to rotate the hips beyond the central line, particularly for the very flexible wanting to extend the length of the punch. This is shown schematically in figure 12.10.

A cautionary note on this continued hip rotation is that it could result in off-axis forces on the spine as it becomes more difficult to adequately engage the spinal support musculature. Remember this when undertaking repetitive training with reverse punches in free space. We train to improve, not to damage the body.

In summary, rotating about the left pivotal point will allow the hips to move forward, thereby moving the center of gravity of the body towards the target, which is exactly what we desire to impart more mass into the strike. If actually striking a physical object, the hips can, naturally, be allowed to push forward in a rotational or lateral manner; although this actual physical movement may be prevented or limited by the reaction to the object being struck. If no object was struck and this further rotational or lateral movement was allowed then the attack could be over extended. Body control must therefore be exercised.

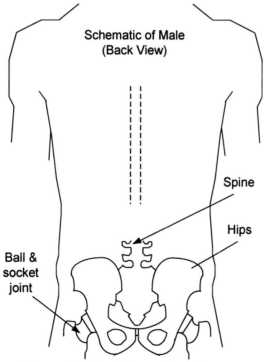

Figure 12.11: Schematic of human anatomy - with specific reference to the hips.

12.10   The Third Force Component: Penetration Distance

In previous chapters we have nominated the speed and the mass of the striking weapon as the two primary components to develop in order to increase the effectiveness of a strike. Repeatedly the importance of speed and mass has been stressed, relating both to the kinetic energy equation. From a force, rather than energy perspective, there are a couple of other considerations. First, let's consider the distance over which the impact occurs and the concepts developed in section 5.4.

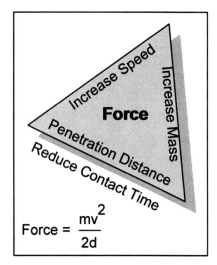

$$\text{Force} = \frac{mv^2}{2d}$$

Reviewing the theory again: since the product of force and distance is work, which equates to energy, we know that Force is equal to Energy divided by Distance (d):

$$\text{Force} = \frac{Energy}{d} \qquad\qquad \text{Energy} = \frac{mv^2}{2}$$

$$\text{Hence, force} = \frac{mv^2}{2d} \qquad \textit{Equation (10.1)}$$

So here we have our third component of interest, the distance 'd' in which the striking velocity is reduced to zero and energy transfers are complete. The above equation can also be derived from Newtons Law – see Appendix A. This shows that the ways to increase the peak force involved with a strike are:

- o   Increase the mass, 'm'.
- o   Increase the velocity, 'v'.
- o   Decrease the distance, 'd' over which the forces are expended

The distance referenced, for the transmission of the energy from the striker to the target is the distance over which the kinetic energy of the strike is absorbed by the target. Hence, the shorter the distance over which the energy is imparted into the target the greater the involved peak force(s). Here we have a scientific basis for so much of the material that we are taught during training and learn from our experiences.

How do we increase these peak forces, how can we reduce the distance over which the energy is absorbed? We know all the usual lessons about hitting perpendicular to the face of the target and this book has discussed the differences between hard and soft targets and has shown how a blow that is 'ridden' reduces the peak forces by elongating the time and distance of contact. This knowledge is critical to maximizing the force transmitted into a target but there is another way of increasing the peak force experienced; simply by reducing the "give" in the target. This has been noted elsewhere: Stull and Barnham (1988) said, "The force of the impact and therefore the potential damage done to an opponent or object struck can be increased by reducing the 'give' during the impact by either the karateka or the opponent or object being struck."

Allow me to illustrate by way of an example. Within the range of Shotokan kata there are repeated instances where the elbow of one arm strikes the palm of the other arm. In these examples at the instance of the strike the hips and body are turned in a classic synchronized manner so that the body is behind the blow and the stance is made strong.

What is happening here? One application is that, with a right arm elbow strike, the left hand has grasped and wrapped itself around the opponent's head or body, bringing the target to the strike point and allowing the target no escape—reducing the "give" or backward movement in the above force and distance equation. Simultaneously the shift of body and establishment of stance and focus ensures that there is minimal 'give' in the fighter that is doing the striking. Furthermore, hitting with the bony end of the elbow is a strike with one of the hardest points of the body, so again there is little 'give' in the attacking weapon. This is a technique which has the capacity to finish a confrontation. An elbow used with force will break a jaw or smash a cheekbone, rather than 'just' knock out the opposition. Note that in training or kata the hand that's struck is not passive; the strike should be timed to hit the hand as it is pulling the imaginary target onto the striking elbow.

Figure 12.12 - Elbow Strike

Implications – hitting a man when he's down

Chapter one lists some of the maximum forces measured. It can be predicted from the above that if the head of the measurement dummy had been placed against a wall such that it was unable to move backwards when struck, then the peak force would have been higher. A person on the floor hit with a downward strike is going to suffer a very high impact force. Faced with such circumstances a fighter needs a good ground guard and the ability to get out of trouble.

Don't push it

Often a fighter is told to strike or punch and not to push. One of the distinguishing features between a strike and a push is the contact time and distance. A punch is sharp while a push is protracted. A punch is effective over a small penetration distance and short time. A push is executed over a longer distance and elongated time period. Therefore the peak forces with a push are smaller than those with an equivalent energy strike; if necessary return to chapter seven, for example section 7.3, to better understand these principles.

12.11 The Fourth Force Component: Impact Contact Time

If we punch a target then the fist is stopped or slowed by the target that is struck and the force involved is the product of the mass behind the punch (m) and the deceleration of the fist (a) [where 'a' is negative]. Mathematically this law is quoted as $Force = m \times a$ or $Force = m \frac{\Delta v}{\Delta t}$ and this shows that the greater the mass, or the higher the striking speed or the shorter the time taken for the strike speed to drop to zero, then the higher the force experienced. This is referring to the time taken to absorb the punch; it is not promoting an artificial reduction in contact time by pulling the punch back too early; which could prevent the fist from dispensing all its energy into the target. If, however, the energy is fully transmitted to the target in a shorter contact time then the peak force will be greater. The shorter the distance over which the energy is imparted *into* the target, the greater the involved peak force. As always, time and distance are related.

This can be thought about from another perspective. As chapter 2 states, the more power you have the more work you can do in less time. The more power you can put into a strike then the greater the energy transmitted to the target in less time. If that transmission or absorption time is too short for that energy to be absorbed by the target without damage, then damage must result. Earlier discussions have related these aspects to contact time, collision object characteristics, hardness and padded gloves, riding a punch or catching a high speed cricket ball with a hand and arm that momentarily follows the trajectory of the ball, extending the contact time and thereby reducing the peak forces. A bare-knuckled punch to the face is essentially a bone on bone strike and the contract time is therefore going to be short; shorter than hitting the stomach and shorter than striking the face wearing a well padded glove. Reduce the time over which the power of the strike is absorbed for a high peak force and more devastating effect, but the bones of the fist can be injured and open hand techniques are often very effective.

12.12   Relative Time: Application to Real Circumstances

Power equals work divided by time (section 2.3.5). Where time is not limited a person can prepare, develop and deliver power 'at their leisure'. They can start with a preparatory wind up or pull back of a fist to maximize the delivery speed of the punch and then drive through the target without concern over the time taken or any urgent need to recover.

The above is often seen in performances involved in breaking a board or similar. It refers to two different 'packages' of time, one being preparation time (e.g. wind up) and the other as the application and contact time (e.g. the drive through). The relationships quoted earlier concentrated on contact time, not preparation or follow through, but this subsection will cover this full range of considerations.

In a real and dangerous situation time is not an affordable luxury to be used at leisure. In a fight there is little safe prospect of prolonged preparations such as 'wind-up' and a critical need to recover quickly after any technique has been thrown. The optimization of time is of the utmost importance to a fighter. Unlike a board-breaker, fighters may not have the time to ensure that the strike is at the maximum, peak, kinetic energy at the moment of impact and they are careful about not over-extending themselves. It could be said that here are two opposing ends of the practice of the martial arts: Firstly, where time is unlimited, such as a controlled exercise, e.g. a breaking demonstration, and the next where time is seriously constrained, for example in a fight.

1   *Time is a priority, speed is the dominator:*

In a fight, a bare-knuckle blow to the face will probably be launched from the free style or sparring hand position. On striking the focus is short and sharp; to execute the blow quickly, penetrate, deliver the power and energy into the opponent and withdraw.

In these real circumstances a very fast action may be used to set up the opponent (get him confused or groggy etc.) so that the second strike can be 'longer' in duration, allowing time for enhanced body weight to be applied. Numerous combinations cover this type of set-up—the classic front hand jab followed by the reverse hand punch or 'cross', or, for example, a front foot snap kick, perhaps to the groin, followed by a fully delivered reverse punch or uppercut. In the case of a strike to the face in 'real' circumstances, speed is a priority. If we can also get plenty of body weight behind the blow then that's all to the good, but often we will not elongate the time or reduce the speed in order to 'push into the blow', particularly with the initial 'jab'. In a fight, time may be very limited with no allowance for preparation, hesitation or elongation. This is especially true when faced with the prospect of multiple opponents or the suspicion of a weapon being carried by an attacker.

2   *Time is not limited, work is the priority,*

Now assume that there is no time constraint. Perhaps in a breaking demonstration we have 'all the time in the world' to prepare for, and follow through with, the strike; effectively our priority goes to power or the work done over time.

Hence the board breaker can deliberately elongate the contact time to allow him to 'push through and in' with everything he has, even if it takes a little longer. This is often seen during the multiple board breaking types of demonstration where the wooden blocks or tiles are rigidly supported and separated by pencil thin spacers, and the striker attempts to

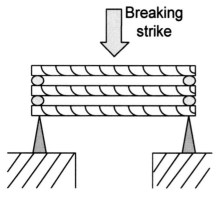

Figure 12.13: Multiple board breaking - elongated contact time and increased striking distance

drive the power of the first break through the other boards. This is not a short, sharp, strike—for the fist, elbow or foot needs to continue to move and carry the power over the length of the stack. Time is not a limit here; the priority is on the work required to break all the boards.

The rigid supports of these boards allow a person to elongate the strike time and hence 'punch through'. If a tile or board is free standing or hanging from the ceiling by a cord then you have only the first instance of the strike to be effective. Once contact is achieved either the board breaks or it is driven away, so with free standing board breaking the priority goes to speed not power: See the Chapter 7 including section 7.8.

We have here the two ends of a spectrum. At the one end are the problems in facing multiple opponents on a dark night – at the other is the breaking of multiple boards without concern over the time to prepare or complete the strike action.

Boards may indeed 'hit back' but they don't tend to carry a knife.

12.13   Summary

With any stance find where the strengths and weaknesses are, which muscles are in tension, and how the body is connected to the floor. Understand from where the forces are derived when punching or kicking. When stepping (forward or backward) or turning notice how the forces comes from the floor.

Optimize energy and momentum with fluid movements and know how and when to impart that energy into the opponent. Use any momentum gained, rather than squander such a valuable source of energy.

To increase speed of movement be relaxed. To increase the mass behind a strike synchronize the impact with the delivery of body weight and ensure that the technique and striking structure can transmit that body mass. A weak wrist, elbow or shoulder will result in a punch shedding energy because that joint cannot take the strain of impact.

Many fighters contemplate the 'one strike' concept; with a conflict ending in a single blow and moment. This one life, one strike idea is not just about technique—it is a philosophical attitude.

The usage of the hips in the martial arts is crucial. Ensure that the push from the floor and the movement of the hips contributes to the effectiveness of a technique or combination. Understand the different ways that the hips can be utilized, with the available choices in how we can apply both rotation and forward motion. Know where the center of gravity of your body is and how it can be moved into an attack.

For training purposes some styles teach the practice of becoming tense during the execution of a technique, such as at the completion of a punch. This can be taken to the extreme where the whole body aims to become virtually rigid, with connection from the floor through to the fist. Science shows that a high impact collision requires a missile (the fist) to have high speed and mass. Body tension from a fighter that will reduce the impact speed of the punch should be avoided. Tension can add mass to the strike but should not prevent the necessary penetration of the target. There is a difference between training and actually hitting something hard

There are numerous components to consider when striking, including four key variables: Speed of strike; the weight or mass behind the strike; the distance penetrated by the impact; the contact time of the strike.

In life-threatening conditions time may be of the highest priority, with no time for preparation, delay or recovery from over extension.

Breathe - and know life in a single breath

Chapter 13: Conclusions

'Do not forget that karate-do begins and ends with rei'
Master Funakoshi

13.1   At the Core

For a forceful strike the kick or the punch has to have both mass and velocity. When learning and relearning how to strike with force always ask how can the striking speed be increased and how to put more mass into the impact. A strike that impacts a small area will do more local damage than the same energy being dissipated over a larger area. A higher peak force is attained when the contact time is small compared with an impact that is spread out over a longer time (punch, don't push). A higher peak force is registered when the energy of the strike is spent within a short contact penetrative distance – a hard surface being hit by a hard object.

13.2   In General

If this summary was being written in the weightless environment of an orbiting space-shuttle I could still grip a pencil, make my wrist and arm move and hold a writing pad. A pencil would need to be used because pen and ink doesn't like zero gravity but I could still write. If my cosmonaut colleague and I wanted to try to fight while floating in zero gravity we could, but a lot of my training would be of limited use. Locks and holds would work but if I were to punch my opponent the impact force and reaction would cause both he and I to be pushed away from each other. If I am floating in space my punching power would be reduced because I could not push from the floor or any other solid surface; rather like fighting while floating in an ocean, except the sea water has more to push against than air. Not being connected to the floor, having no weight through gravity and having nothing to push from does not stop all forces: I still have mass and could still apply a choke hold, but I'm really going to struggle to get through a kata or one-step sparring.

Having weight and gravity allows me to push against a floor and I know that the floor will push back with equal force. This is how we learned to walk, run and jump. Newton's third law formally explains what is happening here but it's been known instinctively and intuitively since childhood. As children we naturally learnt to bend at the knees and push away from the floor in order to jump. In the martial arts we develop and adapt this intuitive knowledge to allow us to launch an attack or initiate evasion by deriving power from our base, from the earth. Years of study and instruction can teach the body how differing stances and body positioning will develop the most effective attack or evasive move. Fighters hone their skills to be able to move instinctively into and out of stances to suit conditions and intensions—perhaps from a strong and stable stance to a lighter and more dynamic one, as circumstances dictate.

When changing from one stance to another, be aware of the position of the hips. An object with a low center of mass (or center of gravity) is more stable and thereby more difficult to 'uproot' or topple. A stance that deliberately lowers the hips will lower the center of mass of the fighter and help to gain force from the floor. Fighters need to be able to dynamically shift from one position to another quickly and efficiently. They need to have accumulated a wide-ranging repertoire of stances so that the most effective choice comes naturally. In combat a person is not static.

For a strike to carry energy it needs speed and mass. For both speed and mass to be applied in an optimal manner at the time of impact the body and movement needs to be coordinated. For maximum force the instance of impact should coincide with maximum speed and highest effective mass transmission. As an example a stepping punch should, at impact, carry the speed of the step and the speed of the extending punch. The strike should occur just before the step is completed. Striking **after** the step lands means that some momentum is lost; speed is reduced and the available mass behind the strike has lowered, because the body is no longer in full motion. Good coordination, body alignment and focus can put a proportion of the mass of the stepping body behind the punch. This kind of coordination and timing is only accomplished through hard, long and diligent training with an instructor that can spot mistakes and instigate corrective actions.

A natural way of increasing the body mass carried by or 'behind' a punch is to physically move or push forward into the strike; in other words, have the body's center of gravity moving towards the opponent when the strike hits. This is an option, not a compulsory action, for trained fighters will exercise control or caution since they will not normally want to be overextended or off-balance, especially if there is a risk that the strike will not be fully effective.

Increasing the striking mass of a punch or kick, over and above the mass of the fist or foot, demands that additional body mass is transmitted into the target through that striking fist or foot. This means that the delivery mechanism must be capable of transmitting that additional mass. If a straight punch is delivered with a weak wrist or loose elbow then that joint can buckle and some of the potential force will be lost because the full weight behind the wrist or elbow cannot be transmitted into the target. If you spend a lot of time working a heavy punch bag, you will see that there are times when, as you get more tired, it becomes more likely for the wrist to suddenly 'fold' on impact.

Certain schools have taught martial artists to focus and tighten or 'squeeze' muscles for a fraction of a second at the point of impact, with an applied tension virtually throughout the body. There are benefits to that practice as a training aid, but trying to tense muscles at the point of impact can tend to reduce the speed of the punch. I haven't seen any experimental work that scientifically tries to compare the difference between applying and not applying this maximal contraction method. However, within these pages is a discussion on the differences between hitting a stationary or retreating target, compared with hitting and trying to stop an opponent that is rushing in towards you. 'Focus' and the tensioning of supplementary muscles *after* impact is not the same thing as contracting muscles *before* impact. For many the 'focus' is to get the breathing, timing and penetration right, rather than trying to make the body 'rigid' for that fraction of a second.

To increase the speed of the strike demands good form, good instruction, endless practice and a relaxed movement. In virtually all strikes the use of the hips is crucial. Good footwork and easy, well-timed, hip rotation helps to increase speed, assists balance and aids the technique's biomechanics that drive more of the body's center of mass into the strike. Using the hips properly facilitates the 'release' of the strike; not using the hips can oppose the natural motion of the technique. This is true for both punches and kicks. An increase in speed is of benefit and we have seen that the kinetic energy associated with a moving object is directly proportional to the mass of the object and the square of the velocity: Increase the speed at impact by 40% and the energy of the punch will double. This is very difficult to achieve and as section 7.10 points out fighters should not sacrifice too much punching mass for the sake of increased speed.

Typically the striking object, the fist or the foot, reaches maximum velocity at around three quarters of its total reach or trajectory distance. That is the point at which to make impact. Impact too early in the strike and the speed will not have reached its peak, too late and the speed will be dropping towards the zero, full extension, point. High speed physical movement requires a relaxed bodily action, yet in times of combat stress levels tend to become high, resulting in tension and stiffness—the opposite of what is needed. This alludes to one of the major advantages of training in the martial arts. After years of working with opponents, in controlled but stressful conditions, a fighter is better equipped to deal with the stress and fear of a street confrontation. In my view there is truth in the suggestion that students should feel a degree of unease or stress whenever entering a training hall; a good instructor will even create occasions of fear—in controlled conditions of course. Nevertheless, as is always the case, there is no substitute for real experience and a proven street fighter is a very dangerous opponent. The difference between sparring during class and fighting in the street is an opponent that doesn't care if you suffer permanent physical injury – or worse; and no one is there to prevent it but yourself.

Hitting a bony part of an opponent's body warrants high-speed action. Minimal contact time should be expected, as the kinetic energy is quickly dissipated and inflicts (breaking) damage. Hitting a softer part of the opponents' body—or striking through heavy clothing— warrants more of a follow-through type of action, with a little more thrust. With a soft cushioning protective layer guarding the real target, such as a heavy stomach, you may need to go deeper and stay longer to do serious damage. There is a difference between hitting a soft target, perhaps the stomach, compared with hitting a hard target such as the ribs or face of an opponent: Bones can break, a head strike is usually trying to achieve a knockout, a punch to the stomach is very different and expert fighters will modify their techniques accordingly. Important parameters such as penetration and contact time are affected by the characteristics of the target. As a rule of thumb:

When hitting the face go for speed, when hitting the body go for 'weight'.

There is also a difference between hitting an opponent that is moving towards you compared to hitting one that is static or in retreat. With an in-rushing opponent a counter strike from a strong or rooted stance may be important. With an opponent in retreat you may need to launch an attack by charging forward or even be 'in-flight' with a jumping technique—the antithesis of a rooted stance. With an in-rushing opponent an evasive option is often best, striking the attacker without being in his line of attack.

In combat balance is essential. This is not restricted to the physical balance of the body only. A balance needs to be continuously maintained with regards to the timing and delivery of strikes. In combat perfect positioning is often not practical and the 'setting-up' of a move or a strike such as retraction of the fist before punching is probably an unaffordable luxury. It is interesting that whenever a person is asked to break a board the individual will prepare himself, check the distance, take time to be fully ready and then when striking push through the break point and not return immediately. Combat is not the same as breaking a board. In a fight you risk being hit, as well as risk signaling an intension to strike if you take time to prepare a punch. In combat the target does not stay still and wait patiently while you measure the distance; and it has an unfortunate habit of wanting to hit you first.

A higher pressure is experienced by a strike impacted over a smaller area than the same force spread over a larger area. That's one reason why a strike with only two bare knuckles creates more localized pressure than the same punch would have while wearing a large padded glove. The peak force of a strike is reduced by the elongation of the contact time, so striking with bare knuckles creates more localized damage than the same punch would if wearing a padded glove (which would elongate the contact time and reduce the peak force). More breaks and cuts can be expected in a bare knuckle fight. In these unfortunate times blood in a street fight has to be considered as a health risk.

A strike path that is perpendicular (at a right angle) to the face of the target is more forcefully penetrating than a similar energy striking the target at an angle. As a defender, if you can't avoid being hit then try and 'ride' the blow and turn the face of the target away from the strike path in order to reduce the maximum force experienced.

The above comments are based upon known science and observations from training in the martial arts. Knowledge and understanding of the science helps the conscious mind but it is the body and mind in harmony that needs to assimilate that knowledge. Under pressure trained fighters react in the way that they have trained to become instinctively. Training has to be appropriate, has to be correct, for bad habits are still bad habits even after years of repetitive training—they are just errors performed well.

Discussions amongst fighters occasionally reference 'muscle memory' which can best be thought of as a description of movements that do not need conscious thought. We can walk, talk, brush our teeth or perform a punch without having to engage in a step by step conscious set of mental instructions. We need this ability to survive; it is a classic evolutionary survival of the fittest attribute. Without it we could not perform as well as we do, run as fast as we can or fight as effectively. It can basically be considered as the mechanism by which neural pathways are gradually built up by repetitive practice, so that eventually the neural route for performing this physical act is established and becomes effectively instinctive. The brain activity when first performing a task is far greater than is needed after the physical task has been practiced a very large number of times. Hence the action becomes faster, more precise and more accurately repeated. This is exactly what a martial artist (or a musician or golfer, etc.) needs. One point for all instructors to keep in mind is that if a particular technique is incorrectly instructed or copied then the muscle memory developed by the student through incorrect repetition will retain these errors. Unlearning this behavior takes a massive investment of repetitive training of the right technique; the wrong neural pathways have to be overwritten and the right ones created. Obviously the phrase muscle memory is misleading; in this context the muscles cannot memorize anything.

Part of the training of a fighter should include hitting things. The use of bag work or similar is strongly recommended. A good instructor is essential; the more constructively critical the better. Years of training are essential. As it states above one dojo floor that I train at: *"The more you train in here, the less you bleed out there,"* (Master Viola). Or a phrase that I have held in mind for years: *Train Hard, Fight Easy* (paraphrase from Suvorov).

It was once said that the throwing and grappling arts are more 'hands-on' and practical in nature compared with striking arts that are mainly theoretical. This reasoning was based upon a view that striking techniques that are supposed to maim and disable cannot be fully tested and therefore the training has to be accepted on trust. Most of us involved in karate or similar have accumulated sufficient bruises, stitches and occasional breaks to contest this 'purely theoretical' notion; we have a good idea of what works and what is suspect, and who is really dangerous. Many of us have witnessed individuals that appear more 'elegant' in their execution than others and, equally, have trained with individuals that to some may appear to be anything but elegant, despite being devastatingly effective.

With the advent of Mixed Martial Arts (MMA), many myths have been rightfully dispelled. Official MMA competitions do have some restrictive rules to take into account but the lessons learned through MMA over the last decade are fairly clear and have provided a significant contribution to the martial arts. Perhaps the most important lesson is the clear advantage of being a **mixed** martial artist: A fighter well versed in grappling, locks, holds, chokes, guards, throws, kicks, punches and elbow or knee strikes. The competitive nature of the MMA may be considered to be detrimental to the ideals of some of the traditional schools that are not interested in winning competitions against others. Certain traditional schools may hold onto a concept that the martial arts are ultimately about understanding the self. These same schools may have a heritage that dates back to times of war and see a relationship between warrior-ship, self understanding and self control. Whatever your background it should be acknowledged that the upper level MMA fighters are amongst the most highly trained and best conditioned weaponless warriors this planet has ever seen. A true martial artist will, without hesitation, recognize and acknowledge this assertion and give these fighters the respect that they have earned and deserve.

It should always be recognized that the purely competitive side of fighting is not for all people; that the traditional fighting arts that do not over concentrate on competition will retain an appeal to a wide range of people. We all know innumerable martial artists who just keep on coming to every class and simply want to continue their lifelong pursuit of mastery of certain techniques or kata. They just train, just carry on dealing with their own demons and never really care if the younger student behind them is faster or stronger. A martial artist may consider their art to be a lifelong endeavor; a champion competition fighter could consider retirement at a relatively early age.

13.3   In Theory

A scientific theory can provide a model to help understand what is actually happening in nature and thereby predict results. Experimental or practical work can then provide numerical results and allow those predictions to be tested. The model and numerical results can give a framework of reference and permit comparisons; showing numerically what is faster or more forceful. Numbers are always useful, for if something cannot be measured then how can we be sure what size it is (whatever 'it' is).

This book has described a wide range of theories or scientific principles, covering such topics as:

Newton's laws of motion	The conservation of energy
Force, contact time and penetration	The conservation of momentum
Elastic & inelastic collisions	The kinetic energy equation

Newton's laws are known to scholars as a way of understanding how mechanical objects behave. The principles of the conservation of energy, mass or momentum tell us, scientifically, that there is balance and you cannot get something for nothing. Understanding the difference between elastic and inelastic collisions provides an insight into the different kinds of strikes, such as snap or thrust, the characteristics of the target and missile – such as hard or soft - and how all these affect the consequential force felt. This scientific understanding aligns with our intuitive or natural reasoning. Science describes the difference between a thrust and snap technique. It explains what happens when you put on gloves and how the impact force impulse will change compared to an equivalent bare-handed strike. It helps one understand how a bare-handed strike action from an expert can be more akin to a strike from a snake—rather than the slower but possibly heavier blow from an untrained heavy adult.

The theory shows the importance of mass, speed, penetration and contact time in a strike. This reinforces the lessons that we have received from respected instructors: Lessons that cover instruction on how to increase the speed or the 'weight' behind a technique and how and when to 'focus'. By describing how to hit hard, technical theory also provides advice on how to reduce the force of an opponents' blow, how the diversion or deflective blocking of a kick or punch needs only a fraction of the force that the strike may carry.

13.4   Peak Forces

All of these theoretical aspects align with the experimental results, and they match our everyday experiences. They would have to—there is no mysticism involved. The only magic to be seen is how incredibly effective we can make our bodies. The experimental results show what approximate speed and peak forces can typically be attained by the advanced exponent of the martial arts:

o   Peak force for a punch   5,000 Newtons (1,100 pounds force)

o   Peak force for a kick   7,000 Newtons (1,570 pounds force)

o   Highest Speed for a punch   12 meters per second, or 27 mph

o   Speed of a roundhouse kick   16 meters per second, or 35 mph

As you would expect, the highest force is from kicking rather than punching. What you may not expect is that a fighter can hit with around half a ton of force—it makes little difference if that's an imperial or metric ton, it's still an enormous force.

The experimental results show that experience counts, the most prevalent correlation that indicated causality was that (weight for weight) the grade of individual and length of time training was what promoted the greatest force of strike to be

> **Exceptions**
> Dedicated and exceptional athletes, performers and fighters are the ones that set records and win world titles.

achieved. The expert is generally better than the intermediate, the intermediate generally better than the novice or less skilled. Caution is needed in drawing too many conclusions from results obtained from relatively small samples. The measurement of force is not easily undertaken in a strictly controlled manner, comparison of results between different experimenters can be problematic. Velocity measurements are generally more reliable.

13.5   And Yet . . .

All of this is far from the end of the story. Striking a stationary object, a bag, brick, board, dummy, or force transducer, is only a small part of the whole, it is not the full story—nowhere near. The traditional martial arts are not about how many boards we can break; the amount of force we can create is not an overall judgment criterion of 'The way'. As Funakoshi wrote in *Karate-do Nyumon*, "Karate-do is a noble martial art, and the reader can rest assured that those who take pride in breaking boards or smashing tiles, or who boast of being able to perform outlandish feats like stripping flesh or plucking out ribs, really know nothing about karate. They are playing around in the leaves and branches of a great tree, without the slightest concept of the trunk."

In fighting or sparring hitting hard and fast is only part of an equation that involves timing and distance, anticipation and reaction, accuracy and control, rhythm and breathing, mind and no-mind. It is of little use being able to hit hard if you cannot catch your opponent. And if your opponent can only hit half as hard as you but hits you many, many more times, then the chances are that will be enough for him to beat you—especially if you are hit in the vital or more vulnerable areas. The traditional martial arts are sometimes considered to be split into the three parts of basics, forms or kata and fighting. These are not independent parts; they may be taught in a systematic manner that deliberately puts different attributes into (apparently) separate categories but that's only for ease of teaching. In the end everything comes together.

But returning to Master Funakoshi's concept of the trunk of a great tree: I don't train five times a week out of fear of being attacked. If I needed to overcome such a fear I might carry a stick and spend an hour a week checking that I was still proficient in the dozen Escrima techniques needed to survive most encounters. No – it isn't about being able to fight: It might have been once, but that passed.

13.6   And in the Future?

We are at a unique point in the development of technology. The availability of powerful laptop computers and high speed multi-shot or video digital cameras is unprecedented. There are now ways of testing the effectiveness of techniques that has previously been impractical or cost prohibitive and it is now easier to undertake a comprehensive technical, *measured* study of the martial arts. Such a study would have to be pre-planned and reviewed by an authoritative panel that would be respected and accepted by the martial arts and scientific community. A systematic study of a large population of martial artists, measuring speed and force of techniques, could provide a step forward in the quantification and understanding of the efficacy of the arts.

However, the martial arts are not solely concerned with effectiveness of technique. Karate, for example, is in truth Karate-do—the *way* of the empty hand—and its founder is well known for pointing out that karateka should '*seek perfection of character*'.

This emphasis on character is not an empty gesture. I have personally seen how people young and old have grown in character and spirit as they have progressed through years of training. Many of us know that in traditional martial art schools at least the bully doesn't last; he either stops being a bully or he leaves. We know how those that grew to be amongst the very best appeared to check their ego—when you have nothing to prove you don't have to prove anything. I have fought and trained with some truly outstanding fighters and have found that, in my experience, the best trained fighters can be trusted.

Excellence in the Martial Arts is achieved by understanding and applying the innumerable incremental improvements that accumulate to make the difference, there are no fast tracks, no easy passes.

My experience is mainly within a traditional style and school. The sparring competitions engaged in were controlled with reasonable contact only - and part of the art was to be able to fight with spirit and force but remain in complete control. This is different from putting on gloves and aiming to knock your opponent out, as is the case in a boxing match, Muay Thai or Mixed Martial Arts full-contact fighting. The relatively recent upsurge in mixed martial art contests will continue to have an impact on the development of the martial arts. History will (probably) show that this has been mostly positive in its effect on the development of the martial arts. Some negative side effects however are to be expected, if only because of the potential adverse consequences of commercially orientated endeavors. The greatest teachers have emphasized that budo is more than self-defense, strength or fitness; it's about the cultivation of spirit and the refinement of character.

As a traditional karateka an extensive amount of my time has been devoted to the study of kata or forms and I have been fortunate in being taught by people that had a direct lineage back to the masters of the art, such as Masters Enoda, Kanazawa, Kase, Nishiyama or Okaziki. To me it is clear that the dynamic moves within true Shotokan kata completely align with the methods explained in this book of how to use the laws of physics to a fighter's advantage. The slower moves assist in a fighter's training and development and the faster moves, performed properly, help increase the speed and mass behind a strike

13.7 And in the End?

We are all mortal, our time alive is finite and all that we see or have is impermanent. Life is only a journey. Living the martial way means that the harder path is often chosen. Just as the rainbow is seen after the rain, the fruits of life's journey taste so much sweeter when they are earned and deserved. The view from a peak is very different for the person who climbed to reach it, compared to that seen by those that gained ground without effort.

> The question: *"Why I do Karate"* isn't even a question any longer
> I am part of Karate and Karate is part of me
> It's a simple as that.
>
> *Christopher Harrop, 2005*

An authentic Japanese sword is forged from differing steels to combine hardness with the ability to absorb impact. This forging is worked and hammered to squeeze out impurities. The inner structure of the finished material is locked in by the forge-master and the blade is polished using finer and finer grains of stones.

A true warrior is made in a similar way.

APPENDIX

Derivation of the Kinetic Energy Equation

Newton's second law states that Force equals mass times acceleration: $F = ma$ If we start from zero speed then the acceleration (a) equals the speed attained (v), (which equals the change in speed Δv) divided by the time taken (t), (which equals the change in time Δt).

Hence Force $\qquad F = ma = m\dfrac{\Delta v}{\Delta t}$ (Δv is change in velocity, Δt is time taken)

If 'v' changes from v_i to 0 then $\Delta v =$ 'v'
If 't' changes from t_i to 0 then $\Delta v =$ t

Hence, $\qquad F = m\dfrac{\Delta v}{\Delta t} = m\dfrac{v}{t}$

Energy = Force x Distance

Hence Energy $\qquad E = m\dfrac{v}{t}d$

Distance (in the linear case) $\quad = \dfrac{1}{2}\,velocity \times time = \dfrac{1}{2}vt$

Hence Energy $\qquad E = m(\dfrac{v}{t}) \times \dfrac{1}{2}vt = \dfrac{1}{2}mv^2$

or $\qquad E = \dfrac{1}{2}mv^2$

Also, since $\qquad F = ma = m\dfrac{\Delta v}{\Delta t} = m\dfrac{v}{t}$

And in the linear case - Distance $= \dfrac{1}{2}\,velocity \times time = \dfrac{1}{2}vt$

Hence Force $\quad F = \dfrac{mv}{2d} \qquad Or\ F = \dfrac{energy}{distance} = \dfrac{(1/2)(mv^2)}{d} = \dfrac{mv^2}{2d}$

All of the above uses the simple case where the start and finish is taken as a baseline so that the final velocity is zero and the initial time is zero.

Appendix B

The Deformation Energy Involved in a Collision between two Objects

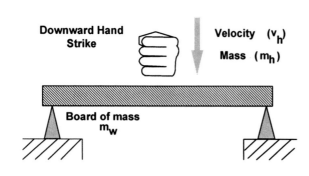

Downward Hand Strike

Velocity (v_h)

Mass (m_h)

Board of mass m_w

This appendix derives the equation that is used to determine the energy needed to break a board. If an object (the wooden board) that we are about to break has a mass of m_w and the projectile that is about to hit that board (our hand) has a mass of m_h and velocity v_h, we can use the laws of physics to determine the amount of energy lost to deformation damage during a strike.

Starting with the **Conservation of Energy**, we know that the kinetic energy of the hand, before impact, will equal the kinetic energy of the hand at or just after impact plus the kinetic energy of the wood at that time, plus the 'deformation' energy used to break the wood, plus any energy 'losses', such as sound. We can ignore the very small energy losses to sound or heat and write out the above statement mathematically as follows:

$$\left[\frac{1}{2}m_h(v_{h1})^2\right]_{initial} = \left[\frac{1}{2}m_h(v_{h2})^2\right]_{post} + \left[\frac{1}{2}m_w(v_{w2})^2\right]_{post} + \Delta E \qquad \text{Equation (B1)}$$

[Initial KE of hand] = [subsequent KE of hand] + [KE of wood] + Deformation Energy

ΔE = *Deformation Energy*
m_h = *effective mass of the hand*
m_w = *mass of the wood*

v_{h1} = *initial velocity of the hand*
v_{h2} = *post strike velocity of the hand*
v_{w2} = *velocity of the wood*

If we make a fairly reasonable assumption, that at the point of breaking the velocity of the wood is the same as the velocity of the hand, then v_{h2} and v_{w2} become equal and can be simply represented as v_2. The hand velocity can also be simply represented as v_1 and the above equation will then simplify to:

$$\left[\frac{1}{2}m_h(v_1)^2\right]_{initial} = \left[\frac{1}{2}m_h(v_2)^2\right]_{post} + \left[\frac{1}{2}m_w(v_2)^2\right]_{post} + \Delta E \qquad \text{Equation (B2)}$$

And by rearranging this equation it can be shown that the deformation energy, that is the energy available to break the wood, is given by the following:

$$\Delta E = \frac{1}{2}m_h(v_1)^2 - \frac{1}{2}(v_2)^2(m_h + m_w) \qquad \text{Equation (B3)}$$

Now using the **Conservation of Momentum** we know that the momentum of the hand before impact will equal the momentum of the hand at or just after impact, plus the momentum of the wood at that time. We can write out this statement mathematically as:

$$m_h v_1 = m_h v_2 + m_w v_2$$

Hence: $\qquad\qquad v_2 = \dfrac{m_h v_1}{(m_h + m_w)} \qquad\qquad \text{Equation (B4)}$

Substituting this into equation (B3) gives:

$$\Delta E = \frac{1}{2}m_h(v_1)^2 - \frac{1}{2}\left[\frac{m_h v_1}{(m_h + m_w)}\right]^2 (m_h + m_w) \qquad \text{Equation (B5)}$$

This simplifies to: $\qquad \Delta E = \dfrac{1}{2}\left[\dfrac{m_h m_w}{(m_h + m_w)}(v_1)^2\right]$

or $\qquad\qquad \Delta E = \dfrac{m_w}{(m_h + m_w)}\left[\dfrac{1}{2}m_h(v_1)^2\right] \qquad \text{Equation (B6)}$

Note that the $\frac{1}{2}m_h(v_1)^2$ term is the kinetic energy of the striking weapon. Other work by experts (Channie, J. (1999); Walker , J. D. (quoted in Arementi (1999)) and Blum, H. (1977) provide a slightly modified relationship that takes account of the elasticity of the collision, using a restitution coefficient 'e' to show that the amount of energy lost to deformation damage (ΔE) is given by the equation:

$$\Delta E = (1 - e^2)\frac{m_w}{(m_h + m_w)}\left[\frac{1}{2}m_h(v_1)^2\right] \qquad \text{Equation (B7)}$$

The coefficient of restitution 'e' is determined by the elasticity of the collision and is a function of the hardness or softness of the colliding objects. An object which collides with perfect elasticity has a coefficient of restitution of 1, while 0 represents a totally inelastic collision. In our considerations of breaking objects the collisions will involve fairly hard objects so if we assume that the 'e squared' term is very small then we effectively return to our previous equation (B6), because $(1 - e^2)$ approximately equals one.

When you enter a training hall and stand among fighters you either have to have earned the right to be there or you have to pay later; or both.

BIBLIOGRAPHY

Armenti, A. (1997); *The Physics of Sports*. American Institute of Physics.

Atha, J., Yeadon, M.R., Sandover, J., and Parsons, K.C. (1985); The Damaging Punch. *British Medical Journal*, 291.

Burgar, B. (2004); Does the front leg really pull? *Shotokan Karate Magazine*, Issue 81, October 2004. pp. 1756-1757

Blum, Haywood (1977); Physics & the Art of Kicking & Punching, *American Journal of Physics*, Vol 45, No. 1

British Medical Association (1993) *The Boxing Debate*. London: British Medical Association.

Chananie, J. (1999); The Physics of Karate Strikes, *Journal of How Things Work*, Vol. 1

Cheetham, J. (2003); The Proof of the Pudding, *Shotokan Karate Magazine*, Issue 77, October 2003.

Cheetham, J. (2005); The Power of Kage Zuki – the hook punch, *Shotokan Karate Magazine*, Issue 82, October 2005.

Cheetham, J. (2004); Hirokazu Kanazawa – a lesson with a master. *Shotokan Karate Magazine*, Issue 78, January 2004. pg. 19

Combo, B. (2005) *Shoshin Ryu: Practitioner's Guide Book*, Shoshin Ryu, Second Edition. Senior Editor: Brian Combo

Feld, M.S., McNair, R.E., and Wilks S.R. (1979); The Physics of Karate. *Scientific American*, Vol. 240 (4). (Also within the book *The Physics Of Sports* edited by Angelo Armenti. and Feld, M.S., McNair, R.E., and Wilks S.R. (1983); The Physics of Karate. *American Journal of Physics* 51 (9), pg. 783-790).

Funakoshi, G. (published 1994); *Karate-Do Nyumon: The Master Introductory Text*. Kodansha International.

Funakoshi, G., Teramoto, J., Oshima, T. (translation published 2001); Karate Jutsu: The Original Teachings of Gichin Funakoshi (illustrated english edition of Rentan Gishin Karate Jutsu), Kodansha International.

Gulledge, J., Dapena, J. (2008); A Comparison of the Reverse and Power Punches in Oriental Martial Arts. *Journal of Sports Sciences*, January 15, 2008

Hooper, D.; *JKA Thoughts from Japan Back to Basic*. Dragon Times. [Online] Available at: http://www.dragon-tsunami.org/Dtimes/Pages/articlek.htm [Accessed: August 27, 2010]

Medical News Today. *'Hitman' Hatton Packs A Mighty Punch*. [Online] (Updated 27 Jun 2007). Available at: http://www.medicalnewstoday.com/articles/75128.php [Accessed: December 30, 2009].

Nakayama, M. (1966) *Dynamic Karate*. Kodansha International, pp 298, Also re-printed: 1986

Ohmichi, H; The Body's Centre of Gravity in Budo Science - From the Biomechanical View. (Possibly within Budo Studies: An Anthology of Research into Budo in the 21st Century - First edition. - Katsuura : Institute of Budo/Sports Science Research, International Budo University, 2000)

Okazaki, T., Stricevic, M.V. (1984); *The Textbook of Modern Karate*. Kodansha America, Inc. 1st Edition.

Oyama, Master Masutatsu (1965); *This is Karate,* Japan Publications Trading Company [previously available in Britain through Ward Lock & Company].

Pearson, J. N. (1997); Kinematics and Kinetics of the Tae Kwon Do Turning Kick. Bachelor of Physical Education Honors degree dissertation [Online] Available at: http://www.itfnz.org.nz/ref/essays/Study_of_Turning%20Kick.pdf [Accessed: January 5th 2010]

Pheasant, S. (1996); *Bodyspace: Anthropometry, Ergonomics and the Design of Work.* Taylor & Francis Ltd; 2nd Revised edition

Pierce, J.D., et al (2006); *Direct Measurement of Punch Force During Six Professional Boxing Matches.* Berkeley Electronic Press.

Pieter, F., Pieter W. (1995); Speed and Force in Selected Taekwondo Techniques: *Biology of Sport,* Vol.12 No. 4.

Redman, R.(2005); Build your own Makiwara, *24 Fighting Chickens* [online] (Updated 29th Sept 2005) Available at: http://www.24fightingchickens.com/2005/09/29/all-about-makiwara/ [Accessed 25th August 2010]

Ristimaki, T. (2009); Hidetake Nishiyama 1928-2008. Interview & Seminar Report. *Shotokan Karate Magazine,* Issue 99, April 2009.

Rokah, A. (2009); Nishiyama: My Sensei. *Shotokan Karate Magazine,* Issue 99, April 2009.

Schmidt-Olsen, S., Jensen, S.K., Mortensen, V. (1990) Amateur Boxing in Denmark. The effect of some preventative measures. *American Journal of Sports Medicine.* Vol. 18(1), pp. 98 – 100.

Scwartz, M.L,. Hudson, A.R., Ferie, G.R., Hayashi, K, Coleclough, A.A. (1986); Biomechanical study of full-contact karate contrasted with boxing. *Journal of Neurosurgery.* 64 pp. 248-252

Serina, E.R., Lieu, D.K. (1991); Thoracic Injury Potential of Basic Competition Taekwondo Kicks, *Journal of Biomechanics,* Vol.24 No.10, pp. 951 – 960.

Smith, M.S. et al (2000); Development of a Boxing Dynamometer and its Punch Force Discrimination Efficacy. *Journal of Sport Sciences,* Vol 18, pp. 445 – 450

Stricevic, M. V., Dacic, D., Miyazaki, T., Anderson, G (1989); *Modern Karate: Scientific approach to conditioning and training,* Miroto Karate Publishing Co., Inc.

Stull, R. A., Barham, J. N. (1988); An analysis of work and power produced by different karate styles in the karate reverse punch in front stance. *International Symposium of Biomechanics in Sports.*

Terranova, T. (2004); We Are What We Experience, Not What We Learn, *Shotokan Karate Magazine,* Issue 80, July 2004.

Unterharnscheidt, F. (1975); Injuries due to boxing and other sports, in Vinken, P.J., Bruyn, G.W. (eds): Injuries of the Brain and Skull, Part 1. *Handbook of Clinical Neurology,* Amsterdam: North-Holland. Vol 23. pp 527-593.

Walker, Jearl D. (1975) Karate Strikes. American Journal of Physics 43, 845-849; (Also within the book The Physics Of Sports edited by Angelo Armenti.

Whiting, W.C. et al (1988); Kinematic analysis of human extremity movements in boxing, *American Journal of Sports Medicine,* Vol. 16, Issue 2, pp. 130 – 136.

DETAILED CONTENTS

Chapter 13   Conclusions

Credits

Photography: Page   91   Fiona Harrop
Pages   109, 237 & back cover: Ray Adams
Page   147   Mark. A. Davies
Page   219   Nick Biemans

Artwork   Cover   Huang Hai
Internal   Grenville Harrop

Editor   Rebecca Harrop

CPSIA information can be obtained at www.ICGtesting.com
Printed in the USA
BVOW05s1009301013

335002BV00006B/337/P